T0329958

Financial Expert
Witness Communication

Financial Expert Witness Communication

A Practical Guide to Reporting and Testimony

BRADLEY J. PREBER

WILEY

For general information on our other products and services or for technical support, please contact our Customer Care Department within the United States at (800) 762-2974, outside the United States at (317) 572-3993 or fax (317) 572-4002.

Wiley publishes in a variety of print and electronic formats and by print-on-demand. Some material included with standard print versions of this book may not be included in e-books or in print-on-demand. If this book refers to media such as a CD or DVD that is not included in the version you purchased, you may download this material at http://booksupport.wiley.com. For more information about Wiley products, visit www.wiley.com.

Library of Congress Cataloging-in-Publication Data:

Preber, Bradley J., author.
  Financial expert witness communication : a practical guide to reporting and testimony/Bradley J. Preber.
      pages cm.—(Wiley corporate F&A series)
  Includes bibliographical references and index.
    ISBN 978-1-118-75355-2 (hardback)—ISBN 978-1-118-75383-5 (ePDF)—
ISBN 978-1-118-75385-9 (ePUB)—ISBN 978-1-118-91177-8 (oBook)
    1. Forensic accounting—United States.   2. Evidence, Expert—United States.   I. Title.
  KF8968.15.P74 2014
  347.73'67—dc23
                                                                      2014007535

Printed in the United States of America

10 9 8 7 6 5 4 3 2 1

Dedicated to my wife, Lois, and my children, Heather and Cameron, with thanks to the many great professionals I have worked with over the course of my career.

Contents

PART III: FINANCIAL EXPERT WITNESS REPORTS AND TESTIMONY

Disclaimer

T HIS BOOK WAS WRITTEN TO serve as a nonauthoritative educational resource for nonattorney financial experts retained to assist with U.S.-based civil litigation or alternative dispute resolution proceedings. It is based on the author's experience as a business professional, Certified Public Accountant, and financial forensic specialist. The author is not an attorney and is unqualified to provide legal advice or opinions. Therefore, nothing in this book should be considered, construed, or referenced in any way as legal advice or opinion, or as a substitute for the financial expert's professional judgment.

The author designed this material to assist the financial expert to provide useful and appropriate communication in connection with commercial disputes and civil actions to be resolved through U.S. civil litigation or alternative dispute resolution. Nonfinancial experts and others may also find this book helpful in connection with business disputes, criminal proceedings, or the communication of matters to boards of directors, corporate officers, or regulatory authorities.

Caution should be exercised when considering the relevance, applicability, and appropriateness of using the author's approaches, methods, procedures, and practices, as there may be significant differences between his experiences and your own. Assignments, professional services, facts and circumstances, and jurisdictional and forum rules, among other matters of importance, may differ significantly from those described in this book. Accordingly, financial experts and others are encouraged to seek the advice of legal counsel when performing services intended for use in U.S. civil litigation or alternative dispute resolution.

1. Accounting pronouncements:
   This book is based on general concepts and terms, is not a comprehensive analysis of the subject matter covered, and is subject to change in part because any existing or proposed accounting and other literature summarized herein may be amended or may change before being issued in

final form. The views and interpretations expressed in the book are those of the author, and the book is not intended to provide accounting or other advice or guidance with respect to the matters covered. All relevant facts and circumstances, including the pertinent authoritative literature, need to be considered to arrive at appropriate conclusions. Accordingly, this book should not be used as a basis for any decision or action that may affect the reader's business. Neither the author nor Grant Thornton LLP or its affiliates or related entities shall be responsible for any loss sustained by any person or entity relying on this book. For additional information on the matters covered in this book, contact an appropriately qualified professional.

2. Tax pronouncements:

Tax professional standards statement

This book supports Grant Thornton LLP's marketing of professional services and is not written tax advice directed at the particular facts and circumstances of any person. If you are interested in the subject of this book, we encourage you to contact us or an independent tax adviser to discuss the potential application to your particular situation. Nothing herein shall be construed as imposing a limitation on any person from disclosing the tax treatment or tax structure of any matter addressed herein. To the extent this book may be considered to contain written tax advice, any written advice contained in this book is not intended by Grant Thornton LLP to be used, and cannot be used, by any person for the purpose of avoiding penalties that may be imposed under the Internal Revenue Code.

Supplemental tax disclaimer

The information contained herein is general in nature and is based on authorities that are subject to change. It is not, and should not be construed as, accounting, legal, or tax advice provided by Grant Thornton LLP to the reader. This material may not be applicable to, or suitable for, the reader's specific circumstances or needs and may require consideration of tax and nontax factors not described herein. Contact Grant Thornton LLP or other tax professionals prior to taking any action based upon this information. Changes in tax laws or other factors could affect, on a prospective or retroactive basis, the information contained herein; Grant Thornton LLP assumes no obligation to inform the reader of any such changes.

Foreword

THE PAGES THAT FOLLOW ARE the product of Mr. Preber's 30-plus years of experience as an expert witness and reflect his unique ability to both walk the walk and talk the talk. While many professionals possess the requisite intellectual firepower to qualify them as experts, it's Mr. Preber's rare combination of intellect, poise, grace under fire, professionalism, and the ability to communicate complex concepts, facts, and analysis in simple, easily understandable terms that sets him apart.

As one of the lead Department of Justice attorneys defending the largest class action ever filed against the United States, with damages estimated in the billions, I was responsible for identifying and hiring the experts who would perform the data analysis, provide the forensics, testify, and otherwise assist the United States and, more important, the court in navigating the complexities of the case. The complaint raised myriad issues involving allegations of breach of fiduciary duty stemming from more than a century of accounting and other alleged financial mismanagement. The data sets and other documents necessary to defend the case, to the extent they existed, were voluminous, were strewn across the country, and few, if any, were available electronically. Anticipating the issues that could arise required us to undertake an analysis that only Rube Goldberg could appreciate.

The process of identifying potential experts was itself daunting, but was one of the most important decisions we had to make in those early stages of the case. When we were ready, or so we thought, we began interviewing dozens of prospective experts. One group stood out from the rest for one principal reason: There was a person on that team who, no matter what we said or what we assumed, kept challenging us. Initially, I didn't fully appreciate Mr. Preber's tenacity, but after each conversation, interview, and restless night struggling with trying to make some sense of it all, I came to the realization that Mr. Preber's intellect, diligence, and his relentlessness in asking again and again "why" was what would, at the end of the day, cause us to hire his team as our experts and would make him an invaluable member of our defense team and a lifelong friend. Through that case, which started nearly two decades ago in 1996, Mr. Preber drove home one of the most important lessons I've learned in my career: you can't get to *how* unless you know *why*.

There are hundreds of how-to books available on the market on topics ranging from how to read financial statements to how to write a winning Supreme Court brief. My observation is many of these so-called expert treatises are filled with clichés and lack useful, practical guidance. This book is different. Each chapter starts with an overview that puts the concepts that follow in context. Each concept is then broken down into its core elements with a concise explanation of each element. Throughout, Mr. Preber explains not just the "how" but the "why" of each concept. The reader is left with an understanding of not only what is required of a successful financial expert and those who support him or her, but why those things are critical to the expert's, and ultimately his or her client's, success.

Beyond a guide for financial experts, this book is a must-read for attorneys who engage financial experts. Mr. Preber's insights, drawn from years of experience in working with attorneys, good and bad, provide a peek behind the curtain of how successful experts prepare, how they work to maximize value, and how they strive to work in partnership with their clients and the court. Mr. Preber's outlines, checklists, and templates for preparing an expert report, deposing financial experts, presenting testimony at trial and for cross-examination, among others, are a must read (and follow) for every attorney, no matter how accomplished one is in his or her career. This book has already become a critical reference guide that occupies a portion of the precious real estate on the corner of my desk, less than an arm's length away.

Lewis S. Wiener
Chair, Financial Services Litigation Group
Member, Executive Committee
Sutherland Asbill & Brennan LLP
Washington, DC

Lewis Wiener, a corporate defense attorney with more than 25 years of trial and advocacy experience, leads Sutherland Asbill & Brennan LLP's Financial Services Litigation Team and serves as a member of the firm's executive committee. Mr. Wiener's extensive civil litigation and trial experience includes serving as class-action defense counsel and arbitration counsel, conducting large internal investigations, handling complex litigation matters, and defending entities in connection with investigations and enforcement actions brought by government agencies. Mr. Wiener was a decorated former trial lawyer with the U.S. Department of Justice, twice recognized by the attorney general for special achievement in the handling of significant litigation matters on behalf of the United States. Mr. Wiener was the lead government counsel in the largest class action ever filed against the United States.

Preface

THIS BOOK WAS WRITTEN FOR practitioners having specialized expertise in, without limitation, accounting, auditing, economics, digital forensics, finance, financial forensics, taxation, and valuation, and who are planning on providing, or are currently providing, services in connection with formal litigation or alternative dispute resolution. For ease of reference, I refer to these professionals as financial experts, regardless of whether they serve as expert consultants or expert witnesses. The design of the book is to inform the financial expert about the many things that financial experts learn from the school of hard knocks. In other words, this book alerts the financial expert to the mistakes that I, and others I have observed, have made in the past and the resultant lessons learned. As such, this book is not fraught with technical seriousness and formalities. Instead, it is a book of anecdotal wisdom presented in a casual, accessible way.

The text has been organized into four parts. Part One is entitled "Dispute Resolution and the Financial Expert." This part of the book provides an overview of U.S. civil litigation and explains how to get engaged, start work, and create value in litigation and alternative dispute resolution. Part Two, "Financial Expert Witness Rules, Case Precedent, and Ethics," covers the federal rules regarding expert reporting and testimony. In addition, it sets out a number of cases potentially important to the financial expert witness and professional ethics. Part Three dives into the heart of this book, "Financial Expert Witness Reporting and Testimony." This part of the book provides practical tips and pointers for the financial expert witness related to expert reports and testimony. "Part Four, Alternative Dispute Resolution Services," explains the provision of services in mediation, arbitration, and neutral decision-making proceedings.

PART I

Part I of this book includes five chapters. Chapter 1 attempts to explain the reasons why a financial expert would want to serve as a consultant or expert witness in litigation or alternative dispute resolution. To do this, it describes the value created by the financial expert in the dispute resolution process. Chapter 2 identifies and explains the roles suited for the financial expert when serving as a consultant or expert witness. Chapter 3 provides insights into the identification and retention of the financial expert. Chapter 4 covers getting started as a financial expert. Chapter 5 provides an overview of the U.S. civil litigation process.

 PART II

There are four chapters in Part II. Chapter 6 outlines the Federal Rules of Evidence followed by Chapter 7 on the Federal Rules of Civil Procedure. A number of case studies are included in these chapters to reinforce the meaning of the rules. Chapter 8 gives the financial expert basic knowledge about laws and other rules applicable to the financial expert witness. This chapter includes the *Daubert v. Merrell Dow Pharmaceuticals* and *Kumho Tire Co. v. Carmichael* cases, plus a description of reasonable certainty. Chapter 9 is a summary of the professional ethics obligations attached to the financial expert providing services for litigation or alternative dispute resolution.

 PART III

"Financial Expert Witness Reporting and Testimony," Part III of this book, is made up of nine chapters. Chapter 10 concerns the preparation of the financial expert witness report. It provides practical advice toward the goal of writing a compliant and effective expert report. Chapter 11 covers the task of rebutting an opposing expert witness' report. Chapter 12 digs more deeply into litigation discovery, describing financial expert witness deposition. Chapter 13 helps the financial expert witness prepare for deposition. Chapter 14 gives practical counsel on financial expert witness deposition testimony. Shifting gears slightly, Chapter 15 describes financial expert witness involvement in motions and hearings. Chapter 16 moves into financial expert witness trial testimony, while Chapter 17 focuses on direct examination and Chapter 18 is dedicated to cross-examination.

PART IV

The final part of this book consists of three chapters on alternative dispute resolution. Chapter 19 is a summary of mediation. Chapter 20 covers arbitration proceedings. Finally, Chapter 21 describes the financial expert's role serving as a neutral accounting arbitrator.

 WHAT IS YOUR STORY?

The objective of this book is to share practical knowledge about financial experts serving clients in litigation or alternative dispute resolution. To communicate this knowledge, subject matter seldom taught by formal education or training is identified and explained. In essence, this book acknowledges that personal experience is one of the best ways to learn how to effectively communicate in connection with dispute resolution services. However, practical knowledge on this subject doesn't end with the few topics covered here. The story continues with your own individual experiences, mistakes, and observations. So, what is your story?

Acknowledgments

No one who achieves success does so without acknowledging the help of others. The wise and confident acknowledge this help with gratitude.

—*Alfred North Whitehead*

T HERE ARE MANY TO THANK for the practical tips and techniques expressed in this book. Learning how to serve sophisticated clients, with world-class legal counsel, in a dispute setting largely comes from real-life experience. There are few books or educational opportunities available to teach what can be learned on the job. That adds significance to the people engaging and supporting you in this business. I am blessed to have had great people guiding my career and caring about my success. For this, I am truly grateful.

Foremost, to my friends and family, thanks for your patience, understanding, and acceptance of the time and effort needed to serve clients in dispute resolution. You were often on my mind and always in my heart. Special thanks to my wife, Lois Preber, and my two children, Dr. Heather Preber and Cameron Preber. I also wish to thank my mother, Mary Preber, my aunt, Jeanette Verre, my mother-in law, Elizabeth Cowper, sisters-in-law, Ann and Carolyn Cowper, and in-laws Nancy and Ralph Trevino. To my dearest friends, and you know who you are, thanks for listening to my stories and offering unconditional support. For John Blumberg, you have always inspired me with your caring way and values-driven life. Thanks for the life compass.

The professional experience earned in order to write such a book comes from the many opportunities afforded me by my clients and the talented attorneys who represent them. Thank you for the vote of confidence expressed each time you engaged me. Also, thank you for the chance to learn from so many exceptional professionals. Quality clients and legal counsel made service an honor and pleasure.

Of course, the support and technical talent of my Grant Thornton LLP partners and principals, present and former, assured that my personal shortcomings were minimized and client success reigned triumphant. I would like to thank Stephen Chipman, Grant Thornton LLP's CEO, for supporting quality, learning, and innovation expressed through a set of global values. Steve Lukens, the national managing principal of Grant Thornton LLP's Advisory Services, saw the value of this practical guidance to the profession. Many of my Forensics and Valuation Services partners and principals assisted with quality assurance. I am humbled by their skill and grateful for their partnership and "one firm" spirit. In particular, Ed O'Brien was always there to lend a helping hand—he has been a true partner and friend. A special shout-out to Larry Redler, a retired former partner and boss. He showed me that a sense of humor, mixed with encouragement and trust, can make a tough job a little easier.

Thanks also to the Grant Thornton LLP Risk, Regulatory, and Legal Affairs team for keeping me out of trouble with all the legal terminology included in this book. I work often with this group of exceptionally talented attorneys and staff and have never been disappointed by their professionalism and candor.

There is also a group of professionals in the Grant Thornton LLP Phoenix office who deserve recognition. I personally recruited, trained, and nurtured this group. In turn, they made sure the work was top-shelf and beyond reproach. This is a special team of professionals with enormous talent. So, hats off to Mike Fahlman, now my partner at Grant Thornton LLP; Meredith Murphy; Holly Daetwyler; Eric Lee; Zachary Snickles; and Fran Procopio. Of course, there are many others who work with me now, or have in the past, for which I am thankful and eternally appreciative.

My wife is a teacher by profession. Therefore, I could not write an acknowledgment without expressing my sincere appreciation to the many teachers and professors that touched my life. Their caring way and dedication to education sparked lifelong learning that burns as a bonfire for me every day. In particular, thanks to professors John Yeakel and Perry Mori from the University of New Mexico. They were tough but fair, just like life should be.

Finally, I want to thank my profession for a wide range of career opportunities, outstanding peers, and an unparalleled standard of professional excellence. In particular, the American Institute of Certified Public Accountants has been a go-to organization for my professional development, peer interaction, and connection to the profession.

PART ONE

Dispute Resolution and the Financial Expert

CHAPTER ONE

Value of the Financial Expert in Litigation and Dispute Resolution

 WHY BE A FINANCIAL EXPERT WITNESS?

Before reading any further in this book, you must be able to answer this question: Why do I want to be a financial expert witness? For those of you who do not aspire to be a testifying expert witness, this is still the ultimate question as you will likely be supporting someone who will be serving as a financial expert witness. Serving as a financial expert witness, or as a consultant assisting one, is a stressful, challenging, and tough business.

The financial expert witness will be in the public eye, with his or her personal and professional life exposed for the world to see. Personal opinions will be used to assist a trier of fact to decide important disputes. In some cases, those decisions impact the survival of an enterprise, future rights, or the livelihood of others. Let's not forget grueling deadlines, incomplete data sets, and irrational adversarial disputing parties.

The quality of the financial expert witness's work product is paramount, as it will be critiqued by opposing experts and attorneys who will be dedicated to finding ways to exclude your opinions. If successful, it could adversely impact the financial expert's ability to get engaged as an expert witness in the future, depending on the reasons the testimony was deemed inadmissible. The cherry on top—the financial expert witness is often the last witness to testify at the end of an arduous trial.

But, for the financial expert witness such great responsibilities come with great rewards. Serving as an expert witness is an important role in our society. Expert witnesses are specifically provided for by federal civil litigation rules. Expert witnesses provide necessary assistance to triers of fact to allow them to make well-informed determinations outside their own personal expertise and experience. That is critical for the disputing parties to have a fair trial.

Serving as a financial expert witness also recognizes personal professional expertise. Being qualified as an expert by the court is official recognition of your professional skills, knowledge, education, experience, and training in your field. It is an affirmation that you possess superior expertise compared to the average citizen in your chosen profession. This may enhance your ability to be retained in the future and is a justification to charge premium rates for financial expert witness services.

VALUE OF THE FINANCIAL EXPERT WITNESS UNDER FEDERAL RULES

Fortunately for all expert witnesses, including financial expert witnesses, the Federal Rules of Evidence (FRE) and Federal Rules of Civil Procedure (FRCP) describe the value of an expert witness in a federal case.[1] The FRE and FRCP are the official guidance for civil litigation proceedings adopted by the federal courts and numerous state jurisdictions. Among other matters, the federal rules govern expert witness testimony and admissibility. The financial expert witness should be familiar with the FRE and FRCP when performing dispute resolution services in a federal setting.

Under the FRE, Rule 702, Testimony by Expert Witnesses, a qualified expert must have "scientific, technical, or other specialized knowledge" obtained "by knowledge, skill, experience, training, or education" that will "help the trier of fact to understand the evidence or to determine a fact in issue." Based on this rule, the federal courts are instructed to value the qualifications of financial expert witnesses because they possess technical and specialized knowledge that may be helpful to the trier of fact when making decisions about disputed issues. For financial expert witnesses, that means undergraduate and advanced degrees in accounting, finance, economics, and other areas have value. In addition, professional credentials, like Certified Public Accountant or Chartered

Financial Analyst, are valuable, together with the continuing education these designations typically require. Last, but certainly not least, the courts recognize the value of financial expert witnesses' experience serving clients, the profession, and the community.

Examples of Valued Financial Expert Credentials

- Advanced education degrees
- American Academy of Financial Management:
  - Chartered Wealth Manager (CWM)
  - Chartered Asset Manager (CAM)
  - Chartered Trust and Estate Planner (CTEP)
  - Chartered Portfolio Manager (CPM)
- American Institute of Certified Public Accountants:
  - Certified Public Accountant (CPA)
  - Certified in Financial Forensics (CFF)
  - Accredited in Business Valuation (ABV)
- American Society of Appraisers:
  - Accredited Senior Appraiser (ASA)
- Appraisal Institute:
  - Member Appraisal Institute (MAI)
- Association of Anti-Money-Laundering Specialists:
  - Certified Anti-Money-Laundering Specialist (CAMS)
- Association of Certified Fraud Examiners:
  - Certified Fraud Examiner (CFE)
- Association of Insolvency and Restructuring Advisors:
  - Certified Insolvency and Restructuring Advisor (CIRA)
- Certified Financial Planner Board of Standards:
  - Certified Financial Planner (CFP)
- Chartered Financial Analysts Institute:
  - Chartered Financial Analyst (CFA)
- Institute of Internal Auditors:
  - Certified Internal Auditor (CIA)
- Institute of Management Accountants:
  - Certified Management Accountant (CMA)
- Information Systems Audit and Control Association:
  - Certified information Systems Auditor (CISA)
- National Association of Certified Valuators and Analysts:
  - Accredited Valuation Analyst (AVA)
  - Certified Valuation Analyst (CVA)

The FRE, Rule 702, allows expert witnesses to testify in trial only if their testimony is "based on sufficient facts or data" and "is the product of reliable principles and methods" that the financial expert witness "has reliably applied . . . to the facts of the case." As such, the federal courts value financial expert witnesses' abilities to understand and identify relevant case evidence, especially accounting, financial, and economic facts and data commonly dealt with by the financial expert. Also valued are reliable and generally accepted principles and methods used by financial expert witnesses to analyze relevant financial facts and data. Industry standards, such as generally accepted accounting principles, and audit and valuation standards, are frequently accepted by the courts as reliable principles and methods for use in trial. Furthermore, courts have acknowledged that many of the procedures used by financial expert witnesses in the normal course of business are reliable methods that can be used to review and analyze relevant facts and data in a case. Procedures commonly used by financial expert witnesses include, but are not limited to, the following:

- Analytical tests
- Budgeting
- Compliance and control tests
- Comparative financial and ratio analysis
- Corroboration
- Data analytics
- Examinations
- Financial modeling
- Forecasting
- Inspection
- Interviews
- Inquiries
- Observations
- Projections
- Recalculations
- Reconciliations
- Regression analysis
- Reperformance
- Research
- Statistics
- Substantive tests

Turning now to the FRCP, it is clear that the federal courts also value the communication talents of financial expert witnesses. Under FRCP, Rule 26(b)

(4)(A), financial expert witnesses are required to produce "a written report— prepared and signed by the expert." After submission of the written expert report, an opposing party "may depose any person who has been identified as an expert whose opinions may be presented at trial."[2] During the trial, financial expert witnesses are required to orally testify about their opinions and the bases for them if called to do so. Obviously, financial expert witnesses with effective written and oral communication skills will be more valuable to the trier of fact and the client.

Professional Standards and Value

As professionals, financial expert witnesses hold themselves to a higher standard of behavior and performance than an amateur or average layperson. In many cases, through professional affiliation and membership, financial expert witnesses are bound to adhere to professional standards governing acceptable behavior and service delivery. For example, the American Institute of Certified Public Accountants, the largest industry membership organization for CPAs, promulgates professional standards of conduct through a codification of professional standards. Adherence to professional standards governing professional services is valuable to clients and triers of fact because it evidences conformance to generally accepted industry requirements for the standard of professional due care, quality, ethics, integrity, and objectivity, among other matters.

The courts recognize the importance of professional standards toward meeting the FRE, Rule 702, requirements related to expert testimony. Triers of fact may also find such standards compelling when assessing the qualifications and reliability of financial expert witness testimony. Clients understand this value and often seek to engage financial experts whose work will be performed in compliance with professional standards. For these reasons, the adherence to professional standards adds value to the work of financial expert witnesses.

Value Perceptions and the Financial Expert Witness

The perceived value of financial expert witnesses' technical, specialty, and communication skills was validated in a study entitled the *Characteristics and Skills of the Forensic Accountant* sponsored by the American Institute of Certified Public Accountants (AICPA).[3] Although this study was designed to solicit feedback related to CPAs serving as financial expert witnesses, it is instructive to others. In this study prepared by two professors at California State University and the Managing Partner of Ueltzen & Company, LLP, a public accounting firm, forensic accountants'[4] areas of specialty, traits, characteristics, and skills were assessed by three constituencies: (1) attorneys, (2) academics, and

(3) Certified Public Accountants (CPAs). A summary of the AICPA study can be found in Exhibit 1.1.

Related to areas of specialty, attorneys ranked "financial statement misrepresentations" as the number one specialty, followed by "economic damages calculations," "fraud prevention, detection, and response," and "valuation." Academia ranked "fraud prevention, detection, and response" first, with "computer forensic analysis" second. "Economic damages calculations" and "valuation" were next in line. In line with academia, CPAs chose "fraud prevention, detection, and response," "economic damages calculations," and "valuation" as the top areas of specialty needed. CPAs selected "financial statement misrepresentations" as the fourth-ranked specialty. Using these results, it is clear that financial expert witnesses should pay attention to "financial statement misrepresentations," "economic damages calculations," "fraud prevention, detection, and response," and "valuation" as areas of specialty driving the potential value of financial expert witnesses.

As for traits and characteristics, the AICPA Study reported that attorneys, academics, and CPAs all believed "analytical" was the number one trait and characteristic for a forensic accountant to have. Following this, attorneys responded the top traits to be "detail-oriented," "ethical," "responsive," and "insightful." Academics thought "ethical," "skepticism," "inquisitive," and "persistent" were important beyond being "analytical." CPAs placed "inquisitive," detail-oriented," "ethical," and "persistent" after "analytical" in the rankings of traits and characteristics. Therefore, to create value, financial expert witnesses should at a minimum be analytical, ethical, and detail-oriented, traits and characteristics that attorneys, academics, and CPAs all agree are important.

The perception of core skills needed by the forensic accountant varied among attorneys, academics, and CPAs, except "critical/strategic thinker" and possessing "investigative ability," which all constituents ranked in the top five. The number one skill attorneys want a forensic accountant to have is the ability to be an "effective oral communicator." In addition, attorneys responded that they need the skills to "simplify the information" and "identify key issues" using "auditing skills." Academia agrees that "auditing skills" are critical, but also thinks forensic accountants need to "synthesize results of discovery and analysis" and "think like the wrongdoer." CPAs seemed a bit out of sync with attorneys and academics on this topic, selecting "effective written communication" and "investigative intuitiveness" as required core skills. Regardless, if financial expert witnesses are going to create value in the litigation and dispute resolution process, they must be critical/strategic thinkers with investigative

Areas of specialty needed	Attorneys	Academics	CPAs
Financial statement misrepresentations?	1	1	4
Economic damages calculations	2	3	2
Fraud prevention, detection, and response	3	1	1
Valuation	4	4	3
Essential traits and characteristics	**Attorneys**	**Academic**	**CPA**
Analytical	1	1	1
Detail-oriented	2		3
Ethical	3	2	3
Responsive	4		
Insightful	5		
Inquisitive		4	2
Intuitive			5
Persistent		5	
Skeptical		3	4
Core skills	**Attorneys**	**Academic**	**CPA**
Effective oral communicator	1		3
Simplify the information	2		
Critical/strategic thinker	3	1	1
Identify key issues	4		
Auditing skills	5	2	
Investigative ability	5	3	4
Effective written communicator			2
Investigative intuitiveness			5
Synthesize results of discovery and analysis		4	
Think like the wrongdoer		5	
Enhanced skills	**Attorneys**	**Academic**	**CPA**
Analyze and interpret financial statements and information	1	3	1
Testifying	2		4
Knowledge of relevant professional standards	3	5	
Audit evidence	4		
Fraud detection	4	1	3
Asset tracing	5		
Electronic discovery		4	
General knowledge of rules of evidence and civil procedure		4	5
Interviewing skills		2	2

EXHIBIT 1.1 AICPA Study

Source: Davis, Charles, Ramona Farrell, and Suzanne Ogilby. "Characteristics and Skills of the Forensic Accountant." AICPA FVS Section 2010, accessed January 3, 2014, www.aicpa.org/InterestAreas/ForensicAndValuation/Resources/PractAidsGuidance/DownloadableDocuments/ForensicAccountingResearchWhitePaper.pdf.

abilities that can simplify information using effective communication, especially oral communication.

The AICPA Study also inquired about the enhanced skills necessary for the forensic accountant to possess. All constituents, attorneys, academics, and CPAs agreed that the forensic accountant must be able to "analyze and interpret financial statements and information" and assist with "fraud detection." Attorneys also perceived the enhanced skills of "testifying," "having knowledge of relevant professional standards," the use of "audit evidence," and "asset tracing" as important. Academics rated "testifying" and "audit evidence" lower than attorneys, leaning more toward "electronic discovery," "general knowledge of rules of evidence and civil procedure," and "interviewing skills" as critical for the forensic accountant. CPAs selected the same enhanced skills as attorneys and academics, but ranked them differently. CPAs ordered enhanced traits needed by the forensic accountant to be "analyze and interpret financial statements and information," "interviewing skills," "fraud detection," "testifying," and "general knowledge of rules of evidence and civil procedure." In most cases, the enhanced skills needed from financial expert witnesses to provide value to the client and the trier of fact will align with the responses of CPAs in the AICPA Study.

The Financial Expert as Teacher

One of the best ways to add value in your role as an expert witness is to approach and deliver oral and written testimony as if you were an effective teacher. Each of us can recall a special teacher in our lives, one who made learning interesting, engaging, and memorable. The financial expert witness often tries to capture the magic between a great teacher and his or her class when testifying to a judge or jury.

Of course, great teachers share some common traits that can be studied and replicated by the expert witness. Personally, I have observed that effective teachers are prepared, dynamic, empathetic, positive, and energetic people who truly enjoy what they do. They have a knack for storytelling and use analogies and demonstratives to reinforce key concepts and make them memorable. In addition, effective teachers are students themselves, constantly seeking new information and ways to teach.

An effective teacher (i.e., the expert witness) knows the subject matter to be taught, together with the teaching techniques best suited for student (i.e., judge or jury) learning. The great teacher is ready, willing, and able to explain difficult and complex matters in a clear, concise, and easy-to-understand way, often using stories, examples, analogies, visual aids, and anecdotes to make matters approachable and understandable. They also never forget what it is like to be a student learner (i.e., *juror*) and use this empathy to craft relevant teaching techniques and methods.

Learning objectives (i.e., what the financial expert witness wants the judge or jury to learn and remember) are made clear by the teacher and reinforced throughout the learning experience. At times, it may be necessary for the teacher to provide the learner with: (1) context by describing past, present, and expected future states; (2) contrast by introducing differing theories, or (3) comparison by showing concepts from related fields.

Effective teachers display true enjoyment about what they do. By their human nature, great teachers are dynamic and enthusiastic people who ooze self-confidence. To student learners, this positive and energetic way can act as a magnet for attention and a catalyst for memories. Like effective teachers, financial expert witnesses also must be passionate about their profession and assignments and be able to confidently and appropriately show that passion through their testimony.

An effective teacher (and testifying financial expert witness) is also a talented speaker who can tell when others are not following along or understanding the material. Concerned about the quality of instruction, an effective teacher stimulates the audience using variations in pace, gestures, and other communication methods. This means finding a way to connect with each juror or the judge during testimony. This can be accomplished by using appropriate eye contact, displaying a relaxed and open body frame, and responding to noticeable lapses in attention with changes in vocal pace and tone. Perhaps this concept is best expressed by this quote from Benjamin Franklin:

Tell me and I forget, teach me and I may remember, involve me and I learn.

—*Benjamin Franklin*

The Seven Cs of Financial Expert Value

It may be helpful to remember the keys to a financial expert's value in litigation and dispute resolution by using the seven Cs, which consist of (1) competence, (2) credibility, (3) compliance, (4) creativity, (5) care, (6) confidence, and (7) convincing. Each of these words has deep and far-reaching meanings beyond the obvious.

Competence refers to the qualifications of the financial expert witness to accept and faithfully, professionally, and successfully complete litigation and

The Seven Cs of Value

1. Competence
2. Credibility
3. Compliance
4. Creativity
5. Care
6. Confidence
7. Convincing

dispute resolution assignments. Competence relates to the financial expert witness's skills, knowledge, education, experience, and training, together with the personal talent and necessary resources required to responsibly do the work in a professional manner.

Credibility is earned by the financial expert witness. It requires the financial expert witness to be unbiased, objective, and intellectually independent, in fact and appearance. In addition, credibility refers to the character traits of personal integrity and trustworthiness. Credibility is also dependent on competence and due care.

Compliance with laws, rules, policies, and professional standards is critical for the financial expert witness's testimony to be deemed admissible. Therefore, it is essential that the financial expert witness be knowledgeable about relevant civil laws, rules, and regulations, and professional standards applicable to the financial expert witness. This includes an awareness of statutory requirements related to allowable civil claim relief and damages, which can vary based on the type of dispute and be influenced by case precedence. It is also important to understand and comply with local rules for jurisdictional and courtroom processes and the individual preferences of each presiding judge.

Creativity recognizes that the financial expert witness has been engaged to do what the client cannot do himself or herself—provide out-of-the-box thinking on complex disputes. It requires sharing the financial expert witness's unique thought processes in the form of business advice, methods for effective communication (visual and oral), and solutions to issues and problems. Creativity can build value that sets the financial expert witness apart from others participating in litigation and dispute resolution.

Care is a direct reference to the exercise of due professional care by the financial expert witness. It includes a dedication to quality and accuracy. It also encompasses confidentiality. A well-known legal treatise defines professional due care as:

> Every man who offers his services to another and is employed assumes the duty to exercise in the employment such skill as he possesses with reasonable care and diligence. In all these employments where peculiar skill is requisite, if one offers his services, he is understood as holding himself out to the public as possessing the degree of skill commonly possessed by others in the same employment, and if his pretentions are unfounded, he commits a species of fraud upon every man who employs him in reliance on his public profession. But no man, whether skilled or unskilled, undertakes that the task he assumes shall be performed successfully, and without fault or error; he undertakes for good faith and integrity, but not for infallibility, and he is liable to his employer for negligence, bad faith, or dishonesty, but not for losses consequent upon pure errors of judgment.[5]

Confidence is to have a strong, assured belief in yourself and the certainty of your opinions. The financial expert witness must be an advocate for his or her opinions—not an advocate for the client or the client's positions. Confidence is markedly different from arrogance. One way to reinforce the difference between the two is to remember the following saying:

> Confidence is believing you have something to teach. Arrogance is believing you have nothing to learn.[6]

To be **convincing** is to master the art of persuasive communication. The financial expert witness must be able to get others to believe that his or her opinions are true, right, and reliable. Of course, the financial expert witness is most convincing when he or she has followed the other six of the seven Cs.

 ## ENHANCING VALUE USING THE LITIGATION PROCESS

Clearly there are many ways financial experts can add value to the litigation and dispute resolution process. However, there are inefficiencies built into the process that may adversely impact the effectiveness of the financial expert.

The American Institute of Public Accountants (AICPA)[7] established a task force to study these issues. The AICPA Study revealed five recommendations to "maximize both the effectiveness of financial experts and efficiency of their use in the civil pretrial process":[8]

1. Judges should implement early and consistent active case management;
2. Clients and attorneys should involve experts early in the process;
3. Attorneys should target, focus, and streamline expert depositions and discovery;
4. Attorney's *Daubert*-like challenges should be appropriately targeted and acted on promptly by the court; and
5. Attorneys and the court should develop a process for the collaboration and cooperation of opposing experts where appropriate.

 ## COMING UP

Chapter 2 addresses important matters related to the retention of the financial expert.

 ## NOTES

1. Federal Rules of Evidence, December 1, 2013, available at www.uscourts .gov/uscourts/rules/rules-evidence.pdf and Federal Rules of Civil Procedure, December 1, 2013, available at www.uscourts.gov/uscourts/rules/civil-pro cedure.pdf.
2. FRCP, Rule 26(b)(4)(A), TITLE V, DISCLOSURES AND DISCOVERY, Discovery Scope and Limits, Trial Preparation; Experts, Deposition of an Expert Who May Testify.
3. AICPA, *Characteristics and Skills of the Forensic Accountant* (2010), available at www.aicpa.org/interestareas/forensicandvaluation/resources/practaidsguid ance/downloadabledocuments/forensicaccountingresearchwhitepaper.pdf.
4. As used in this study, a "forensic accountant" is defined similarly to a financial expert witness as used in this text.
5. D. Haggard, *Cooley on Torts*, 4th ed. (1932), 472.
6. "True arrogance is the belief that you have nothing left to learn, while true confidence is the belief that you can help others to learn as you continue learning yourself." Michael Haberman, *Arrogant versus Confident*, quoting Alan Weiss, available at http://omegahrsolutions.com/2012/05/arrogant-versus-confident.html.

7. The AICPA is "the world's largest association representing the accounting profession." AICPA, *Another Voice: Financial Experts on Reducing Client Costs in Civil Litigation* (2013), available at www.aicpa.org/interestareas/forensican dvaluation/newsandpublications/advocacy/downloadabledocuments/finan cial-experts-on-reducing-client-costs%20in-civil-litigation.pdf.

8. Ibid.

CHAPTER TWO

Roles Suited for the Financial Expert

THE "BIG THREE": LIABILITY, CAUSATION, AND DAMAGES

In civil disputes to be resolved by formal litigation or alternative dispute resolution, such as mediation or arbitration, there are three areas that the financial expert witness may be asked to take on as assignments. They are liability, causation, and damages—the "Big Three" as listed in the sidebar. All three must be legally proven for monetary damages to be awarded to an injured party.

> **The Big Three Areas for Financial Expert Testimony**
> 1. Liability
> 2. Causation
> 3. Damages

Liability

Civil liability is the legal determination that a party is responsible or accountable to another party for an injury caused by the first party's wrongful act or omission. Typically, the responsible party is required to pay damages for the harm that it caused. In some cases, there are obligations other than damages, such as injunctions requiring or restraining certain parties' actions. In layman's terms, civil liability attaches when one party is to blame for causing harm to someone else. In legal terms, liability requires proof that the responsible party committed a wrongful act or omission that was the proximate cause of a harm or injury. In civil disputes, the plaintiff has the burden of proof, which is established by a preponderance of the evidence.

Liability is an "ultimate" issue that must be determined by the trier of fact, who could be either the judge or a jury. The financial expert witness will not be permitted to give an opinion on whether a party is liable, though he or she typically will be permitted in trial to explain an analysis of the financial evidence and to provide views on the potential significance of that evidence to the trier of fact related to liability. Often, the financial expert will be asked to opine on a factual question that is very closely related to the ultimate determination of liability, such as whether a party properly disclosed financial information in accordance with generally accepted accounting principles, or whether a disputed asset was accurately valued for purposes of a sale or financing transaction.

Causation

Legal causation is the bridge between civil liability and damages. It represents the relationship of cause (i.e., liability) and effect (i.e., harm resulting in damages). Legal causation is often best understood by applying the "but for" test. This test uses the words "but for" in a sentence to describe a causal factor. For example, the "but for" test might be expressed like this: "But for the fraud committed by Mr. Doe, Company A would not have suffered the loss of $1,000,000." The fraud committed by Mr. Doe in this example is the legal causation for the harm, or loss, to Company A that can be measured in monetary damages.

Causation shakes hands between a legal issue and economic reality. Like liability, the fact of causation is an ultimate issue for the trier of fact; but, to be directly linked to damages, causation must reasonably fit the economics of the case at hand. Similar to liability, the plaintiff carries the burden to prove causation. At times, the financial expert witness may be well suited to assist the trier of fact with causation issues. For example, the financial expert witness may be able to assist in the proving of losses caused by fraudulent acts.

The financial expert witness should not blindly accept requests to prepare an estimate of damages, typically made by the client attorney, wherein it is assumed that causation will be proven in trial. The linkage to economic realities must be evaluated. Causation assumptions divorced from reality are likely to raise serious challenges from opposing attorneys. Therefore, at a minimum, the financial expert witness should make inquiries and perform those procedures deemed necessary to determine that any causation assumptions are professionally reasonable.

Damages

Damages are the award of money by the court to an injured party in order to compensate for harm done by a liable party. If you will, it is the price tag on the dispute to compensate a damaged party and punish a wrongdoer. In general, damages are designed to place an injured party in the position they would have been in if the party liable had not committed the harmful act or omission. However, damages also can be nominal, compensatory, and/or punitive.

Nominal damages are just what they sound like, a small award of money by the court. Nominal damages acknowledge liability, but are typically awarded when an injured party is unable to prove a compensable loss under the law. Compensatory damages are monetary awards by the court for the direct and natural legal consequences of unlawful acts or omissions proven against a liable party. Punitive damages, or exemplary damages, are court-ordered awards over and above compensatory damages designed to punish a liable party and deter others from engaging in the same kind of unlawful activity.

 FINANCIAL EXPERT ASSIGNMENTS

Financial expert witnesses may be asked to consider assignments that involve disputed facts about the Big Three—liability, causation, and damages. Financial expert witnesses must be careful not to take on assignments to provide opinions on matters of law or the ultimate question of liability, which is the purview of the ultimate trier of fact. Unless the financial expert witness is a licensed attorney, he or she is not qualified to offer legal opinions, which are rarely proper in any event.

At times, the provision of professional opinions by financial expert witnesses requires careful consideration in order to prevent crossing the line into legal matters. Liability, causation, and damages combine to create a delicately balanced formula. Financial expert witnesses must understand this formula, and each of its components, in order to participate successfully in the dispute resolution process. To gain this understanding, financial expert witnesses should read the complaint, case pleadings, and court records. They should also discuss each case and related assignment with the client legal counsel. If the case involves a jury trial, the financial expert should understand the jury instructions that will be given on the issues relevant to the expert's expected testimony. The goal is to understand the causes of action, the governing legal standards, and the remedies available under the law.

By way of example, assume that a financial expert witness has been engaged to perform financial forensic procedures and to compute damages related to alleged fraudulent actions claimed in a complaint. In this case, the unlawful act is civil fraud. The financial expert witness should be careful not to overreach and offer any opinion on whether fraud occurred as a fact of law. That is a job for the trier of fact (i.e., the judge or jury). However, in most cases the financial expert witness would be allowed to testify at trial about financial forensic procedures performed and the evidence analyzed that provide the basis for the trier of fact to form opinions as to whether the results of such procedures and analyses indicate evidence of financial fraud.

ROLES FOR THE FINANCIAL EXPERT

Financial expert witnesses can serve in several different roles in connection with formal dispute resolution. Some of these roles are described by the Federal Rules of Civil Procedure (FRCP) and the Federal Rules of Evidence (FRE), while others are designed to meet the specific needs of each disputing party. Following are summarized descriptions of roles financial expert witnesses are commonly asked to take on in formal civil dispute resolution:

Financial Expert Roles

- Expert witness
- Expert consultant
- Lay (or fact) witness
- Percipient witness
- Neutral

- **Expert witness.** The FRCP describe an expert witness as "one retained or specially employed to provide expert testimony in the case or one whose duties as the party's employee regularly involve giving expert testimony."[1] In addition to the guidance provided by the FRCP, the FRE state "[i]f . . . scientific, technical or other specialized knowledge will help the trier of fact to understand evidence or to determine a fact in issue, a witness qualified as an expert by knowledge, skill, experience, training, or education, may testify in the form of an opinion or otherwise."[2] Financial expert witnesses are formally disclosed to the opposing party based on a schedule approved by the court.
- **Expert consultant.** Although not expansive, the FRCP describes an expert consultant as "an expert who has been retained or specially employed . . . in anticipation of litigation or to prepare for trial and who is not expected to be called as a witness at trial."[3]
- **Lay (or fact) witness.** The FRE describe a lay witness as one "not testifying as an expert" and whose "testimony in the form of an opinion is limited to one that is:
  (a) rationally based on the witness's perception,
  (b) helpful to a clear understanding of the witness's testimony or to determining a fact in issue, and
  (c) not based on scientific, technical, or other specialized knowledge within the scope of Rule 702."[4]
- **Percipient witness.** Percipient witnesses testify about first-hand perceptions of witnessed events. In layman terms, this is an eyewitness.
- **Neutral.** In some cases, like post-acquisition dispute resolution proceedings, financial experts may be retained by disputing parties to serve in a neutral fact-finding role (e.g., an independent arbitrator). In this role, the fact finder must be a disinterested party and impartial.

 ## MATTERS SUITED FOR THE FINANCIAL EXPERT

It is impractical to attempt to describe all the matters for which financial expert witnesses are well suited because each professional's qualifications and experiences vary. In general, technical or specialized knowledge shared by many financial expert witnesses includes the following subject areas:

- Accounting
- Auditing

- Damages
- Economics
- Finance
- Financial forensics
- Financial fraud, waste, and abuse
- Forensic data collection, processing, and analysis
- Statistics
- Taxation
- Valuation

There are a number of professional organizations that offer advanced specialization in these areas through certification programs. Professionals attaining such credentials are typically required to adhere to standards of performance, ethical behavior, and educational advancement. Technical knowledge concentrated into specialized subject areas are part of the qualifications needed to testify as a financial expert witness. Accordingly, financial expert witnesses should recognize these areas of specialized expertise and be able to articulate their value in oral testimony.

 ## FINANCIAL EXPERT LITIGATION SERVICES

Financial experts may be asked to provide services beyond the expected financial analysis, expert reporting, and oral testimony. In some cases, the financial expert is asked to assist the client with an assessment of potential claims and damages before a complaint is filed. In virtually every case, the financial expert will be asked to participate in discovery activities above and beyond the preparation of an expert report and attendance at deposition as an expert witness. It is not unusual for the financial expert to be asked to prepare support for certain motions, or to attend settlement discussions or hearings. Finally, financial experts may be requested to assist with post-settlement or post-trial activities, including the calculation of individual awards to beneficiaries.

Early Case Assessment and Complaint Drafting

Throughout the life cycle of litigation, there are a number of services that financial experts may be asked to provide. In ideal circumstances, financial experts are contacted in the early stages of a dispute, thereby allowing an early case assessment to be performed. Among other things, an early case assessment is used to estimate the time, cost, and level of effort expected for alternative courses of dispute resolution. Involvement of financial experts at the initial stages of a dispute may also provide the opportunity for financial experts to assist legal counsel with the drafting of the complaint by identifying and validating facts, and preparing preliminary estimates of possible monetary damages. However, just to be clear and practical, it is uncommon for financial experts to be retained before a complaint is filed.

Financial Expert Litigation Services

- Early case assessment
- Complaint drafting
- Discovery
- Motions
- Hearings
- Settlement
- Trial preparation
- Trial
- Post-trial

Discovery

In most cases, the majority of the work performed by financial experts occurs during discovery. During discovery, facts and materials relevant to the dispute are identified, requested, and produced. Discovery is also the time when financial experts conduct analyses of produced materials and perform any research needed to provide the bases to form opinions in the case. Financial experts play an important role in this process due to their specialized technical knowledge about sources of financial evidence and the weight that can reliably be afforded differing types of such evidence. Therefore, financial experts may be asked to assist the client legal counsel with the drafting of interrogatories and production requests to be delivered to an opposing party. Conversely, financial experts may be directed to assist legal counsel with responses to interrogatories and requests for production received, including the identification and production of relevant electronic data—a process often referred to as e-discovery.

Under the federal rules, prescribed expert witness information is required to be disclosed in writing to an opposing party. Usually, this disclosure requirement is satisfied by an expert report signed by the financial expert witness.[5] The specific requirements of the expert report are discussed in a later chapter. Note that there is no requirement to disclose the opinions of an expert that is retained solely as a consultant; disclosure is required only as to experts whose opinions will or may be offered as evidence at trial or in some other evidentiary proceeding.

Absent a stipulation or court order to the contrary, financial expert reports are due ninety days before the scheduled start date of trial and rebuttal reports are due thirty days after the disclosure of such reports.[6] Often, however, the court will order phased disclosures in which the plaintiff is required to produce expert reports before the defendant.

After the financial expert report is produced to the opposing party, there is often a critique of that expert report. This critique may be in the form of a written rebuttal report issued by an expert witness retained by the opposing party or a motion *in limine* filed by opposing legal counsel. A rebuttal report challenges the work, findings, and opinions disclosed in the opposing party's financial expert report. A motion *in limine* requests that the court exclude and bar certain testimonial evidence to be given by the financial expert witness at trial.

The financial expert witness may be requested to issue a written surrebuttal to the opposing expert's rebuttal report. A *surrebuttal* is a type of supplemental expert report prepared to respond to an opposing expert's rebuttal report.[7] Supplemental financial expert witness reports may be prepared and issued for a number of reasons in addition to a response to a rebuttal report. For example, they may be required to disclose additional work that has been performed or material new evidence that has been considered, to correct significant errors, and report any previously undisclosed opinions. A written surrebuttal may be considered when it is perceived that the defendant's expert rebuttal report has the potential to harm or limit the plaintiff's ability to present important expert testimony during trial. A written surrebuttal may also be considered if it is determined that the opposing expert's rebuttal report is flawed and unreliable for use by the trier of fact.

After expert reports are exchanged, discovery provides for the deposition of financial expert witnesses prior to trial.[8] As such, the financial expert witness must prepare for and attend the deposition to be questioned by opposing legal counsel. Because of the financial expert witness's expertise, it is common for financial expert witnesses to be asked by retaining legal counsel to assist with the preparation of inquiries and key materials to be used for the deposition of opposing financial expert witnesses and fact witnesses.

Motions

Throughout the course of litigation, the opposing legal counsel will prepare motions asking the court to rule on matters and facts in dispute. In many cases, financial expert witnesses may be asked by retaining legal counsel to provide written statements of support for these motions in the capacity of a financial expert witness. This written support typically is prepared and filed with the court in the form of a declaration or sworn affidavit signed by the financial expert witness. The preparation of such support will be subject to scrutiny and examination by opposing legal counsel.

Hearings

In connection with the court's deliberations regarding pending motions or other matters, a judge may request a hearing. Hearings usually are conducted in the courtroom; however, telephonic hearings are not uncommon. Hearings are civil litigation proceedings designed to assist the court in its determination of legal or fact issues in dispute, oftentimes involving the presentation of evidence. A typical hearing in civil litigation resembles a bench trial, with the opposing parties' legal counsel appearing to make oral arguments and present evidence. At times, the financial expert witness may be asked to appear at a hearing to present testimonial evidence to the judge.

Settlement

Settlement is an ongoing activity in civil litigation beginning with the initial dispute and, in certain cases, continuing well after the completion of a trial. In most federal cases, pretrial mediation or settlement conference is required to encourage resolution by the opposing parties before trial begins. Financial expert witnesses and consultants may be asked to assist with the accumulation and preparation of materials intended exclusively for use in such proceedings.[9] Depending on the formality of the discussions and the desires of legal counsel, financial experts may be asked to attend these proceedings in order to handle anticipated technical questions and issues, or to address a neutral mediator.

Trial Preparation

Preparation for trial is intense and requires a significant level of effort by the legal teams and the financial experts. Working with legal counsel, financial experts must determine the necessary evidence that must be available during the trial to support the financial expert witness's testimony. Such evidence must be logged and disclosed to the court prior to trial. Furthermore, this evidence must be organized so that it can be easily retrieved and referenced during the proceedings, for example, in trial binders. In some cases, evidence is magnified, summarized, or otherwise constructed into demonstrative exhibits to assist the trier of fact during the proceedings.

In addition, the financial expert in the role of an expert witness must work closely with legal counsel to prepare for direct and cross-examinations. This not only includes the topics and order of the questions and answers, but also any demonstratives and exhibits expected to be used at trial by the financial expert witness to help the trier of fact understand the testimony. Financial experts may also be asked to assist with the preparation of questions for the cross-examination of opposing financial experts and fact witnesses. It is common for there to be multiple trial presentation preparation sessions in advance of the trial.

In rare cases, financial experts will be asked to participate in a mini-trial, or mock trial, before the actual trial begins. A mock trial simulates an abbreviated version of a forthcoming courtroom trial proceeding. To enhance the experience, a mock trial may employ an individual or panel to preside over the proceedings and use professionals as opposing legal counsel and witnesses. A mock trial is designed to allow the convening party to better understand how impartial persons will interpret the intended presentation of the case. Any perceived strengths can then be repeated in the actual trial, and weaknesses addressed and corrected before trial.

Trial

The trial is the formal proceeding used by the disputing parties to present their evidence to the trier of fact so that they may decide the controverted facts and issues. Trials involve the introduction of evidence by the disputing parties. One form of the evidence to be presented in trial is the sworn oral testimony of the financial expert witness. Therefore, the financial expert witness plays a vital role in a civil trial. Trials always are conducted before a judge and may or may not include a jury.

Post-Trial

After the trial, there are several things that the financial expert may be asked to do. In many cases, the parties will submit written briefs or proposed findings after trial. The financial expert may be asked to assist with these. For judgments involving large awards in connection with class actions or large numbers of beneficiaries, the financial expert may be engaged to serve as a claims administrator or otherwise assist with the identification of the individuals entitled to share in the award, quantification of individual awards, award distribution, and accounting for all such activities. In rare cases, the financial expert may be asked to assist with an appeal or post-trial settlement action.

COMING UP

In the upcoming chapter, we will look at the process for finding and retaining a financial expert for litigation and dispute resolution.

NOTES

1. FRCP, Rule 26(a)(2)(B).
2. FRE, Rule 702.
3. FRCP, Rule 26(b)(4)(D).
4. FRE, Rule 701.
5. FRCP, Rule 26(a)(2).
6. FRCP, Rule 26(a)(2).
7. FRCP, Rule 26(a)(2)(D).
8. FRCP, Rule 26(a)(2)(E) and Rule 26(e).
9. FRE, Rule 408.

CHAPTER THREE

Retention of the Financial Expert

 ## FINDING FINANCIAL EXPERTS

There are many ways for a prospective client to find a financial expert consultant or witness that will be right for a case. Some methods are formal; however, the vast majority are informal and interpersonal. It is important to understand how financial experts are found and the types of information used to locate, recruit, and assess the fitness of a financial expert for a particular assignment. This understanding will aid the financial expert with client engagement acceptance, increase the chances for retention, and decrease the risk of discovering too late in the process that the assignment is poorly suited to the expert's background and qualifications.

Referrals and relationships are the source of choice for many attorneys looking for a good financial expert. However, there is no better way to find a suitable financial expert than to have worked with him before or to have seen him in action as an opponent's expert. Of course, there still exists a version of "you scratch my back, I'll scratch yours" when it comes to finding financial experts. In addition, the Internet may come into play with its available research tools and the many expert subscription services available. The financial expert witness can also help others find him or her by publishing thought leadership and conducting self-promotion. Each of these methods is described in more detail in the following sections.

Finding Financial Experts
▪ Referrals
▪ Relationships
▪ Prior work
▪ *Quid pro quo*
▪ Research
▪ Subscription services
▪ Retained searches
▪ Publications, training, presentations, speeches, and instruction
▪ Advertising and self-promotion

Referrals

In 2011, the American Institute of Certified Public Accountants (AICPA) issued the results of a survey on forensic and valuation services. This survey reported that financial experts who testified on damages were selected in the following manners:[1]

- 50 percent by a referral from an external auditor.
- 25 percent by a referral from external counsel.
- 17 percent by a referral from internal counsel.
- 8 percent by a referral from private equity investors.

This survey demonstrates why referrals are, by far, the most common way for prospective clients to locate a financial expert witness. There are corollaries with the selection of financial expert consultants.

Referrals are typically based on the perception of a positive personal experience from a prior engagement using the financial expert, or on the word of mouth from others with such experiences. Referrals can be internal or external. Internal referrals are those shared amongst the same company or law firm. External referrals are sourced from third parties outside the law firm or potential client-seeking financial expert candidates. It is common for attorneys in different law firms to share intelligence about financial experts, which can lead to referrals.

Relationships

Of course, many financial experts are engaged because they have a personal relationship with an attorney or client decision maker (e.g., corporate legal counsel). As such, business networks consisting of former and prospective clients and referral sources can be an important source of business for the financial expert. However, direct engagements with close relationship parties can potentially be problematic for the financial expert serving as an expert witness. It can lead to a perception of bias that could impair the credibility of the financial expert witness in the eyes of the trier of fact. Therefore, the financial expert must exercise caution when considering an expert witness assignment involving a close interpersonal relationship.

A similar phenomenon may occur after the financial expert, serving as an expert witness, completes a large case requiring a significant level of effort and fees. In these circumstances, many attorneys believe that a cooling-off period is required before they can use the financial expert as an expert witness again. This practice is utilized to reduce the risk that the financial expert witness will be perceived as being "in the back pocket" of the attorney. In these situations, even though the relationship is sound and the service delivery outstanding, an attorney may wait a few months or several years after concluding a large matter before using the financial expert as an expert witness again.

Prior Work

The financial expert witness's body of work may also be used by prospective clients to locate the financial expert. The financial expert witness's prior expert reports and testimony in deposition and trial that resides in the public domain can be used to identify relevant opinions, positions, and issues in common with the case at hand. Alternatively, prior work can be used to identify potential weaknesses in the financial expert, such as excluded testimony, and opinions contrary to positions held by the engaging party. For this reason, the financial expert should remain cognizant about positions and opinions expressed in prior reports and testimony.

Quid Pro Quo

Quid pro quo is Latin for something done for something else in return. Although not spoken about much, it is a method for identifying financial experts, especially amongst large institutional law firms and their large financial and accounting services clients. In exchange for client loyalty and future fees, the law firms use a largely exclusive arrangement to refer financial expert work to clients. Of course, both organizations are smart enough to know that the financial expert must fit the bill, be objective, and be able to provide quality services.

Research

In this age of technology and the Internet, research is increasingly becoming the means to locate financial expert candidates, especially expert witnesses. That means the financial expert must increasingly be sensitive to what is in the public domain of data accessible through free or subscriber-based search tools. Professional postings and information can be a valuable source for inquisitive researchers tasked with finding a suitable financial expert. However, social networking services like Facebook, LinkedIn, Twitter, Instagram, Flickr, and others are fair game for an opposing researcher looking for dirt on the financial expert. A best practice would be to Google yourself every few months to ensure your personal Internet integrity remains accurate and intact. In addition, websites and paid subscriptions services should be monitored periodically. There are a number of sites and services that track motions and associated orders to exclude expert testimony and others that offer dossiers and history profiles of experts.

Subscription Services

There are also a number of free or subscription-based referral services. In some cases, the financial expert pays a service organization to have his information promoted and distributed or made available to a proprietary subscriber list of attorneys. In others, the law firms or attorneys pay a service organization to conduct a formal search for a suitable financial expert. In any case, these subscription services attempt to match case needs with financial experts—a kind of dating service for financial experts looking to be matched with attorneys.

Retained Searches

Attorneys may also retain an expert search organization to locate a potentially suitable financial expert witness. In such instances, the attorney will initiate a retained search for a fee. Among other arrangements, fees may be fixed, commissioned, or based on incremental fees charged based on the ultimately engaged financial expert witness's hours or billings. The retained search organization will then use its network of experts and research to locate and recruit eligible expert candidates to submit to the retaining attorney. This process is very similar to what a headhunter might do for an employment search.

However, retained searches can be awkward for financial expert witness candidates. Frequently, the retained search organization will not disclose the attorney who initiated the search, case details, or looming deadlines. Therefore, robust engagement acceptance due diligence is not possible before the financial expert witness candidate's name and curriculum vitae is disclosed to the retaining attorney. If the financial expert witness is selected for possible engagement by the retaining attorney, he or she must deal with both the potential client attorney and the search organization for contracting the services. If selected to serve, the financial expert witness may also be required to report ongoing engagement progress and fees incurred to the search organization, which can cause issues related to conflicts, confidentiality, and discovery.

Publications, Training, Presentations, Speeches, and Instruction

Some financial experts provide thought leadership related to their areas of expertise. Thought leadership may be in the form of publications, such as articles and textbooks, or training, presentations, speeches, and instruction. In today's world, this may also include webcasts, podcasts, and blogs. Thought leadership can strengthen the credentials of the financial expert, especially if the financial expert's knowledge and experience is cited and acknowledged by professional peers. Strong credentials may result in greater success for retention.

The preparation, delivery, and publication of thought leadership can also create risks for the financial expert. Thought leadership can, and will, be used by crafty opposing counsel to impeach the credibility of a financial expert witness. Furthermore, thought leadership, especially published or web-enabled content, has a very long tail on it, thereby leaving a legacy of risk well into the future. So, word of caution to the financial expert, be careful about the thought leadership you prepare, publish, and present—it may come back to haunt you.

> Mind your speech a little—lest you should mar your fortunes.
>
> *—William Shakespeare*

Advertising and Self-Promotion

The financial expert must realize that he is always on stage. This is particularly true for financial experts serving as expert witnesses. Habits, hobbies, idiosyncrasies, and conversations are monitored as the financial expert is a servant of the public trust in the civil litigation system. Therefore, extreme care must be taken to avoid unprofessional advertising and self-promotion.

The most common form of advertising and self-promotion for the financial expert is the curriculum vitae, or CV. Before any financial expert is engaged, the prospective client attorney will almost always request a CV. So, whether the financial expert admits it or not, the CV is a marketing tool—a special marketing tool that carries significant weight for the financial expert. Unlike a résumé, the CV is designed to identify the financial expert and provide a summary of his qualifications and experience. Keeping in mind the Federal Rules of Evidence, it is an overview of the financial expert's skills, knowledge, education, experience, and training. Financial experts take two different approaches to the CV: a standard CV and a customized CV.

The standard CV is consistent about the information provided, usually updated only as required to meet the Federal Rules of Civil Procedure.[2] The customized CV is one tailored to be as relevant as possible to the case needs. The customized CV attempts to disclose information about the financial expert that will help the reader better understand the relevance of the financial expert's qualifications and experience to the matters in dispute. However, the customized CV should still be consistent from case to case, with the exception of the unique qualifiers used to describe the financial expert's relevance to a present case. Whether standardized or customized, it is critical that the financial expert not over-reach or brag in the CV. Such transgressions can be exploited by opposing counsel to disqualify or discredit the financial expert at trial or in pretrial motions.

As far as aggressive marketing and sales campaigns go, proceed with caution. Remember this is a communication to sell the financial expert as a dependable, reliable, and professional servant to the court. The general public sees this as a conservative and honorable role and any messaging inconsistent with that image may raise concerns about integrity, bias, and objectivity. Also stay away from claims about predetermined or guaranteed results or success. For example, advertising claims along these lines appear biased and lacking in objectivity:

- "Our mission is to find fraud."
- "We won't stop looking until we find fraud."
- "We catch the crooks who cook the books."

These types of advertised claims may create the perception that the financial expert is biased against any party accused of civil unlawfulness.

If unknown, the financial expert should ask a prospect how he or she was discovered as a potential expert for a case. This allows the financial expert to better understand how he or she is identified by the marketplace, which, in turn, can direct the financial expert to the most effective methods for expert matchmaking. In addition, referrals and other favors can be acknowledged and the sources thanked for their professional generosity.

Perhaps most important of all—be top of mind. Attorneys often identify a financial expert based on the need or desire to make a quick decision to engage a financial expert for a pending case in progress. In other words, if an attorney has a business need today for a financial expert and you contact that attorney on that day, she is likely to share the expert requirements with you in an effort to immediately address their need. So, frequency of contact with litigation attorneys is essential for being considered for financial expert assignments.

> There are four ways, and only four ways, in which we have contact with the
> world. We are evaluated and classified by these four contacts: what we
> do, how we look, what we say, and how we say it.
>
> —*Dale Carnegie*

PROSPECTIVE CLIENT DUE DILIGENCE

After financial expert candidates have been sourced, it is likely that the prospective client attorney will perform some type of due diligence to select the best financial expert for the case. Pre-engagement due diligence can range from informal inquiries to formal inquisitions. The financial expert should expect pre-engagement due diligence and prepare for it accordingly. Following are a few of the due diligence techniques the financial expert may encounter.

The CV

Without question, every financial expert will have their CV analyzed by prospects during the due diligence process. Therefore, it is critical that the CV be well-written, complete, precise, accurate, and grammatically correct. Typographical errors and inaccuracies can create the perception of sloppiness and a lack of attention to details—fatal flaws for a financial expert in litigation. The CV should not be used to puff or sell the financial expert's qualifications and experience. However, a professional-looking CV that clearly communicates the financial expert's skills, knowledge, education, experience, and training can be the best tool to get noticed and engaged.

As a test for the CV, the financial expert should scrutinize every entry and be prepared to explain why it is there and the relevance to the matter at hand. Emeritus or honorary degrees, awards, or memberships should be labeled as such. Publications, speeches, and training courses should list coauthors or editorial roles. Certifications, licenses, and professional designations should be active and current, listing any restrictions. The financial expert witness should be able to describe how such certifications, licenses, and designations were awarded or earned and any regulatory requirements to maintain them. Memberships should typically be limited to exclusive professional organizations. The financial expert should be able to describe how the membership was conferred, any requirements to remain active and in good standing, and any applicable professional standards.

> ### The Financial Expert Witness CV
> - Name (required)
> - Title (optional but recommended)
> - Firm or employer (optional but recommended)
> - Contact information (optional but recommended)
> - Employment history (optional)
> - Post-secondary education and degrees awarded (optional but recommended)
> - Other formal education and training (optional)
> - Professional qualifications, such as certifications, designations, and awards (optional but recommended)
> - Professional memberships (optional)
> - Relevant civil and community activities (optional)
> - Authorships (required disclosure for past 10 years)
> - Testimony (required disclosure for past 4 years)

The following paraphrased request provides an example of the due diligence an attorney may conduct on the financial expert's CV. After receiving and reading the financial expert's CV, the attorney may comment something along these lines:

> We received your CV and would like to begin our due diligence evaluation. In that regard, please send us a list of all cases in which you have provided damages testimony (deposition or trial) as identified in your CV for the types of matters identified below:
>
> - breach of contract, business interruption, intellectual property, fraud, fiduciary duty
>
> Also, please send any cases having to do with antitrust, in general.
>
> Further, please send us copies of the following 10 articles listed under the "publications" section of your CV and any publications related to the types of matters described above.
>
> Once we have reviewed these materials, we will let you know if a telephone interview will be arranged.

The Interview (That Feels Like a Deposition)

Every seasoned financial expert knows about the due diligence interview that feels like a deposition. Sure, there can be niceties exchanged—What is your position? How long have you been there? Who have you worked with in the past? But, that quickly changes into a battery of questions fired at the financial expert with unbridled fervor like they were an opposing expert in deposition. Make no mistake about it, this is a test.

The prospective client attorney is assessing the financial expert's communication skills, qualifications and experience, demeanor, reaction to stress, and likability. Yes, likability. After all, if the trier of fact finds the financial expert likable, that can help the case. But, there is also a personal motive for the attorney related to the financial expert's likability. She understands that many hours will be spent with the financial expert—so, it might as well be spent with someone you like. This shared chemistry can be described as a "foxhole" qualification. All qualifications and experience being equal between financial experts, who would the prospective client attorney rather be in a foxhole with?

An interview is like a minefield.

—*Michelle Williams*

Professional References

Professional references are referrals that the financial expert hand-selects to speak to prospects. Professional references consist principally of existing or former clients who have worked directly with the financial expert and can, therefore, personally vouch for the financial expert's work and services. However, the financial expert should not be surprised if a client attorney prospect takes case information from the financial expert's CV and contacts a number of former clients, including some that may not have been on the list of professional references provided by the financial expert.

Knowing that any former client may serve as a professional reference, the financial expert should do a couple of things. First, have handy a short list of two to three recent matters and the name of the client legal counsel to produce as professional referrals when asked. Second, the financial expert must have satisfied clients. Nothing impairs the financial expert's ability to be selected and engaged as an expert witness more than an unhappy former client, whether because of bad work, excessive billings, or excluded testimony.

Research

Also high on the financial expert due diligence list for prospective client attorneys is research. In its basic form, research is conducted using free Internet search engines. It is now well-known what helpful, or harmful, information you can find on the Internet—especially from social networks. Upping it a notch are searches performed using paid subscription services to do background searches and prepare proprietary dossiers or work histories.

Research-Related Due Diligence

- Internet searches
- Subscription services
- Prior testimony
- Excluded or limited testimony
- Authorships
- Training attendance and instruction
- Character references

Many attorneys will also research the cases listed on the financial expert's CV to obtain public records on the case and the financial expert's testimony. Of particular concern are cases where the financial expert's testimony was excluded or limited by the court in the past. There are several web-based services that track and report motions to exclude testimony and the ultimate decisions of the courts, making this information readily available. Therefore, in an abundance of caution, the financial expert should voluntarily disclose any prior exclusion of testimony, together with the facts and circumstances around the situation, prior to accepting any engagement to serve as a financial expert witness. In most cases, an exclusion of prior testimony is not fatal for the financial expert in the eyes of a trier of fact. But consideration of this possibility must necessarily be the responsibility of the client attorney, after full disclosure by the financial expert.

Other matters that may present additional concerns related to prior case work include the following:

- Substantive repeat work for a single attorney or law firm.
- A disproportionate majority of work for either the plaintiff's or defendant's side.
- Differing opinions and testimony for similar fact patterns.
- Reprimand or admonishment by the court.
- Failure to demonstrate a professional demeanor.

The financial expert's list of materials authored, not limited to those disclosed in the CV, may also be read and assessed prior to making a decision to engage a financial expert. Publications authored by the financial expert can be helpful to establish qualifications, especially if the pieces are directly relevant to the case or if the financial expert is quoted or cited as a luminary or industry expert. On the other hand, prospective client attorneys will be cautious about engaging financial experts who are excessively outspoken, known for radical or entrenched positions, or have a propensity to flip-flop.

Most financial professions encourage or require continuing education. The financial expert should keep this in mind when it comes to selecting and engaging financial expert witnesses. A steady diet of technical training relevant to subject matters that frequently arise in litigation and disputes can greatly add to the qualifications of the financial expert. Furthermore, instructional materials prepared and delivered by the financial expert, especially when the financial expert acts as an instructor for peers and other professionals in the field, demonstrates superior subject-matter knowledge that can be an important factor when selecting and engaging a financial expert.

Character reference research may also be conducted by prospective client parties before engaging the financial expert. Using all of the techniques mentioned above plus other techniques as extreme as private investigation, the due diligence process might identify family members, known associates, business relationships, hobbies, travel experiences, political activities, national affiliation, and other personal information that can be explored to evaluate potential impacts on the case. Adverse findings and appearances may exclude the financial expert from consideration.

 ## PRE-ENGAGEMENT COMMUNICATIONS

There are some important things that the financial expert needs to know before being engaged. Pre-engagement client communications can be critical to making an informed and reasonable decision about engagement acceptance. However, pre-engagement communications also have risks, such as the risk of "tainting," which can get the financial expert removed from a case. Confidentiality is paramount and must be maintained at all times by the financial expert. Finally, the financial expert needs to know what to do with materials obtained or created prior to formal engagement.

Know Your Client

Top of the list—know your client. Insist on meeting the prospective lead attorney responsible to the underlying client, who is typically one of the named parties in the litigation or alternative dispute. In addition, ask to meet the underlying client in person, if possible. From these encounters, get an understanding of the dispute, issues, and concerns. Find out if there are worries about fees, unreasonable time constraints, missing or lost records, or overly aggressive positions taken. These matters can be important determining factors for engagement acceptance.

It is useful to ask the client attorney and underlying client to define success. Success is the ultimate outcome desired for the dispute. Success may be settlement and conciliation. Alternatively, it may mean all-out war so that a party can get justice by their day in court. In any event, setting expectations up front is critical to delivering quality service and relevant financial expert witness opinions.

Tainting

The financial expert must also be concerned about tainting prior to engagement. Tainting primarily affects testifying experts. However, tainting may cause ethical issues for the financial expert consultant, as well. Tainting is caused by the financial expert obtaining confidential information that is potentially harmful to an opposing party in the dispute. Tainting causes a conflict of interest or potential unfair advantage to one of the disputing parties that can result in the removal of the financial expert from the case by the court because testimony would be inadmissible.

Tainting may occur when the financial expert witness inadvertently fails to discover actual conflicts of interest during client acceptance. It can also happen when existing or former clients of the financial expert witness merge with a party in a dispute. There are also situations that appear to demonstrate intentional tainting. Intentional tainting happens when an attorney or law firm contacts a financial expert as a candidate for an expert witness assignment and confidential case information is communicated to the financial expert in an effort to intentionally remove the financial expert from consideration by an opposing party. This is a "poison the well" strategy used to gain advantage in litigation and alternative dispute resolution. Therefore, in order to avoid the possibility of intentional tainting the financial expert must be careful about asking too many case-specific questions or allowing the exchange of too much information prior to clearing conflicts and entering into a formal engagement.

Confidential Information

Any information obtained by the financial expert must be kept in strict confidence. This is a widely accepted professional obligation. The names of the disputing parties and the nature of the dispute are confidential information unless it is known as a verifiable fact by the financial expert that such information is in the public domain. Even if the information is public, the fact that the financial expert has been contacted and is being considered to serve is confidential. The financial expert may also be required to keep pre-engagement information confidential by court order or applicable professional standards. It will often be advisable for the financial expert's engagement letter to specify the process by which counsel will identify confidential information and the expert's obligations or expected practices with respect to safeguarding, retaining, and eventually returning or destroying confidential information that is provided to the expert in the course of the engagement.

Pre-Engagement Materials

It is likely that the financial expert will get information and be provided materials from the prospective client attorney in anticipation of retention. For example, the financial expert may be given the complaint or a brief description of the dispute and parties. This is normal and necessary for the financial expert to perform conflict-checking activities and usually will not present a serious risk of tainting the financial expert, as described earlier. In addition to the materials and information received from the prospective client attorney, the financial expert may generate notes and other materials.

There can be confusion and healthy debate about whether such information and materials obtained and used prior to formal engagement are potentially discoverable to an opposing party. One view is that such information and materials were obtained and used by the financial expert prior to formal engagement solely to aid with client acceptance and, as such, these facts and data were not considered by the financial expert witness to form opinions in the case. Therefore, pre-engagement information and materials received by the financial expert are not discoverable. The opposite view is that any information and materials used by the financial expert witness, regardless of whether a formal executed engagement contract existed at the time, is subject to discovery by an opposing party. For example, if a financial expert received a copy of the complaint prior to formal engagement, it is disingenuous to suggest that it was not considered by the financial expert when forming opinions in the case. It is also common to ask a financial expert witness during deposition how he was hired, who made the initial contact, and what materials were provided—all pre-engagement activities.

Due to the controversies surrounding the discoverability of pre-engagement information and materials received by the financial expert witness, it is recommended that such facts and data be retained by the financial expert witness, unless specifically instructed otherwise by a client attorney. The safest course of action is for the financial expert witness to retain pre-engagement information and materials and consult with the client legal counsel about whether to disclose or produce pre-engagement facts and data to an opposing party. The discoverability of pre-engagement facts and data is a legal question for attorneys to answer, not the financial expert witness.

 ## SELECTION OF THE FINANCIAL EXPERT WITNESS

The selection of a financial expert witness can be part science and part art. Depending on the complexity and size of the claims and the experts anticipated to be engaged by an opposing party, prospective clients may believe that a unique specialist is required. In these cases, it is not unusual for the opposing parties to retain financial experts who have a long list of professional credentials and college degrees earned. On the other hand, a financial expert witness who is a generalist may be able to handle complexities together with a broader range of expected disputed issues. Some camps believe that a practicing professional with no testimonial experience is preferable as a financial expert witness. Conversely, for "bet the company" cases, most attorneys believe that an experienced and seasoned testifying financial expert witness is mandatory. However, the vast majority of attorneys prefer to go with known commodities—financial experts they have worked with before and seen in action.

Highly Specialized

In general, cases with numerous complex issues and significant claimed monetary damages will drive decisions to engage highly specialized financial expert witnesses with narrow, but deep, technical and industry qualifications and experience. Through intelligence-gathering, the parties to such lawsuits expect each opposing party to engage a luminary or recognized specialist to serve as their financial expert witnesses. In many instances, this means that the opposing experts will each have a long list of professional licenses, credentials, and designations after their names. Accordingly, the pitting of these experts against each other is often called the "battle of the professional acronyms." An example of the post-nominals of such an expert might look like this:

John Q. Public, Ph.D., CPA, CFA, CFF, ABV, AVA, CIA

General Expertise

For the vast majority of other cases, generalized financial expert witness qualifications will suffice. The foremost financial expert in a very specialized field will not necessarily be needed to assist the trier of fact in many cases. Instead, a broad-based financial expert witness with superior expertise in the field as compared to the average layperson, or juror, will suffice. Selection of a financial expert witness with broad and wide-ranging generalized experience and qualifications is often helpful because this type of financial expert witness is likely to be able to provide admissible opinions not only for known issues at the start of the dispute, but also any unforeseen issues that may arise in their area of expertise during the dispute resolution process.

Practitioners as Testifiers

Based on attorney preferences and perceptions about triers of fact, an attorney may seek to engage a financial expert witness who has never testified. In these situations, legal counsel seeks an expert who has meaningful qualifications and experience as a practicing professional outside of the world of dispute resolution. Examples might include an audit partner in a public accounting firm, a corporate income tax preparer, a former financial officer, or a director designated as a financial expert on a public company board of directors. The belief is that practicing financial expert witnesses have an advantage over dedicated litigation and dispute professionals because they can explain firsthand the application of principles, instead of just explaining them to the trier of fact. There may also be a perception that the trier of fact will find the novice testifier to be less of a "hired gun" than the experienced financial expert testifier.

Experienced Testifiers

Experienced financial expert witnesses bring to the table personal practical experience with the litigation and dispute resolution process. In other words, they know the business. This knowledge and experience allows the experienced financial expert witness to more quickly identify critical sources of information, facts, and data in order to understand disputed issues. With that understanding, an experienced financial expert witness is better able to effectively and efficiently source and analyze the evidence needed to form admissible opinions. Experienced financial expert witnesses also are familiar with the antics and techniques used by opposing counsel in deposition and trial, often resulting in better showings. Experienced testifiers also have real-life experience to be able to convincingly and confidently communicate opinions in an expert report or to the trier of fact in trial. Like most things in business, experience counts for the seasoned financial expert witness.

Known Commodities

Known-commodity financial expert witnesses are individuals who have worked directly with an attorney before, or been opposite of that attorney, thereby giving the attorney firsthand experience with the expert's work. The attorney knows the shortcomings of the financial expert witness and uses that knowledge to place the financial expert witness in roles that are best suited to their personal strengths. By the nature of their experience, these financial experts have been deposed before and may have testified in trial. These financial expert witnesses provide legal counsel with a level of comfort and performance predictability that often results in selection of the financial expert witness to serve in a case.

> The ability to deal with people is as purchasable a commodity as sugar or coffee and I will pay more for that ability than for any other under the sun.
>
> —*John D. Rockefeller*

 COMING UP

Now that we have addressed retention of the financial expert, Chapter 4 provides some helpful information on getting started on the engagement.

 NOTES

1. AICPA, *The 2011 Forensic and Valuation Services (FVS) Trend Survey* (2012), available at www.aicpa.org/InterestAreas/ForensicAndValuation/Resources/ PractAidsGuidance/DownloadableDocuments/2011%20FVS%20Trend%20 Survey.pdf.
2. FRCP, Rule 26(a)(2)(A).

4

Getting Started as a Financial Expert

 GETTING STARTED

The financial expert should accept each project in compliance with an internal policy on client and engagement acceptance. Once engaged, the financial expert should obtain information that is mission-critical for the successful completion of assignments. In many cases, this information can only be acquired through conversations with the client and client attorney. In addition, the financial expert serving as an expert witness needs to be particularly cautious about the methods used and documentation prepared while gathering this important information.

Key Communications

Entering into an engagement to serve as a financial expert in litigation or alternative dispute proceedings requires a solid understanding about the key types of communications typically expected. Prior to beginning any work, the financial expert must complete a conflict check and communicate the results to the prospective client. If selected to serve as the financial expert by the prospect, the financial expert will then communicate official client and engagement acceptance, or decline the work as deemed appropriate. Formal client and engagement acceptance is typically followed by a written engagement letter that may be executed by the financial expert, the client attorney, and an authorized legal representative of the underlying client.

After engagement, the financial expert will have communications with the client law firm about a number of things such as evidentiary needs, document productions, level of effort, costs and expenses, and if serving in the role of an expert witness, disclosures, opinions, and testimony. Many of these communications with the trial legal team, and in some cases the underlying client, will be in the form of e-mails, reports, billings and other forms of written material that must be retained and may potentially be disclosed to an opposing party if the financial expert is serving as an expert witness. Formal communications delivered by the financial expert witness during the dispute resolution process include sworn statements, disclosures and other expert reports, trial demonstratives, and of course, deposition and trial testimony.

Key Financial Expert Communications

- Conflict checks
- Engagement acceptance
- Engagement letter
- Evidence production
- Timekeeping records
- Billings and invoices
- Client and trial team exchanges
- Work papers and files
- Sworn statements
- Reports and disclosures
- Deposition testimony
- Trial exhibits and demonstratives
- Trial testimony

Engagement Acceptance

As a rule, the financial expert should have a policy on client and engagement acceptance. It is a professional responsibility and may be required by professional standards for members of certain trade associations.[1] Matters to be considered in such a policy may include the following, without limitation:

- An evaluation of the integrity, qualifications, experience, and reputation of the prospective client attorney, law firm, and underlying client of the law firm.

- Conflict-checking requirements and procedures (legal, business, and professional practice conflicts, such as financial statement audit independence rules).
- Engagement risk and quality control plan and procedures.
- Identification of client parties and adverse parties.
- Identification of any prior relationship with any adverse parties.
- Understanding the assignment, including deadlines and deliverables.
- Assessment of the financial expert's qualifications, experience, competence, capabilities, and resources to determine suitability for the assignment.
- Definition of the scope of services.
- Agreement on applicable professional standards governing the engagement.
- Identification of the party responsible for payments, including the retainer.
- Expectations regarding the handling of confidential information.
- Engagement letter contracting.
- Compliance with applicable court orders and subpoenas.

General Instructions

Immediately after engagement, the financial expert should make inquiries into several matters of critical importance to the provision of dispute resolution services. The inquiries should be directed to the client attorney. They are designed to be general in nature to allow flexibility and should be made whether the financial expert is serving in the role of a consultant or expert witness. Of course, the inquiries are only the method used to elicit responses from the client attorney. The actions taken by the financial expert after learning the answers is what really matters.

Client Attorney Preferences

It is smart for the financial expert to ask the prospective client attorney for instructions on engagement protocols and preferences before beginning any work. Each attorney will have unique ways to do things. The financial expert must know these ways if he or she is to work harmoniously with the client attorney. In most every case, the client attorney will provide instructions to the financial expert on communications and the need to be mindful of information and materials potentially discoverable by an opposing party as part of legal discovery. Additional instructions may be on a variety of topics ranging from billings to client contact.

Initial Understanding of the Dispute

One of the first orders of business is to gain an initial understanding of the dispute. This can usually be accomplished by having a discussion with the client attorney and the underlying client (under conditions provided by the client attorney); reading case pleadings, filings, and court docket records; and in certain cases, performing research to discover public records on the case. The financial expert witness should not lose sight of the fact that such research may need to be documented and preserved, as it may be subject to discovery by an opposing party. Therefore, the financial expert witness should discuss this with legal counsel before actually conducting any independent research. Regardless of the approach, getting an initial understanding of the claims, issues, and disputes early in the engagement will help to drive more informed inquiries about other matters in the case.

As part of the process used to gain an initial understanding of the case, the financial expert should ask the client attorney about applicable laws, rules, and procedures. The financial expert must have a working knowledge about the legal claims and, if damages are part of the assignment, the available legal remedies. In addition, it is often helpful to understand relevant case precedence. In many cases, legal remedies are defined or restricted by law and failure to comply with statutory requirements can lead to the exclusion of expert witness opinions and testimony by the court.

Sources to Gain an Initial Understanding of the Dispute

- Inquiries of client legal counsel and underlying client
- Matter pleadings and filings
- Public records searches
- Applicable law and relevant legal precedence
- Court docket records

Court and Ruling Body Directives

The financial expert must also be aware of any directives from the court or ruling body presiding over the case. Expected directives are scheduling and protective orders. Scheduling orders set out the calendaring of the proceedings. Protective orders shield confidential information from disclosure. Failure to comply with court or ruling body directives can potentially result in serious problems for the financial expert, including but not limited to exclusion, removal, sanctions, and fines.

Scheduling Order

Virtually every federal litigation case in which financial experts are involved will have a scheduling order.[2] Scheduling orders include time limits for parties to join the lawsuit, amend pleadings, complete discovery, and file motions. They may also include: (1) modifications to the timing of disclosures, including the financial expert witness's report; (2) the extent of discovery; (3) providing for the discovery of electronic data; (4) agreements between the parties related to privilege and confidentiality; (5) dates for pretrial conferences and trial; and (6) other matters. In most cases, alternative dispute resolution proceedings will also have the equivalent of a scheduling order. Scheduling orders frequently are modified by the court during the course of the case. The client attorney should be able to provide guidance on whether modification is likely in a particular case.

Protective Order

Either party to the dispute, or any person from whom discovery is sought, may also request a protective order. A protective order protects a party or person from "annoyance, embarrassment, oppression, or undue burden or expense, including one or more of the following:

- Forbidding the disclosure or discovery;
- Specifying terms, including time and place, for the disclosure or discovery;
- Prescribing a discovery method other than the one selected by the party seeking discovery;
- Forbidding inquiry into certain matters, or limiting the scope of disclosure or discovery to certain matters;
- Designating the persons who may be present while the discovery is conducted;
- Requiring that a deposition be sealed and opened only on court order;
- Requiring that a trade secret or other confidential research, development, or commercial information not be revealed or be revealed only in a specified way;
- Requiring that the parties simultaneously file specified documents or information in sealed envelopes, to be opened as the court directs.[3]

Protective orders have particular relevance to financial experts because they may be required to read and sign such an order acknowledging awareness and agreeing to comply with the terms of the order. Once again, alternative dispute resolution may also have directives similar to a protective order.

Agreements with Opposing Legal Counsel

Oftentimes, legal counsel representing each of the disputing parties will agree to matters concerning the dispute resolution proceedings among themselves. These matters can be about the timing, form, and requirements for disclosures, discovery, and legal privilege, among many other things. Some of these agreements must be affirmed by the court. In certain instances, these lawyer agreements may directly affect the financial expert and the work to be performed. For example, it is common for disputing parties to agree to waive the requirement for an opposing party to pay reasonable fees and expenses to the financial expert witness for time spent responding to a request for deposition.[4] Perhaps this is waived because it is, in essence, a wash if each side pays the opponent's fees and expenses. Regardless, the financial expert needs to ask his client attorney about any agreements with an opposing party that may impact financial expert assignments.

Document Preservation

The extent of a testifying expert's obligation to preserve documents and information in connection with a litigation engagement can be difficult to clearly define and increasingly often can be a source of unwelcome and potentially embarrassing disputes. For any financial expert that either expects or may be requested to offer testimony, the best practice in most cases will be to preserve everything unless the expert receives clear direction otherwise from the client attorney. This includes both written materials and electronic information, such as e-mail and any kind of electronic data or files.

Recent changes to the Federal Rules of Civil Procedure (FRCP) protect an expert's drafts of any report or disclosures from discovery in most circumstances.[5] Nevertheless, it is advisable to discuss how the expert will manage drafts with the client attorney, especially in more complex or contentious matters.

Financial Expert Work Papers and Work Product

The financial expert should strongly consider using standard protocols for the preparation, distribution, and retention of work papers, work product, and other records produced by the financial expert. Standard protocols often include provisions for titling, referencing, and preservation, among other matters. The use of standard protocols can improve quality and usefulness. In depositions, it is often very helpful for the expert witness to be able to rely on standard protocols in answering questions about how the expert handled work product, work papers, and other materials related to the case. Such protocols can also assist client legal counsel with the preservation of legal privilege available to the client.

Titles

All work papers and any work product prepared by the financial expert should be properly headed with the case caption, including the names of the disputing parties, identification of plaintiff and defendant parties, the court or tribunal having jurisdiction over the matter, and the assigned identification number. In highly confidential matters, it may be prudent to label financial expert work papers and work product with a code name instead of the actual case caption. For example, a dispute over a manufacturing contract might be called "Project Widget." For work papers and work product generated from the financial expert's independent research (e.g., website downloads or copies of textbook materials) the financial expert should document the date the research was performed and the information source (such as the web address or the textbook citation). Instead of using a heading for these materials, it is often more convenient to file the results and index the work appropriately.

Financial expert work papers and work product in process, or draft form, should be marked with each, or all, of the terms: *PRELIMINARY, DRAFT, SUBJECT TO CHANGE,* and *FOR DISCUSSION PURPOSES ONLY.* The work product of an expert who acts only as a nontestifying consultant is presumptively privileged against disclosure to the other side. Accordingly, when the financial expert has not yet been formally designated as a testifying expert and disclosed to the opposing party, it is recommended that work papers and work product include a header or footer such as *PRIVILEGED,* or *SUBJECT TO PRIVILEGE* to aid in the identification of facts and data potentially protected by applicable legal privileges.

These markings related to privilege are likely to become irrelevant and, regarding certain materials, inaccurate after designation and disclosure of the financial expert as an expert witness. It is usually harmless to leave indications of legal privilege on the financial expert witness's work papers. However, efforts should be made to remove any such labels from final work product, like the financial expert witness report, disclosed to the court or an opposing party.

References

All work papers and work product prepared by the financial expert should include unique references and be indexed and maintained in a professional manner. References are identifiers applied to work papers and work product.

References are frequently numbers and letters, or a combination thereof. For schedules, exhibits, appendices, tabs, and charts a reference may be a specific number and title attached to the material. Data sets and spreadsheets are often referenced using an electronically generated number, or by a file name. Indexing provides a guide to facilitate the ready location of referenced work papers and work product. The maintenance of the financial expert's work papers and work product requires careful attention to security and confidentiality. The sensitivity of disputed matters combined with protective requirements imposed by the court or a ruling body should cause the financial expert to consider extraordinary access restrictions, such as locked storage facilities and secured data drives.

The financial expert should retain work papers and work product in compliance with: (1) contractual obligations, typically spelled out in the financial expert's retention letter; (2) court or ruling body orders, including any applicable protective order governing confidentiality of discovery materials; (3) the wishes or instructions of the client legal counsel; or (4) the financial expert's normal course retention policies. In many situations, the retention letter or a court order will require the financial expert to confirm the destruction or return of any and all materials produced by an opposing party or otherwise used or referred to in the financial expert's work papers and work products. In other cases, the client legal counsel will provide specific instructions related to the retention of the financial expert's documented work. However, before destroying any work papers and work product, or alternatively subjecting them to the financial expert's normal course retention policies, the financial expert should ask the client legal counsel what course of action should be taken.

Facts, Data, Assumptions, and Evidence

The request, receipt, and handling of facts, data, assumptions, and evidence in connection with a case can be one of the most challenging tasks the financial expert must perform. It requires a disciplined approach to note taking and strict protocols for logging, indexing, filing, and disclosing materials received. The production of facts, data, assumptions, and evidence to the financial expert may vary widely from one case to another. This fact contributes to issues the financial expert may face related to the receipt and handling of such items. Ideally, the expert should be able to identify all of the materials requested, received, reviewed, or relied upon in the course of the engagement, as well as all of the analyses performed and work product created.

Note Taking
Note taking is a sensitive matter for a financial expert and should only be done extensively if the financial expert is assured that he or she will not be asked to testify or has reached a clear understanding with the client attorney. As an expert witness, handwritten and electronically prepared notes often are fair game for an opposing party's discovery request.[6] Once discovered, they can make fertile fodder for deposition inquiries. Accordingly, the financial expert should ask the client legal counsel about preferences related to note taking before any notes are prepared by the financial expert. In most cases, when serving strictly in the financial expert consulting role, the financial expert's notes will be protected from unwanted discovery by an opposing party.

Materials Produced to the Financial Expert
The protocols needed to request, receive, handle, log, index, and maintain materials produced to the financial expert are in many ways similar to the protocols used for financial expert work papers and work product discussed above. They should be designed to help the client legal counsel preserve applicable legal privileges. In addition, such protocols should allow the expert witness to identify and produce for purposes of discovery the materials he or she has "considered" in forming his or her opinions, and to prove a proper chain of custody for admissibility purposes. A chain of custody is important because it is part of the foundation proving that an identifiable person had custody of unaltered authentic evidence.

Requests for facts, data, assumptions, and evidence can be made on either disputing party. Regardless of the method, the financial expert should make such requests solely through the client legal counsel as a best practice. Requests may be made orally, or in writing through an e-mail or letter. For requests aimed at the client, the client legal counsel will deliver the materials or arrange for production of the requested items from the underlying client. For example, the client legal counsel can directly provide to the financial expert any relevant case pleadings and filings, deposition transcripts, and court orders. The financial expert should avoid obtaining any documents or records directly from the underlying client. As a general rule, all materials produced to the financial expert should come through the client legal counsel. For opposing party requests, the client legal counsel will request the materials using appropriate legal communications and filings and deliver them to the financial expert once received. Prior to conducting any independent research for facts and data on which the financial expert might rely, it is advisable to have a discussion with counsel regarding the intended scope of the research and how the results should be tracked and preserved.

For the vast majority of disputed matters to be resolved using litigation or alternative dispute resolution proceedings, facts and data are produced only after being uniquely marked for identification. This process is often called "Bates stamping." Bates stamping affixes a unique identifying number and letter code to each piece of evidence. The name comes from the handheld device that once was used to sequentially number a series of documents. Today, the numbering is usually done by computer on pdf or other image files. "Bates numbers" or production numbers can be applied to hard copies, electronic data sets, and native format electronic files.

An example of a Bates stamp for the first page of the first document produced by the imaginary company ABC, Inc. might be "ABC000001." Each subsequent page produced by ABC, Inc., would be numbered sequentially thereafter. A word of caution to the financial expert: The delivery of produced evidence to the financial expert without Bates numbering will make the identification, reference, and use of the evidence immensely more difficult. Therefore, if evidence is produced to the financial expert without Bates stamping, it is strongly recommended that the financial expert delay acceptance until such stamping can be done, or alternatively, the financial expert should apply appropriate production numbers to the evidence upon receipt.

Timekeeping and Billing Practices

The requirements for timekeeping and billing must be discussed with the client legal counsel before work is commenced by the financial expert. The discussion has both strategic and administrative significance. Strategically, timekeeping and billing information may include important information to an opposing party such as who was staffed on the work, how much time was incurred by each person, the bill rates of those individuals, and the description of the services provided. Therefore, it is critical that such records be accurate, complete, and administratively compliant with applicable rules and procedures.

In certain cases, the client legal counsel may request that the descriptions of the work performed be documented in a highly summarized and generic fashion to avoid the untimely discovery of legal strategies by an opposing party.

In other cases, it is critical that the financial expert provide a sufficient description of the work performed, even to the tenth of an hour. This is particularly true for matters in bankruptcy or subject to reimbursement by an insurance company. For example, Northern District of Illinois Bankruptcy Rule 5082–1 requires that "Such statement [of services] shall be divided by task and activity to match those set forth in the narrative description. Each time entry shall state: (1) the date the work was performed; (2) the name of the person performing the work; (3) a brief statement of the nature of the work; (4) the time expended on the work in increments of tenth of an hour; and (5) the fee charged for the work described in the entry."[7] In any case, the financial expert should discuss timekeeping and billing practices with the client attorney before significant time is incurred on an engagement.

Financial Expert Witness Special Instructions

There are some special instructions that apply specifically to a financial expert who is expected to testify as an expert witness. These instructions are necessary because of the role the financial expert witness plays in the dispute resolution proceedings by providing evidentiary oral testimony. In addition, special instructions are needed to ensure that the financial expert witness is not unintentionally exposed to legally privileged information that is intended to be kept confidential by the client legal counsel. Special instructions applicable to the financial expert witness are discussed next.

Qualifications and Expert Opinions

It is not unusual for the financial expert to not know exactly what qualified him to be selected to serve as an expert witness by the client. Therefore, it is helpful for the financial expert witness to ask the client legal counsel what skills, knowledge, education, experience, education, and training were identified during the due diligence process as relevant to the case at hand. With this information, the financial expert witness can demonstrate those qualifications throughout the proceedings and during the trial. This can enhance the credibility of the financial expert witness to the trier of fact.

The financial expert witness must also obtain a clear understanding about the opinions the client attorney expects the financial expert witness to form after work is complete. Oftentimes, the client attorney will articulate up front the opinions expected from the financial expert witness. This is a normal part of the assignment scoping process. Mind you, the client attorney is not telling the financial expert witness what the opinion is to be, but instead which disputed issues require opinions. If this is not communicated, the financial expert witness should confirm that the objective of the assignment is for the financial expert to do the work deemed necessary to reach an admissible opinion on a specific issue in dispute.

If the client attorney crosses the line and asks the financial expert witness for unreasonable opinions, the financial expert witness should carefully consider any continuing involvement in the case. Under no circumstances should the financial expert subject his judgment to another and agree to offer opinions that are unsupported, over-reaching, overly broad, or unattainable. Any request to form an opinion on the intent of any party or legal matters is inappropriate and should be declined by the financial expert witness.

The Storyline

The financial expert witness will find that every case has a storyline. The client attorney will prepare each case to tell their version of the story. Facts and data will be organized and presented to reinforce the story with the trier of fact. The financial expert witness should understand the storyline and attempt to dovetail his testimony to fit the story being told by the client attorney—always staying true to the principles of truthfulness, integrity, and objectivity. In this way, the financial expert witness's testimony will be consistent, relevant, and understandable in the context of the storyline.

> I've always said I have one skill. That skill—if I have it at all—is storytelling.
>
> —Mitch Albom

Discoverability of Draft Reports and Notes

The federal rules protect financial expert witness draft reports and communications that may be exchanged between the financial expert witness and the client legal counsel from discovery and disclosure to an opposing party.[8] The federal rules "protect drafts of any report or disclosure" prepared by the financial expert witness "regardless of the form in which the draft is recorded."[9] Furthermore, the federal rules "protect communications between the party's attorney and any witness" required to prepare an expert witness disclosure report, "regardless of the form of the communications," with limited exceptions.[10] The exceptions to this rule relate to communications that:

    (i) relate to compensation for the expert's study or testimony;
    (ii) identify facts or data that the party's attorney provided and that the expert considered in forming the opinions to be expressed; or
    (iii) identify assumptions that the party's attorney provided and that the expert relied on in forming the opinions to be expressed.[11]

Regardless of these protections, there can still be controversy about the scope of these exceptions and many state courts and alternative dispute resolution forums do not have similar carve-out rules. Therefore, the financial expert witness should ask the client attorney for instructions about these matters before discarding anything, including draft expert reports.

In a similar vein, there can be differences of opinion about handwritten or typed notes prepared by the financial expert witness. In general, financial expert witness notes are discoverable by an opposing party, if properly requested. Accordingly, most client attorneys will instruct the financial expert witness not to take notes of any kind. However, in some instances that may be impractical. For example, the financial expert witness may be compelled to take notes during an interview of a key witness, or when hearing details of a complicated transaction. In those situations, extreme care should be taken to avoid making comments that potentially reflect bias, incomplete or preliminary conclusions, or important unaddressed matters. If the financial expert witness elects to take contemporaneous notes or type them up later, it is advisable for the content to be strictly limited to facts.

The financial expert witness should be aware that individuals working under their direct supervision and control may also be subject to the same note-taking discovery rules. That means that other staff members' notes may be discoverable by an opposing party. However, there are practical limitations to such requests and production. Regardless, note taking by staff members should be discussed with the client attorney before work begins and such notes should not be produced to an opposing party without the expressed permission of the client legal counsel or an order from the court.

Client Contact

The financial expert witness should not attempt to arrange direct contact with an underlying client of the client legal counsel. This applies to casual interactions as well as case-related interviews and fact-gathering activities performed by the financial expert witness. Failure to follow this protocol may jeopardize applicable client legal privileges. Therefore, the financial expert witness and the underlying client should be clear on the protocols to be followed when such exchanges are necessary.

In most cases, it is preferable that communications between the underlying client and the financial expert be requested and delivered exclusively to the client attorney. The client attorney will decide the appropriate timing and delivery for such communications and the method of response, if any. In some cases, direct access may be granted. If so, reasonable efforts should be made to inform the client legal counsel about such communications so that timely decisions can be made about party participation.

Phone Calls and Electronic Communications

In this high-tech world of communication, the financial expert witness should be cognizant about the discovery of communications delivered via phone, text, instant messenger, and e-mail. In addition, confidential information is under the constant threat of compromise from hackers and data jockeys. Therefore, the financial expert witness should do several things. First, make sure your technology infrastructure has sufficient security protocols and controls to minimize the risk of unauthorized access to confidential information. Next, consider adding verbiage to the engagement letter to confirm with the client the inherent risk of using technology for communicating and transferring facts and data. The financial expert witness should get specific permission from the client to use technology for such purposes. Lastly, talk to the client attorney about communication preferences and protocols. Some client attorneys request minimal electronic communications. Others seem to have no concerns at all, e-mailing the financial expert witness frequently and at all hours.

Regardless of any specific instructions from the client attorney, the financial expert witness should have their own protocols for phone calls and electronic communications. That includes voicemail and texting. Electronic communications to and from the financial expert witness should be carefully considered as they are likely subject to discovery by an opposing party. That applies to exchanges between the financial expert witness and the client attorney, as well as those between the expert and the engagement team. It is preferable to communicate with the financial expert witness by phone because of the firsthand nature of the exchange. Remember, all recorded materials and electronic communications must be saved by the financial expert witness as they are subject to opposing party discovery, except for expert report drafts as discussed previously.

Work Papers and Work Product

In addition to the work paper and work product headings that should be used for all engagements discussed earlier, the financial expert witness should label work as "CONFIDENTIAL," especially if the matter is subject to a protective order or confidentiality agreement. In addition, sensitive and confidential information disclosed by the financial expert witness in the expert report or produced in response to a subpoena *duces tecum* may require redaction at the direction of the client legal counsel. Examples of the types of information to be redacted may include legally protected personal information, bank account numbers, and proprietary client names. Related to financial expert witness reports subject to court-ordered restrictions, it is prudent to mark each page with "CONFIDENTIAL—SUBJECT TO COURT ORDER" to warn the reader about the restrictions and indicate the intent of the financial expert witness to comply with such orders. Ideally, the financial expert should agree in advance on such confidentiality markings and procedures with the client attorney.

It is common for the financial expert witness to be asked by client legal counsel to assist with a number of tasks throughout the dispute resolution process. Requests may include, but not be limited to, preparation of the following items:

- Fee and expense budgets
- Staffing plans
- Resource requirements
- Work programs and procedures
- Identification of facts, data, assumptions, and evidence to be produced
- Witness questions to be asked during deposition or trial
- Rebuttal and critique of opposing expert witness reports and testimony
- Direct examination outline
- Cross-examination questions for opposing experts

Special attention should be paid to these requests for assistance and the resultant work product. The same is true for requests made by the financial expert witness to the client attorney or underlying client. To the extent these matters are documented, the materials are likely available to an opposing party through discovery, which may create problems. As such, the financial expert witness should double-check with the client legal counsel before memorializing any response to such requests, or before making any requests in writing.

Authenticity of Evidence

It will be important in some situations for the financial expert witness to be able to establish the authenticity of the facts, data, and evidence on which he or she relies. All evidence is required to be authentic in order for it to be admissible in trial.[12] The Federal Rules of Evidence (FRE) permit an expert to rely on facts and data that are not admissible as evidence, so long as "experts in the particular field would reasonably rely on those kinds of facts or data in forming an opinion."[13] This is often referred to as the expert witness exception to the federal hearsay rules. However, there often may be other reasons that it is important to establish that the materials on which an expert relies are authentic copies of what they purport to be.

Therefore, the financial expert witness must maintain a proper chain of custody for any materials to be relied upon in forming expert opinions to be offered in court. A proper chain of custody accurately documents the source, movement, location, and custodianship of facts, data, and evidence from the time they are obtained by the financial expert witness until such materials are used in court. The ability of the financial expert witness to establish a proper chain of custody lays the foundation to establish authenticity by proving such materials were not altered, amended, substituted, or compromised.

Get Paid Before You Testify

Unpaid bills for services rendered by the financial expert witness at the time of testimony create an undue risk of collection. In addition, the trier of fact may perceive bias, thinking that the financial expert witness is to be paid contingent upon testimony favorable to the client—in essence, a hired gun held hostage by the threat that bills won't be paid. Accordingly, the financial expert witness should consider a policy or contractual term that requires the payment of all outstanding invoices before testimony is given. This is in the client's interest as well, but sometimes is easier said than done. So, it is important for reminders to be delivered well before scheduled deposition or trial testimony. If for some reason payment cannot be received before testimony, formal arrangements should be made for payment using scheduled remittances or written agreements that may include collateral security.

Special Considerations for Combined Consulting and Expert Witness Engagements

Client legal counsel may decide to engage a consulting financial expert as well as a testifying financial expert witness. This typically happens when a dispute is large and complex. In these cases, the client attorney uses the consulting financial expert for a number of services, but intends for the consultant and associated work to be undisclosed and subject to applicable legal privileges preventing discovery by an opposing party. Alternatively, the financial expert witness is expected to be disclosed to an opposing party and fully open for discovery, except for reports drafts excluded by federal rule.

The practice of engaging two financial experts and keeping legally privileged matters protected is more easily managed when the financial consulting and testifying expert witness are from different organizations. Communications between the consultant and expert witness can be restricted and controlled by the client legal counsel using formal communication protocols. Such protocols usually require all exchanges go through the client legal counsel. This helps to protect legal privilege that may attach to the consultant and prevents any leakage of nonessential information to the financial expert witness who may be compelled to disclose such knowledge to an opposing party.

In circumstances where the client attorney chooses to use the same organization to draw upon both a financial expert consultant and witness, strict attention must be paid to sequester the financial expert witness from the consulting financial expert. Internal protocols are commonly adopted to build firewalls to keep the consultant and expert witness separated. Methods used to accomplish this end may include having the consultant and expert witness in different divisions or offices, using separate data and file storage, and restricting communications related to the matter in dispute. Regardless of the methods used, the controls should be designed to protect applicable legal privileges and avoid untimely disclosures to an opposing party during discovery.

 ## COMING UP

We turn our attention in Chapter 5 to the requirements and obligations of the financial expert.

 ## NOTES

1. Members of the American Institute of Certified Public Accountants should refer to: Statement on Quality Control Standards No. 8, QC Section 10, *A Firm's System of Quality Control*, effective January 1, 2012, for guidance on client acceptance policies and practices.
2. FRCP, Rule 16(b).
3. FRCP, Rule 26(c).
4. FRCP, Rule 26(a)(4)(E).
5. FRCP, Rule 26(b)(4)(B).
6. There are protections afforded the financial expert witness related to the discovery of certain materials under FRCP Rule 26(b)(4)(B) and (C).
7. United States Bankruptcy Court, Northern District of Illinois, effective January 1, 2012, available at www.ilnb.uscourts.gov/sites/default/files/local_rules/Local_Rules_2012.pdf.
8. FRCP, Rule 26(b)(4).
9. FRCP, Rule 26(b)(4)(B).
10. FRCP, Rule 26(b)(4)(C).
11. Ibid.
12. FRE, Rule 901.
13. FRE, Rule 703.

CHAPTER FIVE

Civil Litigation and Dispute Resolution Processes

 ## CIVIL LITIGATION ACTIONS AND PROCEEDINGS

In the United States of America, claims of civil torts and contract causes of action are handled through the federal and state civil court systems. Procedural rules and practices can vary significantly between state and federal courts, and even between different courts in the same state or federal system. However, an increasing number of state courts are adopting rules and procedures that closely follow the federal rules. Therefore, the focus for this book will be on federal civil actions and proceedings.

Federal civil litigation consists of a number of interrelated activities that can be grouped into a process flow. The litigation process flow starts before the litigation has formally started and ends with after-trial activities. Settlement activities, legal motion practice, and hearings occur in furtherance of the resolution of the dispute, with rulings and orders issued by the court throughout the proceedings. This process flow is reflected in Exhibit 5.1.

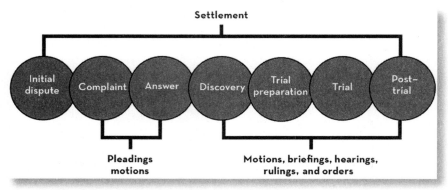

EXHIBIT 5.1   Civil Litigation Process Flow

Initial Dispute

The pre-litigation process includes the identification and initial reaction to a dispute by the parties. This process precedes formal litigation. Activities in this process can be formal or informal and might include:

- Socialization of issues and potential responses.[1]
- Investigations, inquiries, and fact-finding activities.
- Identification and collection of relevant data and records.
- Preparation of suspected causes of action, allegations, and claims.
- Notice, dialogue, demands, and negotiations between parties.
- Meet and confer proceedings.
- Determine preferred and suitable formal dispute resolution actions.

Complaint

At this stage, the first formal pleading is prepared by the plaintiff in the form of a civil complaint.[2] A federal civil complaint identifies the complaining party or parties, their legal counsel, and the defendant or defendants being sued. It is required to set forth a "short and plain statement of the claim showing that the [plaintiff] is entitled to relief" along with a demand for the relief sought, often in the form of monetary damages.[3] Depending on the nature of the claim, and with the exception of certain specialized courts, the complainant generally has the right to request a jury or bench trial. Over the course of civil litigation proceedings, the complaint may be amended. It is critical that the financial expert read the complaint and any associated amendments in order

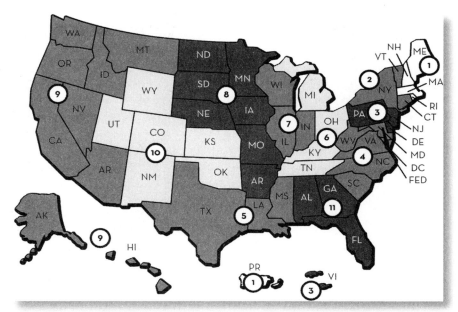

EXHIBIT 5.2   Federal Court System of the United States of America

Geographic boundaries of United States Courts of Appeals and United States District Courts
Source: See United States Courts at www.uscourts.gov.

to ensure reporting and testimony will be relevant, useful, and appropriate within the requirements of civil litigation. The federal court system is shown in Exhibit 5.2.

Answer

Each named defendant is required to formally respond or answer in writing an officially filed and served complaint. The Federal Rules of Civil Procedure (FRCP) provide for a defendant to respond either by filing a motion directed at the complaint, usually a motion to dismiss, or by filing an answer.[4] (Motions to dismiss are discussed further on.) The answer typically admits or denies each allegation in the complaint, or states that the defendant lacks sufficient information to admit or deny the allegation.[5] In addition, the answer may include affirmative defenses, one or more counterclaims against the plaintiff, or cross-claims against one or more other defendants.[6] Defendants also may file third-party claims against one or more additional parties that must be served with the third-party claims and added to the case as third-party defendants.[7]

Discovery

Discovery is the pretrial process whereby the disputing parties are compelled to disclose requested information and knowledge about the pending dispute to the opposing party. Discovery is facilitated by the use of recognized methods available to the disputing parties, some of which are defined by federal rules. These methods include stipulations, requests for admissions, interrogatories, requests for production, witness statements, expert reports, and depositions.

Stipulations are binding agreements about matters relevant to the proceedings entered into voluntarily by and between disputing parties. Among numerous other matters, stipulations may involve practices, protocols, facts, and rules. For example, opposing parties may stipulate to the authenticity of documents, the dates of certain events, the fact of liability, or how to handle the exchange of requested materials.

The most common written discovery tools are interrogatories and requests for production. Interrogatories are written questions prepared in connection with the dispute that are submitted to an opposing party and required to be answered in writing and under oath.[8] Typical interrogatories might ask an opposing party to identify witnesses with relevant knowledge, identify relevant documents, explain the basis of certain allegations or defenses, or answer questions about factual events.

Requests for production request a party to produce relevant or potentially relevant documents or electronically stored information in that party's possession, custody, or control.[9] Alternatively, the party receiving the request for production may allow the requesting party the opportunity to inspect, copy, test, or sample documents or electronically stored information in that party's possession, custody, or control.[10] The proper scope of requests for production and the extent of the responding party's obligation to produce are frequent subjects of discovery disputes. Occasionally, the financial expert will be requested to support the client's request for production by providing a statement that the requested information is important or useful for an analysis the expert has been retained to perform.

Requests for admission are formal written requests served to an opposing party to admit or deny specific propositions about the facts, how the law is applied to the facts, opinions about facts and legal application, or the genuineness of documents relevant to the pending dispute.[11]

Witness statements evidence information, knowledge, and accounts of a witness relevant to the pending dispute. Witness statements are provided outside the courtroom and can be sworn or unsworn. Sworn witness statements are commonly documented in an affidavit. Unsworn witness statements may take the form of a declaration, or may be less formal. Typically, the parties will serve on each other requests for production of any witness statements.

The discovery rules also require written expert witness reports that include specific disclosures to the opposing party under FRCP Rule 26(a)(2)(B).[12] The expert report is to be prepared and signed by the expert witness and must include:

- A complete statement of all opinions the witness will express and the basis and reasons for them.
- The facts or data considered by the witness in forming them.
- Any exhibits that will be used to summarize or support them.
- The witness's qualifications, including a list of all publications authored in the previous 10 years.
- A list of all other cases in which, during the previous four years, the witness testified as an expert at trial or by deposition.
- A statement of the compensation to be paid for the study and testimony in the case.

Expert Report Rules

- Opinion
- Facts and materials considered
- Trial exhibits
- Qualifications
- Publications
- Prior testimony
- Compensation

Depositions are usually oral testimony given outside the courtroom by a witness, normally during discovery.[13] Depositions for oral testimony are convened by an opposing party's legal counsel with notice or by using a valid and legally enforceable subpoena compelling the witness to attend and participate. A deposition session consists of deposing legal counsel asking the witness questions to be answered in real time. Deposition oral testimony is recorded verbatim using a written or videotaped transcript prepared by a court-certified court reporter or videographer. The record of the deposition testimony can be used in discovery or later during trial.

The FRCP also provides for depositions on written questions, but this procedure is rarely used.[14]

Trial Preparation

Trial preparation begins before the initial filing of the complaint and continues through the date the trial ends. In addition to discovery activities, trial preparation includes procedures for the disputing parties and the court to narrow the facts and issues in dispute prior to trial. In most cases, various motions will be filed by the disputing parties in an effort to obtain favorable court rulings and orders related to the trial proceedings. In many instances, the judge may ask for written or oral briefings from the parties to aid in decision making.

Motions, Briefings, Hearings, Rulings, and Orders

Throughout the litigation process, the disputing parties and the court have interactions using oral and written communications designed to resolve or settle a pending dispute, or to reduce the trial proceedings to a clearly defined set of disputed facts and issues that require a formal decision by an impartial trier of fact. Many of these interactions are evidenced by motions, briefs, hearings, rulings, and orders.

Motions are written or oral requests to the judge by the disputing parties for the court to make a ruling or issue an order. Motions often seek pretrial determination of disputed facts or legal issues or otherwise seek to define or narrow the issues for trial. Oftentimes, a written motion is accompanied by a draft order for the judge to adopt and sign if the motion prevails. Orders are authoritative directions issued by the court. Motions usually are accompanied by a brief in support of the motion and followed by a responsive brief from the opposing party asking the judge to deny the pending motion. Depending on the disputed facts and issues at hand, the financial expert witness may be asked by the client's legal counsel to prepare a declaration or affidavit in support of the motion or response to a motion.

Briefs contain written arguments prepared by the disputing parties' legal counsel to assist the court with the determination of legal and factual disputes. Briefs include support for the written arguments, such as citations to relevant case law precedents. The parties also may submit discovery materials and other evidence in support of their arguments. Frequently, the court will convene a hearing to allow the disputing parties the opportunity to orally argue their positions. Hearings are courtroom proceedings presided over by a judge or court-appointed master who hears oral arguments to assist with making decisions about disputed facts and legal issues. The hearing may or may not include witness testimony. Most hearings are attended exclusively by the disputing parties' legal counsels; however, the financial expert witness may be asked to appear or even to testify, depending on the facts and issues in dispute. Similar to trial, hearings may result in the instant or subsequent issuance of orders or rulings.

The financial expert witness should be aware of legal motions likely to be encountered in most cases and their potential role related to supporting such motions. Following is a brief description of common civil litigation motions:

- **Motion to dismiss (or, motion for dismissal).**[15] Most commonly this is a request by the defendant for the court to dismiss some or all of the claims asserted in the complaint.
- **Motion for discovery (and the related motion to compel).**[16] This is a request made by either party that the court require the opposing party to produce legally discoverable materials and data in response to the moving party's discovery requests.
- **Motion to quash or for protective order.**[17] A request that the court invalidate, void, or nullify a pending subpoena, or otherwise provide protection from all or part of a pending discovery request.
- **Motion *in limine*.**[18] A request made by a party often for the court to exclude evidence from being presented at trial by the opposing party.
- **Motion for summary judgment.** A party's request for the court to rule in their favor prior to trial because there is no genuine issue of material fact to be tried in the case and the movant is entitled to judgment as a matter of law.[19]
- **Motion to strike at trial.** A request made by either party for the court to remove objectionable statements or legally inadmissible evidence from the record. This type of motion may also be used to request that the testimony of the financial expert witness be stricken from the record, thereby causing the judge to ask the jury to disregard the testimony if the motion is granted.
- **Motion for judgment as a matter of law (or, motion for directed verdict).**[20] A request by a party for the court to order judgment in their favor before the case is given to the jury because a reasonable jury would not have a legally sufficient evidentiary basis to find in favor of the opposing party.

Common Legal Motions

- Dismiss
- Discover
- Quash
- *In limine*
- Summary judgment
- Strike
- Directed verdict

Settlement

Settlement is an agreement by and between the disputing parties to end or resolve a pending dispute. Settlement can take place at any time after the dispute is known by the disputing parties, including prior to or during trial. Many federal civil proceedings require parties to participate in a mandated pretrial mediation or settlement conference before trial.[21] The overwhelming majority of civil litigation cases settle before trial.

Trial

Trial is the formal courtroom proceeding in which the trier of fact decides the truth about disputed facts. A trial can be conducted as a bench or jury trial based on the rights available to the disputing parties. A bench trial is conducted in front of a judge, without a jury, wherein the judge acts as the trier of fact. A federal jury trial consists of at least six, but no more than 12, jury members with each juror participating in the determination of the final verdict, unless excused.[22] In either a bench trial or a jury trial, the judge decides any disputed issues of law.

Post-Trial

After the trial is complete, the disputing parties may file motions or appeal the verdict and judgment. In some federal cases, a motion may be filed before the case is given to the jury for deliberation and verdict that states there is no sufficient legal basis for a reasonable jury to return a verdict for the opposing party. This is called a motion for judgment as a matter of law and may be referred to as a motion for directed verdict.[23] Alternatively, an adverse judgment against one of the disputing parties may result in a motion for a new trial based on alleged material error made by the trial judge during the proceedings.

An appeal seeks to reverse the trial court's judgment using a higher court. An appeal begins with the filing of a notice by the appealing party. This notice is followed by written brief of the facts and legal arguments supporting a reversal of the trial court's actions. The opposing party, the appellee, responds to the appeal brief with an opposing answer and the appellant may then file another brief in response to the opposition brief.

Based on these briefs and, in certain instances, oral arguments, the appellate court deliberates and determines whether the trial court made material legal errors requiring reversal. If reversed, the case is sent back, or remanded, to a lower-level court. A remand is accompanied by orders to consider the decision of the appellate court, which may amend or correct the trial court's judgment or require the acceptance and consideration of new evidence or the reconsideration of existing evidence. In rare cases a new trial is ordered.

Appellate courts consider only the evidence that was introduced in the trial court and do not consider new evidence from the parties. Accordingly, there is no formal role for a financial expert in the appeal. The expert may, however, be requested to assist counsel in developing their arguments on appeal.

ALTERNATIVE DISPUTE RESOLUTION[24]

There are many ways to resolve a civil dispute outside of formal litigation. In the United States of America there are two commonly used methods—mediation and arbitration.

Mediation assists the disputing parties by attempting to reach a settlement using an independent third-party mediator. Mediation is voluntary and is typically nonbinding to the disputing parties. The mediator identifies disputed facts and issues and helps the disputing parties understand the strengths and weaknesses of each parties' positions, while at the same time trying to negotiate demands for damages and other concessions. In many cases, the disputing parties are separated for much of the mediation, with the mediator shuttling from room to room in an effort to broker a settlement. The mediator does not decide any disputed facts or issues and is, therefore, not a trier of fact.

Arbitration can be voluntary or mandatory and it is usually binding to the disputing parties. In arbitration, the disputing parties agree on a qualified third party, called an arbitrator or arbitration panel, to serve as a neutral trier of fact. The arbitrator presides over the dispute resolution activities, which typically conclude with a formal written decision after an arbitration proceeding. An arbitration proceeding resembles a trial, with each disputing party presenting their respective cases and fact and expert witnesses called to testify. In some cases, the financial expert witness may be asked to testify in arbitration simultaneously with the opposing expert witness—a process called "hot-tubbing." It is also commonplace for an arbitration to be conducted as "baseball" arbitration. Baseball arbitration is loosely based on player salary contract negotiations used in Major League Baseball. In baseball arbitration, the arbitrator is required to choose one side's demands or the other's, as the exclusive decision. As such, it is often referred to as "either/or" arbitration.

 ## COMING UP

In Chapter 6, we discuss roles that are suited for financial experts, including assignments, types of matters, and services to be performed.

 ## NOTES

1. These discussions are typically limited to internal personnel and retained professional consultants.
2. FRCP, Rule 3, Commencing an Action.
3. FRCP, Rule 8(a).
4. FRCP, Rule 12.
5. FRCP, Rule 8(b), Defenses; Admissions and Denials.
6. FRCP, Rule 13, Counterclaim and Cross-claim.
7. FRCP, Rule 14, Third-Party Practice.
8. FRCP, Rule 33, Interrogatories to Parties.
9. *See* FRCP Rule 34, Producing Documents, Electronically Stored Information, and Tangible Things.
10. Ibid.
11. FRCP Rule 36, Requests for Admission.
12. FRCP Rule 26(a)(2)(B), Duty to Disclose; General Provision Governing Discovery, Disclosure of Expert Testimony.
13. FRCP Rule 30, Deposition by Oral Examination.
14. FRCP, Rule 31, Depositions by Written Questions.
15. FRCP Rule 12(b), How to Present Defenses.
16. FRCP Rule 37(a), Motion for an Order Compelling Disclosure or Discovery.
17. *See* FRCP 26(b)(2), Limitations on Frequency and Extent; 26(c), Protective Orders; 45(d)(3), Quashing or Modifying a Subpoena.

18. *In limine* is a Latin term meaning "threshold."
19. *See* FRCP, Rule 56, Summary Judgment.
20. *See* FRCP, Rule 50, Judgment as a Matter of Law in a Jury Trial.
21. FRCP, Rule 16, Pretrial Conferences.
22. *See* FRCP, Rule 48, Number of Jurors.
23. Ibid., Rule 50.
24. Organizations specializing in alternative dispute resolution services include the American Arbitration Association (www.adr.org), JAMS, the Resolution Experts (www.jamsadr.com), and the International Institute for Conflict Prevention and Resolution (www.cpradr.org).

PART TWO

Financial Expert Rules, Case Precedent, and Ethics

CHAPTER SIX

Federal Rules of Evidence for the Financial Expert Witness

EVIDENTIARY RULES ON EXPERT WITNESS OPINIONS AND TESTIMONY

The Federal Rules of Evidence (FRE), ARTICLE VII, OPINIONS AND EXPERT TESTIMONY, Rules 702, 703, 704, 705, and 706 describe the requirements for financial expert testimony.[1] These rules are defined as follows:

Rule 702. Testimony by Expert Witnesses
A witness who is qualified as an expert by knowledge, skill, experience, training, or education may testify in the form of an opinion or otherwise if: (a) the expert's scientific, technical, or other specialized knowledge will help the trier of fact to understand the evidence or to determine a fact in issue; (b) the testimony is based on sufficient facts or data; (c) the testimony is the product of reliable principles and methods; and (d) the expert has reliably applied the principles and methods to the facts of the case.

Rule 703. Bases of an Expert's Opinion Testimony
An expert may base an opinion on facts or data in the case that the expert has been made aware of or personally observed. If experts in the

particular field would reasonably rely on those kinds of facts or data in forming an opinion on the subject, they need not be admissible for the opinion to be admitted. But if the facts or data would otherwise be inadmissible, the proponent of the opinion may disclose them to the jury only if their probative value in helping the jury evaluate the opinion substantially outweighs their prejudicial effect.

Rule 704. Opinion on an Ultimate Issue

(a)   In general—not automatically objectionable. An opinion is not objectionable just because it embraces an ultimate issue.

(b)   Exception. In a criminal case, an expert witness must not state an opinion about whether the defendant did or did not have a mental state or condition that constitutes an element of the crime charged or of a defense. Those matters are for the trier of fact alone.

Rule 705. Disclosing the Facts or Data Underlying an Expert's Opinion

Unless the court orders otherwise, an expert may state an opinion—and give the reasons for it—without first testifying to the underlying facts or data. But the expert may be required to disclose those facts or data on cross-examination.

Rule 706. Court-Appointed Expert Witnesses

(a)   Appointment process. On a party's motion or on its own, the court may order the parties to show cause why expert witnesses should not be appointed and may ask the parties to submit nominations. The court may appoint any expert that the parties agree on and any of its own choosing. But the court may only appoint someone who consents to act.

(b)   Expert's role. The court must inform the expert of the expert's duties. The court may do so in writing and have a copy filed with the clerk or may do so orally at a conference in which the parties have an opportunity to participate. The expert:

(1)   must advise the parties of any findings the expert makes;

(2)   may be deposed by any party;

(3)   may be called to testify by the court or any party; and

(4)   may be cross-examined by any party, including the party that called the expert.

(c)   Compensation. The expert is entitled to a reasonable compensation, as set by the court. The compensation is payable as follows:

(1)   in a criminal case or in a civil case involving just compensation under the Fifth Amendment, from any funds that are provided by law; and

(2) in any other civil case, by the parties in the proportion and at the time that the court directs—and the compensation is then charged like other costs.

(d) Disclosing the appointment to the jury. The court may authorize disclosure to the jury that the court appointed the expert.

(e) Parties' choice of their own experts. This rule does not limit a party in calling its own experts.

Let's explore some of the requirements of the FRE as they relate to financial expert witness reporting and testimony.

SCIENTIFIC, TECHNICAL, OR OTHER SPECIALIZED KNOWLEDGE

The FRE require the financial expert witness to have scientific, technical, or specialized knowledge that will assist the trier of fact. There are two important points about this requirement. Number one, the financial expert witness's purpose is to assist the trier of fact. So, like the saying goes: "Begin with the end in mind."[2] Design ultimate testimony to help the trier of fact. The financial expert witness must ask himself: What will the trier of fact find compelling about my qualifications so that my testimony will be received as credible and reliable? Point number two, the financial expert witness will be allowed to testify in court only if qualified as an expert by the court. Qualifications include the financial expert witness's knowledge, skill, experience, training, or education in the profession relevant to the issues in dispute for which the financial expert witness is expected to testify and give opinions.

To be qualified as an expert, the financial expert witness must prove to the court that he has germane knowledge, skill, experience, training, or education to provide the foundation of credibility necessary for the court to admit the financial expert witness's testimony. In some cases, the financial expert witness will be introduced, qualified, and tendered as an expert in trial with little push-back from opposing legal counsel or the judge. In other cases, opposing legal counsel will attempt to disqualify the financial expert witness prior to trial and, if unsuccessful, ask the court to challenge the expert witness by voir dire at trial. Regardless, there is no hard-and-fast rule about the requisite levels of knowledge, skill, experience, training, or education needed to qualify a financial expert witness in a specified field.

To remember the qualifications requirement, the requisite factors of knowledge, skill, experience, training, or education can be formed into an acronym. By reordering the requirements into the order of skills, knowledge, education, experience, or training, the word SKEET is spelled out. Besides being easy to remember, SKEET seems apropos because the financial expert witness often feels like a practice range skeet target to be shot at by opposing counsel!

The admissibility of a financial expert witness's testimony in court is dependent on the presence of relevant SKEET at levels beyond an ordinary citizen (such as the jurors that serve as the trier of fact in most cases). Financial expert witness SKEET, in essence, assists the trier of fact to reach a decision on factual matters in dispute. Let's now explore more fully each of the financial expert witness SKEET qualifications.

Financial Expert Qualifications ("SKEET")

- Skills
- Knowledge
- Education
- Experience
- Training

Skills

What skills does a financial expert have? Of course, the answer to that question depends on each individual financial expert. Skills are the collection of knowledge, experience, education, and training that gives the financial expert the ability to perform well in a chosen profession or field. Therefore, skills are often identified and described using fields of expertise.

For the financial expert witness, these fields may be related to a technical specialty such as accounting, auditing, finance, economics, forensic investigation, digital forensics, or income taxes, to name just a few. Alternatively, skills may be described as industry-specific, like construction, energy, retail, health care, or not-for-profit. The trick is to identify skills for which the financial expert witness is recognized and that he or she uses on the job in the normal course of business, and that are relevant to the issues in dispute in the case. Typically, that would entail known professional skills that the financial expert witness uses to serve clients on a regular basis for a fee.

Knowledge

From the standpoint of qualifying the financial expert witness, knowledge is the known facts and data that have been processed using experience, training, and education in the financial expert witness's field of expertise. In other words, the combination of known information with specialized expertise and experience creates knowledge. Knowledge is more encompassing than just awareness, as it requires understanding and comprehension. The following quote captures the essence of knowledge.

> We are approaching a new age of synthesis. Knowledge cannot be merely a degree or a skill . . . it demands a broader vision, capabilities in critical thinking and logical deduction without which we cannot have constructive progress.
>
> —Li Ka-shing

Education

Education would appear to be one of the more black-and-white qualification requirements for the financial expert witness. After all, it relates to formal education, something we all have experienced. Formal education is measured by the culmination of a learning process designed for the student to acquire knowledge and competencies. Educational measurement is typically marked by grades and the award of a graduation certificate or educational degree. These grades, certificates, and degrees are the marks of qualifications for the financial expert witness.

As a general rule, university business college undergraduate degree programs provide an education in finance, accounting, economics, valuation, technology systems, and statistics, among other fields of study. These arts and sciences are critical to most financial expert engagements, and the financial expert witness must be prepared to describe to opposing counsel and the trier of fact the importance and relevance of this education to each assignment. In addition to these fields of study, the financial expert may also have a concentration or major in a single field that can further assist in qualifying the financial expert witness.

There may be circumstances where an advanced degree is called for to assist the trier of fact with highly technical issues. In these cases, a master's degree or PhD, especially an advanced degree where the studies and research performed are relevant in relation to the facts and circumstances of the case, is an excellent qualification. In such cases, the financial expert witness should be able to describe the relevance of the advanced education as a qualifier for relevance and credibility in connection with testimony to be given.

Let's not forget teaching, though. One side of the educational coin is learning; the other is teaching. Teachers, professors, and guest lecturers may be uniquely qualified to serve as financial expert witnesses because it is assumed that they have mastered the materials to be taught and others in the field seek them out for instruction. However, a potential downside for a full-time instructor with no other experience is that the trier of fact may see this person as lacking real-world experience. For certain triers of fact, preaching from a professorial "ivory tower" may tarnish the credibility of the financial expert witness who has dedicated a career to teaching alone.

Education Qualifications

- Trade school
- Undergraduate college degree
- Advanced college degrees (e.g., master's, PhD)
- Teaching positions (e.g., professor, guest lecturer)

Experience

Experience is likely the most relatable of all the financial expert witness's qualifications for the trier of fact to understand. Experience is the knowledge gained from events, acts, and outcomes directly dealt with by the financial expert witness. Everyone has experience in something, and the trier of fact appreciates this, especially if the financial expert witness can explain it in a way that is understandable and relevant to the case. Broadly speaking, financial expert witnesses might think of experience falling into three broad categories: (1) real life, (2) work, and (3) public service.

In this vernacular, real-life experience encompasses the financial expert witness's personal experiences outside of professional career work and community service. Real-life experience can come from family life, athletics, friendships, travel, hobbies, or interests. For example, working in a family restaurant could be very helpful and relevant for a dispute in the hospitality industry. Likewise, collecting coins might be useful in a case involving the value of investments in rare coins. In addition, serving on an audit committee of a public company might aid the financial expert in qualifying to testify in a dispute involving the actions of an audit committee when faced with management fraud allegations. The financial expert witness must, however, be able to articulate the weight and relevance of real-life experience in connection with any testimony to be given. This is often a difficult task.

Work experience is the most common experience cited by the financial expert witness as a qualification. Roles, responsibilities, and past performance of the financial expert witness are important factors for the trier of fact to consider when assessing testimony. Once again, the financial expert witness must be able to describe work experiences in a way that qualifies them as an expert in the field. Being able to explain the significance and relevance of day-to-day activities, assignments for other clients, and past major projects in regard to the similarities in size, scope, and complexities of the case at hand is crucial.

The next category of experience is public service. Public service is the time and effort the financial expert witness puts into civic, community, university, and professional organizations, typically as a volunteer. The financial expert witness may serve on a board, committee, task force, or work group for a public service organization. In these roles, the financial expert witness often gains valuable experience into the workings of not-for-profits and small business, while also dealing with a number of business issues large and small. A good example might be a volunteer member of the board of directors of a charitable organization appointed to a special committee to investigate allegations of the theft of donations. This has the potential to build experience with such investigations and the actions considered and taken by board members under the circumstances. That experience may assist the financial witness to qualify as an expert in cases with similar facts and circumstances.

> An expert is a man who has made all the mistakes which can be made, in a narrow field.
>
> —Niels Bohr

Training

Qualifications obtained from training are similar to those achieved by education. It consists of many avenues of learning designed to build skills and competencies, oftentimes using practice as a method of instruction. Much like education, training consists of learners and instructors. The students of training are provided learning content using instructor-led, self-study coursework, or on-the-job experiences.

It is important for coursework to be formalized enough for the student to be able to prove attendance, the learning objectives achieved, the technical content and creditworthiness of such content, and the number of hours credited. This process is normally documented by a certificate of completion issued by an accredited body. For many financial experts belonging to professional associations, there are minimum relevant continuing education requirements. These are important for the training qualification, because failure to meet the minimum training requirements can be a serious issue.

On-the-job training may be the most difficult to prove, and yet most important, part of the training qualification. On-the-job training is rarely formally documented and, therefore, it is challenging to conclusively show what the training accomplished and how it may be helpful to the trier of fact. On the other hand, the ability to clearly communicate what assignments were given to the financial expert witness for purposes of on-the-job training can be an effective tool to convince a trier of fact that the financial expert witness has learned relevant technical skills in real-life projects. Every juror appreciates being taught how to do a hard job and the value of successfully learning how to do it on the job when it really counts.

When it comes to the instruction of training, there are a small number of things that can make a big difference. Teaching peers and others in the profession is a powerful training qualification. It demonstrates that the profession looks to the financial expert witness for the delivery of instructional materials due to superior skills or the mastery of content. Likewise, the preparation, delivery, and publication of speeches, quotes, white papers, books, and webcasts may also be indicative of expertise in the field. Training materials and other thought leadership can be substantive ways to prove training qualifications to serve as a financial expert witness.

Certifications, Designations, Awards, and Citations

We have now taken a closer look at SKEET and the financial expert witness's qualifications. It should now be obvious that certifications, designations, awards, and citations were not included within these confines. Is that because they have no place in the world of expert qualifications? I assure you the answer is, no, they do have a place—and an important one.

Holding a professional certification, designation, award, or citation can be remarkably effective for qualifying a financial expert witness. Earlier in this book, there was a discussion about the value of the financial expert in litigation and dispute resolution. One area of value cited was professional certification, such as Certified Public Accountant, Chartered Financial Analyst, and Accredited in Business Valuation. Each of these achievements demonstrates superior knowledge in the field obtained by education, experience, and examination.

Many professionals holding these types of credentials are licensed and regulated by state authorities. In most situations, licensed practitioners must comply with professional regulations that include practice standards and minimum annual educational requirements to remain actively licensed and in good standing. Furthermore, the vast majority of professional credential holders belong to industry trade associations, like the American Institute of Certified Public Accountants. As members, they are required to adhere to professional standards and agree to be overseen by a governing body of peers. These are strong qualifications for the financial expert witness that can be shared with the trier of fact.

The financial expert witness should avoid collecting awards of achievement from lesser-known organizations or those not recognized widely in the profession. These can take on the appearance of "mail order" awards for which a fee is paid in return for achievement documents. The lack of substance and professional integrity behind such awards will likely be discovered to the discredit of the financial expert witness. In situations whereby the financial expert witness is provided a newly established professional award by a respected professional association after meeting rigorous and substantive minimum qualifications, such as education and experience, such awards are meaningful for qualifying the financial expert witness. However, the financial expert witness should be prepared to handle the inevitable questions from opposing counsel designed to minimize the importance of these professional awards on the premise that the financial expert witness was "grandfathered" into the award.

However, certifications, designations, awards, and citations must be of substance to count with any weight. Honorary degrees, public service awards, personal commendations, among other forms of recognition, may take on less significance to help the financial witness qualify as an expert. That is because there typically are not well-established standards and transparency governing these types of things. Without standards and transparency, it is difficult for the trier of fact to evaluate the weight, relevance, and credibility that should be given to the financial expert witness's testimony. That's not to say that an award for ethics should not be introduced with the belief that it will reflect positively on the character of the financial expert witness—it likely will.

Challenges to Financial Expert Witness Qualifications

Challenges related to the financial expert witness's qualifications may be brought out in motion practice by opposing legal counsel before trial. Alternatively, or in addition, opposing counsel may conduct a process called voir dire of the financial expert during trial. *Voir dire* is Latin for "to say the truth" or "speak what is true."

After the client legal counsel has elicited the financial expert witness's qualifications during direct examination, opposing legal counsel may move to voir dire the financial expert witness before any opinion testimony is heard by the trier of fact. If allowed by the court, opposing legal counsel will attempt to disqualify the financial expert witness by making inquiries designed to expose shortcomings in qualifications. The determination as to whether the financial expert witness is qualified to testify as an expert is made exclusively by the presiding judge. If deemed qualified, the financial expert witness will be allowed to give expert testimony. If disqualified, the financial expert will not be allowed to testify further in the trial.

It is helpful to study how the courts explain their decisions to disqualify financial expert witnesses. It provides interesting insights into the thinking of the courts on case law and federal rules. Accordingly, several case excerpts follow. The names of the financial expert witnesses have been redacted.

The first case following illustrates a financial expert witness found to be unqualified in connection with a cost model.

> The Court agrees with Red Spot that EXPERT WITNESS'S report evidences his lack of expertise to opine on the efficacy of the methodology used in Rogers' opportunity cost model. Under Federal Rule of Evidence 702 ("Rule 702") and *Daubert v. Merrell Dow Pharmaceuticals, Inc.*, 509 U. S. 579, 113 S. Ct. 2786, 125 L. Ed. 2d 469 (1993), the Court follows a two-prong framework: (1) the Court must determine whether "the proposed witness would testify to valid scientific, technical, or other specialized knowledge and (2) [the Court must determine whether] his testimony will assist the trier of fact." *Ammons v. Aramark Uniform Servs., Inc.*, 368 F.3d 809, 816 (7th Cir. 2004) (quotations and citations omitted). The first prong "of this framework evaluates the reliability of the testimony." *Id.* To determine whether EXPERT WITNESS'S opinions are reliable the Court "must determine whether the expert is qualified in the relevant field and whether the methodology underlying the expert's conclusions is reliable." *Id.* (quoting *Zelinski v. Columbia 300, Inc.*, 335 F.3d 633,

640 [7th Cir. 2003]). The Court must "reject 'any subjective belief or speculation.'" *Id.* (quoting *Chapman v. Maytag Corp.*, 297 F.3d 682, 687 [7th Cir. 2002] citing *Porter v. Whitehall Lab., Inc.*, 9 F.3d 607, 614 [7th Cir. 1993]).[3]

The next case is an appeal regarding the exclusion of testimony related to a financial expert witness's qualifications to testify about computer software.

Autotech contends that the district court erred by excluding EXPERT WITNESS'S testimony under Daubert and Federal Rule of Evidence 702. Based on his 26 years of experience in software development, review of the EZTouch software, and review of advertisements about C-More, EXPERT WITNESS testified that the features of C-More could not be developed independently of EZTouch. At no time, however, did EXPERT WITNESS examine the C-More software. Moreover, he never conducted tests on the product. The district court found this methodology unreliable because computer experts must do more than read advertisements. To qualify as an expert on software, an expert should, at a minimum, examine the product and software upon which the expert bases his opinion. Accordingly, we conclude that the district court properly found that EXPERT WITNESS was an unqualified expert and that his opinion was unreliable.[4]

Finally, the case that follows reflects that a financial expert was not qualified as an expert witness because he improperly used averages and reached erroneous conclusions. It also shows the risks of relying on others as a fundamental basis for preparing damages.

EXPERT WITNESS was not qualified to testify as an expert on the damages sustained by Craig's. Like Bloom, EXPERT WITNESS has no logical basis for his method of calculating the bank's ill-gotten gains. He analyzed two samples of 1995 data—one from February of 2,143 accounts and one from November of 970 accounts—and decided that the bank was negligent 51% and 71% of the time. Because he then averaged the results from the two samples, EXPERT WITNESS assumed that the bank acted negligently 60% of the time from January 1994 to October 1996. EXPERT WITNESS did not give weight to the number of accounts handled in each month. He also predicated his conclusions on Bloom's unreliable ones—making his exponentially more unreliable.[5]

Sufficient Facts and Data

The testimony of the financial expert witness may be excluded by the court if the opinions are found to be based on insufficient or irrelevant facts and data. Once again, an examination of exclusions by the court for this reason is instructive. Following are a couple of case excerpts with the financial expert names redacted. Note the courts' explanations for excluding the financial expert witness's testimony.

Challenges to Sufficient Facts and Data

The following case appeal explains the exclusion of financial expert testimony due to improper reliance on insufficient facts and data.

> Two experts were excluded: an economist to project Bahena's future income and a domestic relations lawyer to opine how much of the future income stream Bahena could have been required to pay Trevino's mother as child support. Both opinions were predicated on the assumption that Bahena was employed as a full time mechanic when he was killed. The only foundation laid for this assumption was testimony that (1) Bahena left in the morning and returned in the evening; (2) he gave Trevino's mother money at fairly regular intervals and (3) he was observed on a few occasions working, on cars. There were no pay stubs, no W-2s, no tax returns, no cancelled checks, and no employer testimony offered as foundational evidence. Given the state of the record, it was not manifestly erroneous for the district court to exclude the expert testimony for lack of foundation. See *Shatkin v. McDonnell Douglas Corp.*, 727 F.2d 202, 207 (2nd Cir. 1984) (vague assurances about future support are not an adequate foundation for expert testimony on future income).

The next case excludes financial expert witness testimony in connection with expert opinions on promotions. The facts and data used by the financial expert, in this case in the form of untested assumptions, were deemed by the court to be unreliable.

> While EXPERT WITNESS certainly has sufficient credentials, the expert evidence he purports to offer in this case is unscientific speculation that will not be beneficial to the trier of fact. He has not studied the profitability of promotional agencies in actual supermarket promotions . . . and did not do an analysis of the demand for supermarket promotions in USAir's markets . . . EXPERT WITNESS nevertheless assumes that

RVC would have entered into ten supermarket promotions a year using USAir certificates. His only source for this assumption is Mr. George, who, by his own admission, has no experience in supermarket promotions. . . .[6]

Reliable Principles and Methods Applied Reliably to Case

To be deemed admissible by the court, the financial expert witness must use reliable principles and methods applied to the relevant facts, data, and evidence of the case at hand. Reliable principles and methods encompass a number of proven or provable reliable financial standards and techniques. In the realm of the financial expert witness, these may include the following areas that have published and well-recognized principles and methods:

- Generally Accepted Accounting Principles (GAAP)
- Generally Accepted Auditing Standards (GAAS)
- Digital forensics
- Economics
- Econometrics
- International Financial Reporting Standards (IFRS)
- Financial forensic techniques
- Statistics
- Valuation

The partial case summaries below provide stark reminders about why the financial expert witness's work and opinions must be based on reliable principles and methods applied reliably to the facts, data, and evidence of the case. You will note the number of cases cited herein as an indication of the risks related to this area. Once again, the names of the financial expert witnesses have been replaced with generic terms.

Challenges to Reliable Methods and Principles

This first case involves the inadmissibility of a damages method adopted and used by a financial expert witness.

> In sum, EXPERT WITNESS measurement of losses based largely on prices from what Plaintiffs have consistently asserted are "fire sales," a description with which this Court agrees, renders his methodology unreliable and inadmissible. Without EXPERT WITNESS testimony, Plaintiffs cannot prove loss causation, and therefore cannot prove proximate cause.[7]

The next case relates to the computation of a reasonable royalty and includes the reasons why the model used by the financial expert witness was determined to be inadmissible by the court.

> In summary, the Court finds that Versata's experts' analysis fails to meet the basic criteria established by the opinions of both the Federal Circuit and this Court. Uniloc, ResQNet, and Lucent indicate that a damages model must be based on sound economic principles and reliable data, and that rules of thumb and other methods of speculative approximation should be excluded. For the reasons stated above, Versata has failed to meet this established criteria. Accordingly, the experts' respective reports and testimony regarding the revised reasonable royalty analysis was excluded from the jury trial.[8]

The case immediately following reflects the court's basis for excluding testimony on lost wages because of unreliable methods applied to irrelevant facts.

> Where properly pled and proven, under Louisiana law a plaintiff is entitled to recover past lost earnings and for the loss of future wages or earning capacity. A paramount concern in reparations for loss of future income is to provide the victim with a sum of money that will, *in fact*, replace the money the plaintiff could have earned. The plaintiff's economic analysis extrapolating future lost earnings on the basis of the salary of a dancer in New York for the greater part of her work life expectancy is both unreliable and not grounded in the facts of the plaintiff's work history. In the entirety of the plaintiff's work history, and even factoring in the value of the free ballet lessons earned by the plaintiff in return for teaching ballet, plaintiff's dancing activities did not begin to reap the plaintiff even close to a living wage (i.e., even by southeast Louisiana standards, much less New York's). Although the case law makes it clear that absolute certainty is impossible, considerations of reliability and relevance require that any economic analysis be ensconced with some resemblance to reality. The slender reed on which the economist's projection rests warrants no credence from the gatekeeper.[9]

A flawed methodology was the fatal mistake in the next case. In this case the financial expert witness's testimony was excluded based on an unrealistic sales projection.

> EXPERT WITNESS'S methodology is not reliable. First, as discussed above, EXPERT WITNESS'S conclusion is based on an unrealistic sales

projection. This can be viewed as a methodological flaw. See *Parkway Garage, Inc. v. City of Philadelphia*, 1994 U.S. Dist. LEXIS 10900, at *30, No. 90–7752, 1994 WL 412430, at *7 (E.D. Pa. Aug. 3, 1994) (an expert's opinion should have a reliable basis in the knowledge and experience of his discipline). Second, EXPERT WITNESS makes several significant errors that render his testimony unreliable. See *Raskin v. The Wyatt Co.*, 125 F.3d 55, 67 (2d Cir. 1997) (expert testimony that contains "elementary" error is not helpful); *Wilkinson v. Rosenthal & Co.*, 712 F. Supp. 474, 479 (E.D. Pa. 1989) (same).[10]

In the following case, the financial expert witness issued an expert report that was supplemented to cure deficiencies. However, the court found the supplemental report to be based on inadequate information and excluded the testimony.

On January 28, 2008, Defendants served Plaintiff with EXPERT WITNESS'S First Supplemental Expert Report ("the Supplemental Report"). As with the Initial Report, Defendants had not taken any meaningful discovery with regard to Plaintiff's investment, sales, or gross or net profits. Plaintiff argues that the Supplemental Report suffers from the same deficiencies as the Initial Report. Like the Initial Report, Plaintiff contends that it is based on insufficient data and uses improper damage methodologies to the facts of this case. Plaintiff also argues that Defendants' information is taken from the Proposed Pre-Trial Order (PPTO), which only includes final damages totals as opposed to the raw data which underlie those calculations. Plaintiff states that EXPERT WITNESS essentially "conjured a damages calculation, seemingly from this air."

Defendants argue that the Supplemental Report should not be stricken because each of the alleged defects in the Initial Report have been cured by the Second Supplemental Report, dated March 12, 2008.

Like the Initial Report, the Supplemental Report suffers from the same deficiencies of not having relied on adequate information to calculate the damages. EXPERT WITNESS essentially used the PPTO to guess at Plaintiff's damages amount. Again, EXPERT WITNESS admits that the PPTO "does not provide calculations for FOB's damages, but instead simply assert amounts" and that he was "left to guess about the real calculations that FOB proposes among what would be possible under FOB's vague description." . . . Unfortunately, EXPERT WITNESS'S guesswork cannot constitute reliable expert testimony and will most likely confuse or mislead the jury if it is introduced at trial. *Westberry*, 178 F.3d at 261. As a result, the Supplemental Report will be excluded, and EXPERT WITNESS will be precluded from testifying at trial.[11]

In the last example of inadmissibility due to the unreliable application of principles and methods to the facts of a case, the financial expert witness's testimony on copyright licensing was deemed irrelevant to the trier of fact.

> EXPERT WITNESS'S use of the Georgia Pacific framework for the calculation of a copyright license is unreliable. In determining "actual market value," "[t]he question is not what the owner would have charged, but rather what is the fair market value." On Davis, 246 F.3d at 166. That is an ex ante determination that considers the objective market value of the copyrighted work, as opposed to the Georgia Pacific "book of wisdom" framework, that employs a modified ex post examination of what the specific copyright plaintiff and defendant would have agreed to in a hypothetical bilateral negotiation. EXPERT WITNESS'S methodology is thus the opposite of the one required to determine a lost license fee as a measure of "actual damages" suffered by a copyright owner. It is therefore irrelevant.[12]

In this example, the financial expert is shown to be the mouthpiece of the plaintiff client and the testimony is excluded as it fails to provide an expert opinion based on principles reasonably relied upon by other experts in the field.

> When these principles are applied to the EXPERT WITNESS report, this Court finds that JRL has not met its burden of relevance and reliability under Rule 702. EXPERT WITNESS has merely accepted as true the facts given him by JRL. JRL's assertion that it is not offering EXPERT WITNESS as an expert in causation or statistics but as an expert on the calculation of damages is not enough. EXPERT WITNESS performed no independent analysis of the numbers given him by JRL; in fact, his report is devoid of any analysis of figures other than those provided by JRL. He has failed to show that reasonable accountants would simply and blindly accept such numbers in formulating opinions. His theory cannot be tested, and the rate of error is not known. Basically, the plaintiff is presenting its own estimation of damages in the guise of an expert opinion. EXPERT WITNESS has failed to demonstrate any impartiality in formulating his opinions, and he should be precluded from testifying . . . Motion in limine is GRANTED.[13]

Bases for Opinions

The financial expert witness must disclose the bases for any opinions expressed. The bases consist of the foundation supporting the opinions. The foundation may be relevant facts, data, evidence, and the results of work performed using reliable methods and principles. Unlike lay witnesses, the financial expert witness may base opinions on facts and data that are not admitted into evidence if such information is of the type reasonably relied upon by other experts in the field. The courts have demonstrated that opinions with faulty or unsupportable bases will cause exclusion of the financial expert's opinions. An example of such a case is reported below with the financial expert witness's name replaced with an anonymous label.

Challenges to Bases for Opinions

In the following case, the court rules financial expert witness testimony inadmissible for two reasons. First, it was unpermitted for lack of relevance. Secondly, all of the opinions and the bases for them were not properly disclosed.

> The Court holds that EXPERT WITNESS'S testimony described as "overpayment of the purchase price" is inadmissible for two reasons. First, the witness compares the purchase price with the value of the purchased company as of December 31, 1998. However the comparison between what was paid and what was received generally must be made on the date of acquisition. Neither party has argued that any different date should be applied here. The transaction closed on February 1, 1998, at the latest. EXPERT WITNESS'S testimony, therefore, is not relevant.
>
> EXPERT WITNESS'S testimony demonstrated why courts require the comparison to be made at the time of the acquisition. Making the comparison after the plaintiff has had control of the company raises serious causation questions. Is the company worth so little because it was worthless at the time of the acquisition or because of events after the acquisition, unrelated to the defendants' alleged illegal conduct? EXPERT WITNESS could not answer such questions . . .
>
> With regards to management diversion costs, EXPERT WITNESS'S testimony is inadmissible because it is neither necessary nor reliable. The testimony is unnecessary because the only thing EXPERT WITNESS did was multiply each employee's hours by his or her hourly rate. One does not need accounting expertise to do that. Nor is an accounting expert necessary to tell the jury that consequential damages are an appropriate measure of damages. The Court will instruct the jury on the proper measure of damages that may include consequential damages. The testimony is also unreliable because EXPERT WITNESS was not able to establish a causal connection between the management time claimed in his calculation and the defendants' alleged wrongdoing. If evidence of

management time spent dealing with problems at VHC is to be presented to the jury, it must be through witnesses who can lay a foundation for its admissibility. Such witnesses must be able to explain, among other things, how the time spent relates to any wrongdoing by the defendants.[14]

Opinion on Ultimate Issue

The courts must also decide whether the testimony of the financial expert witness was limited to opinions on issues that ultimately must be decided by the trier of fact. Irrelevant, extraneous, and lay opinions may be excluded as inadmissible by the court. Furthermore, financial expert witnesses are not qualified to offer opinions on legal issues.

Challenges to Ultimate Issue

The following case is interesting because it excludes financial expert witness testimony because the trier of fact could understand the ultimate issues without the assistance of an expert.

> Defendant has not shown that EXPERT WITNESSES would offer any specialized knowledge to assist the jury. The subjects of the proposed expert testimony are solely lay matters that the jury is capable of understanding without the assistance of expert testimony. Moreover, the proposed expert testimony of EXPERT WITNESSES must be excluded because its prejudicial effect substantially outweighs its relevance. Therefore, defendant is precluded from offering expert testimony by EXPERT WITNESSES.[15]

 ## COMING UP

In Chapter 7 we learn some basic litigation knowledge that every financial expert should be familiar with when providing services in litigation and alternative dispute resolution.

 ## NOTES

1. Federal Rules of Evidence, accessed December 1, 2013, www.uscourts.gov/uscourts/rules/rules-evidence.pdf.
2. Stephen R. Covey, *The 7 Habits of Highly Effective People* (New York: Free Press, 1989, 2004), 95.

3. *1100 West, LLC v. Red Spot Paint & Varnish Co.*, 2008 U.S. Dist. LEXIS 16811, 18-19 (S.D. Ind. Mar. 4, 2008).
4. Ibid.
5. *Bank of Louisiana v. Craig's Stores of Tex., Inc. (In re Craig's Stores of Tex., Inc.)*, 247 B.R. 652, 656 (S.D. Tex. 2000).
6. *Real Estate Value Co. v. USAir, Inc.*, 979 F. Supp. 731, 744 (N.D. Ill. 1997).
7. *Bank of Am., N.A. v. Bear Stearns Asset Mgmt.*, 2013 U.S. Dist. LEXIS 125700, 28 (S.D.N.Y. Sept. 3, 2013).
8. *Versata Software Inc. v. SAP Am., Inc.*, 2011 U.S. Dist. LEXIS 102240, 14-15 (E.D. Tex. Sept. 9, 2011), affirmed in part, vacated and remanded in part, *Versata Software, Inc. v. SAP Am., Inc.*, 717 F.3d 1255, 1263 (Fed. Cir. 2013).
9. *Gilmore v. Wwl-Tv, Inc.*, 2002 U.S. Dist. LEXIS 24026, 18-19 (E.D. La. Dec. 12, 2002).
10. *JMJ Enters. v. Via Veneto Italian Ice*, 1998 U.S. Dist. LEXIS 5098, 22-23 (E.D. Pa. Apr. 14, 1998).
11. *F.O.B. Instruments, Ltd. v. Krown Mfg.*, 2008 U.S. Dist. LEXIS 105158, 7-9 (D. Md. May 19, 2008).
12. *Mattel, Inc. v. MGA Entm't, Inc.*, 2011 U.S. Dist. LEXIS 26995, 21 (C.D. Cal. Mar. 4, 2011), affirmed in part, reversed in part and remanded, *Mattel, Inc. v. MGA Entm't, Inc.*, 705 F.3d 1108 (9th Cir. Cal. 2013).
13. *JRL Enters. v. Procorp Assocs.*, 2003 U.S. Dist. LEXIS 9397, 22-23 (E.D. La. June 3, 2003).
14. *Medical Consultants Network, Inc. v. Cantor & Johnston, P.C.*, 2000 U.S. Dist. LEXIS 19279, 9 (E.D. Pa. Dec. 22, 2000).
15. *United States v. Brooks*, 2008 U.S. Dist. LEXIS 44614, 4-5 (S.D.N.Y. June 4, 2008).

CHAPTER SEVEN

Federal Rules of Civil Procedure for the Financial Expert Witness

 PROCEDURAL RULES ON EXPERT WITNESS REPORTING AND TESTIMONY

In general, Federal Rules of Civil Procedure (FRCP), Rule 26(a)(2)(B) governs the disclosure of financial expert testimony. This rule states the following about written reports of the financial expert witness:

> *Witnesses Who Must Provide a Written Report.* Unless otherwise stipulated or ordered by the court, this disclosure must be accompanied by a written report—prepared and signed by the witness—if the witness is one retained or specially employed to provide expert testimony in the case or one whose duties as the party's employee regularly involve giving expert testimony. The report must contain:

> (i) a complete statement of all opinions the witness will express and the basis and reasons for them;
> (ii) the facts or data considered by the witness in forming them;
> (iii) any exhibits that will be used to summarize or support them;
> (iv) the witness's qualifications, including a list of all publications authored in the previous 10 years;

(v) a list of all other cases in which, during the previous 4 years, the witness testified as an expert at trial or by deposition; and

(vi) a statement of the compensation to be paid for the study and testimony in the case.

In order for the financial expert witness to better understand these requirements, each of them is explained in more detail next.

All Opinions and the Bases and Reasons for Them

The proper disclosure of all of the financial expert witness's opinions and the basis and reasons for them is paramount for the financial expert witness to be able to testify. In order to accomplish this duty, the financial expert witness must first understand what represents an opinion. An expert opinion is any personal judgment expressed with reasonable professional certainty by a person deemed by the court to have the requisite skills, knowledge, education, experience, and training to express such judgment in trial.

The failure to disclose all opinions in a timely manner during discovery and provide the basis and reasons supporting them can result in the exclusion of the financial expert witness's testimony by the court. This is best understood by examining how the court has handled such matters in actual cases. In the following case excerpt, the court explains the adverse consequences of failing to timely disclose all financial expert opinions. The name of the financial expert witness has been redacted.

> The second reason why EXPERT WITNESS'S testimony on the purchase price is inadmissible is because his report did not give, as required by Rule 26, "a complete statement of all opinions to be expressed and the basis and reasons therefor." The only statement in the report about the value of the company is: "based on our analysis of VHC, we have determined that there is no current value to its operating assets, and hasn't been since at least December 31, 1998." At the hearing, EXPERT WITNESS explained that the basis for his conclusion that VHC had no residual value was a discounted cash flow analysis he performed. EXPERT WITNESS testified that he considered "large operating losses, a substantial amount of debt and very few prospects of improvement for the future." The expert report, however, does not include an explanation or reference to the analysis discussed at the hearing. Therefore, EXPERT WITNESS'S report does not comply with the requirements of Rule 26 and for that reason as well, his testimony on the topic he described as overpayment of purchase price is inadmissible.[1]

There are instances where the financial expert witness may provide definitive remarks that may not directly be in the form of an expert opinion. The financial expert witness must understand the differences between these expert remarks and opinions if testimony is to be clearly understood, appreciated, and deemed admissible by the court. The following statements, which are not necessarily expressed as expert opinions, are commonly found in financial expert disclosures and reports:

- **Conclusions**—reasoned judgments formed by the financial expert witness roughly equivalent to an expert opinion.
- **Determinations**—statements made by the financial expert witness based on calculation, computation, and research using facts and data.
- **Findings**—statements of fact made by the financial expert witness based on an analysis of the evidence.
- **Observations**—statements of fact made by the financial expert witness based on something personally experienced through the senses.

These terms are intended to be common usage and may not conform to formal definitions. Any of them could be considered by a court to be opinions within the meaning of the FRCP and required to be disclosed. The financial expert witness must be cognizant of the differences intended when such terms are used in place of the literal expression of an "expert opinion" and should be clear and intentional about the terms and intended usage of any such conclusive remarks in expert disclosures and reports.

Facts or Data Considered

The FRCP requires that the financial expert witness disclose all facts and data considered when forming opinions. Sounds easy enough, right? All the financial expert witness has to do is keep track of what is produced to him and used as the basis for opinions. Well, in practice this requirement is oftentimes not as easy as it sounds to comply with, and it can be one of the biggest challenges for the financial expert witness.

When facts or data are produced to the financial expert witness, they can come in many forms. Paper, electronically stored information and images, and videotape are a few that come to mind. These forms may include pictures, documents, records, reports, ledgers, data files, spreadsheets, word documents, e-mails, voicemails, transcripts, and handwritten notes, among many other items. In addition to these facts and data, the financial expert witness generates his own research, work product, and notes. In some cases, facts and data can number in the thousands of documents and millions of pages. Furthermore, with technology advances these volumes are likely to increase significantly in the future. All such facts and data must be identified, recorded, and reported as part of the required disclosure for the financial expert witness.

This issue is complicated even more when facts and data are produced to the financial expert witness without unique identifiers, such as Bates stamps, or in native electronic format. In these cases, the financial expert witness may have difficulty in identifying facts and data produced, which can increase the risk that a proper chain of custody has not been maintained for admissibility. Accordingly, the financial expert witness is encouraged to mark all facts and data as they are received, or request that the client's legal counsel do so before producing them to the expert, and establish a protocol for logging or otherwise tracking all such materials.

In addition to these challenges, the financial expert witness must apply judgment about what he or she has "considered" as facts or data in forming opinions. To make this point, the financial expert witness may look at certain facts and data that are not actually used or relied upon in forming opinions. It may be just as important to the trier of fact, and opposing legal counsel, to know what facts and data you considered but ultimately did not rely upon or use. That means the financial expert witness must carefully consider whether to disclose facts and data not actually used—like Internet searches performed, but deemed to be irrelevant. This also means the financial expert witness must contemplate whether facts and data are required to be disclosed when they are received, but not read; or received and read, but not used or relied upon. In these circumstances, the financial expert witness should consider asking the client's attorney for instructions on these matters.

> [T]here are known knowns; there are things we know that we know . . .
> [T]here are known unknowns; that is to say there are things we now know
> we don't know. But there are also unknown unknowns. There are things
> we do not know we don't know.
>
> —*Donald Rumsfeld*

Exhibits to Summarize or Support Opinions

The financial expert witness is required to disclose, typically in the expert report, any exhibits to be used to support or summarize expert opinions. Besides being a requirement, the financial expert witness will find that explaining complex financial issues can often be best accomplished by using pictures, graphs, and other demonstratives. With that end in mind (i.e., what is most helpful to the trier of fact), the financial expert witness should design the expert report with critical opinions complemented by exhibits. Exhibits can take many forms, from appendices to charts and graphs, as explained in the following sections.

What Is an Exhibit?

Since exhibits can take many forms, the question must be asked: What is an exhibit? The federal rules do not specifically define what an exhibit is; however, the financial expert witness should keep an open mind to allow the maximum amount of flexibility and impact. Some of the most commonly used "exhibits" by the financial expert witness are defined next:

- **Addendum or Appendix**—additional accompanying materials usually placed at the end of a report, disclosure, or other submission.
- **Exhibits**—evidence produced to the court by the disputing parties to prove facts. Such evidence may be used in a trial, hearing, or deposition, or attached to pleadings or sworn statements.
- **Schedule**—facts and data typically arranged in a tabular format, with columns and rows.
- **Table**—facts and data displayed in a tabular format using columns and rows.
- **Chart**—facts and data prepared and organized to be presented visually as a table, process, diagram, blueprint, or other form.
- **Graph**—the plotting of the relationship of variable facts and data into a visual aid.
- **Tab**—the identification of the location of information using a uniquely marked document separation.
- **Map**—the visual depiction of facts and data by organizing unique features.
- **Supplement**—additional materials and information intended to update, amend, enhance, or complete previous reports, disclosures, or other submissions.

Regardless of the "exhibit" form used, the financial expert witness must always keep in mind three things: (1) KISS (keep it simple, stupid), (2) less is best, and (3) pictures tell a thousand words (or numbers). The talent of the financial expert witness is the ability to make complex and highly technical financial concepts simple to understand. KISS means no technical jargon, no lengthy spreadsheets, and no complicated calculations. In addition, the financial expert witness should boil exhibits down to the vital few needed to assist the trier of fact. Triers of fact will struggle to digest too many exhibits and ones loaded with too much material. In trial, that could result in them losing interest and failing to grasp the importance of the financial expert witness's testimony. Professionally prepared exhibits based on images, pictures, and visual impact are more likely to get attention and be remembered by the trier of fact. Ideal visual aids in trial are timelines, process flows, and damage summaries.

A Tale of Too Many Exhibits

In a trial involving complicated and diverse theories of damages, two financial experts squared off. The plaintiff's financial expert witness prepared and presented a handful of exhibits. In direct examination, a visual timeline was explained and the components of lost profits were introduced to the jury in a few short words backed up with a visual exhibit as a reminder. Finally, the damage theory was explained using a small number of visual aids depicting well-known products and retailers that were part of the dispute, together with simple maps.

In contrast, the defendant's financial expert witness prepared and attempted to present to the jury in direct examination a deck of almost fifty slides. Each slide was overwhelmed with words or technical economic theory depicted in the form of graphs and charts. The slides were supplemented by flip-chart drawings and bullet-point lists prepared on the fly by the defendant's legal counsel. The testimony was long and tedious and the judge asked the financial expert witness to move it along, questioning the relevance of much of the materials presented.

At the conclusion of the trial, the jury found in favor of the plaintiff and awarded a multimillion-dollar judgment. A few of the jurors voluntarily agreed to be held over after the trial so that the attorneys could ask them questions about their impressions of the case presentations and witnesses. This is a typical procedure used by legal counsel to get candid feedback directly from jurors after a trial. The jury feedback indicated that the defendant's financial expert witness was viewed as biased, argumentative, and incomprehensible. Although there was nothing specific mentioned about the exhibits used at trial, it seems obvious that they contributed to this undesirable outcome.

Qualifications

In the previous chapter we describe the qualifications of the financial expert witness, labeled SKEET for skills, knowledge, education, experience, and training. The financial expert witness will have several chances to describe his qualifications throughout the litigation process. The financial expert witness likely will be asked to describe personal qualifications during due diligence to select a suitable expert witness. The next opportunity is normally when the financial expert witness disclosure is delivered to the opposing legal counsel in the form of an expert report, unless qualifications were disclosed prior to this time as part of motion practice.

The next time the issue of qualifications is likely to come up is during deposition. Deposing legal counsel is likely to explore the financial expert witness's qualifications to identify shortcomings or fatal flaws. Subsequent to deposition, the financial expert witness may be subjected to qualifications challenges as part of a motion *in limine* or other pleading to the court. The financial expert witness, together with the client's attorney, will defend the financial expert witness's qualifications in an effort to derail any such motions. Last, the financial expert witness may be asked to submit to voir dire as part of the trial proceedings. That is why it is so important that the financial expert witness be qualified and be able to articulate such qualifications convincingly.

Focusing on the initial disclosure of the financial expert witness's qualifications, this is typically done through the combination of a disclosure in the financial expert report, together with the financial expert witness's curriculum vitae (CV). Frequently, the CV is referenced in the expert report as an accompanying attachment. The expert report should include a brief summary of the financial expert witness's qualifications, especially those relevant to the financial expert witness's assignments and the issues in dispute. The CV should support the summary in the expert report, but it will usually include more details covering the financial expert witness's qualifications.

Publications

In addition to other professional qualifications, the CV usually includes a listing of the financial expert witness's publications over the past 10 years. Alternatively, publications authored can be a separate attachment or disclosure. The disclosure of publications authored for the past 10 years should be interpreted broadly by the financial expert witness. Publications authored may include books, white papers, articles, speeches, editorials, training materials, and quoted remarks, to name just a few. Disclosure should include anything published for which you received published attribution as an author, coauthor, or contributor. The 10-year requirement is to be taken literally, and should extend from the date of disclosure backward 10 years. However, many financial expert witnesses choose to disclose publications authored beyond 10 years ago, particularly if they are relevant to the case at hand.

Cases Testified as an Expert

Under the FRCP, Rule 26(a)(2)(B), the financial expert witness is required to disclose "all other cases in which, during the previous four years, the witness testified as an expert at trial or by deposition." Most of the time, this disclosure is made by listing the testimony in the financial expert witness's CV, or in a separate testimony listing provided to opposing legal counsel. The previous four years is a minimum, and many financial expert witnesses voluntarily disclose longer periods. In these cases, the financial expert witness should consider the potential downside of opening up older cases for examination by adversarial opposing legal counsel. Conversely, the disclosure of testimony outside the four-year requirement should be strongly considered if that testimony is relevant to qualify the financial expert witness in the case at hand. In addition to trial testimony, it is recommended that the financial expert witness disclose all binding alternative dispute resolution testimony. These proceedings and the resultant awards are usually legally enforceable and may have been approved by a court.

One thing to keep in mind, the disclosure of prior testimony will be subject to discovery. Many cases may be subject to ongoing disclosure restrictions in connection with confidentiality orders or professional standards. Therefore, the financial expert witness should be careful not to intentionally or inadvertently disclose confidential information orally in deposition or trial, or in written disclosure. In circumstances wherein the financial expert witness is asked to disclose such restricted information, such as in a subpoena *duces tecum* served to the financial expert witness during deposition questioning, or upon cross-examination in trial, the financial expert witness should respectfully decline to provide the requested information, unless ordered to do so by the court. As a precaution, the financial expert witness should retain engagement letters and court orders using normal course retention policies in case proof of confidentiality is challenged. Furthermore, primarily because of the client relationship, the financial expert witness should refer any opposing legal counsel requests for previously issued expert disclosures, reports, testimony transcripts, and trial exhibits to the applicable client or former client legal counsel for permission to release and produce. Ideally, the client or former client legal counsel should respond directly to such requests so that the financial expert witness is not responsible for production.

Compensation

FRCP, Rule 26(a)(2)(B), also requires the financial expert witness to provide a "statement of the compensation to be paid for the study and testimony in the case." However, you will never hear a financial expert witness state that he or she was *paid for his study or testimony.* It sounds biased, as though the client is only paying the financial expert witness for the testimony that will benefit the client. Of course this is not true. So, to avoid misconception the financial expert witness usually describes it as being retained, or engaged, to provide financial expert witness services.

There is disparity in practice regarding the disclosure of financial expert witness fees. That is largely because the federal rules are unclear on the precise meaning of "to be paid." To the financial expert witness, this can mean literally the amounts paid. Alternatively, it could be amounts incurred (billed and unbilled) or the expected budget for the engagement, if one was prepared. In rare cases, it may mean an agreed-upon fixed fee for service. Therefore, the financial expert witness should consult with the client's attorney to confirm what practice to follow.

It is common for the financial expert witness to disclose only rates per hour for the engagement. For example, the disclosure may read something like the following:

> I am being compensated at the rate of $300 per hour. Other personnel under my direct supervision and control are billed at rates ranging from $100 to $250 per hour.

In other situations, the total amounts incurred or billed may be reported. This kind of payment information is normally included with the initial disclosure in the form of the financial expert report. Regardless, the financial expert witness must not forget that billing records may be subject to discovery beyond the billing disclosures required.

COMING UP

In Chapter 8, basic litigation knowledge essential for the financial expert is introduced and explained.

NOTE

1. *Medical Consultants Network, Inc. v. Cantor & Johnston, P.C.,* 2000 U.S. Dist. LEXIS 19279, 10-11 (E.D. Pa. Dec. 22, 2000).

CHAPTER EIGHT

8

Basic Litigation Knowledge for the Financial Expert Witness

 ## LAWS AND RULES

The financial expert witness must know and adhere to relevant laws and rules applicable to expert witnesses. As it relates to the laws relevant to the financial expert witness, we are not referring in this context to personal compliance with lawful behavior requirements. Instead, this knowledge of the law refers to the statutes cited in the complaint and, if the financial expert has been engaged to assist with damages, the legal remedies available. This is the equivalent of the financial expert witness knowing the rules to play a sport. The financial expert witness must know the rules to play the game (i.e., know the laws and rules for admissible and appropriate testimony); however, he is not a referee there to interpret and enforce the rules (i.e., the financial expert witness is not an attorney or trier of fact).

The Federal Rules of Evidence (FRE) explain the rules pertaining to financial expert witness testimony. The Federal Rules of Civil Procedure (FRCP) provide rules for both consulting and expert witnesses. Each of these federal rules is discussed more fully in other chapters of this book.

Relevant Case Law

There are a handful of seminal cases that form the legal basis for the admissibility of financial expert witness testimony. The U.S. Supreme Court opinions on *Daubert v. Merrell Dow Pharmaceuticals (Daubert)*,[1] *Kumho Tire Co. v. Carmichael (Kumho)*,[2] and the Court of Appeals decision in *Frye v. United States (Frye)*[3] are generally recognized as the most notable. In *Daubert*, the U.S. Supreme Court addressed the standard for admitting expert scientific testimony in a federal trial. Even though this opinion was limited to expert scientific testimony, it has been broadly applied to financial expert witness testimony. This is confirmed in the *Kumho* opinion discussed more fully later in the chapter. In most jurisdictions, *Daubert* superseded the *Frye* test, but remnants of it remain relevant. *Frye* is also covered later. The financial expert witness should be familiar with each of these cases and the precedent they set regarding the admissibility of expert testimony.

Important Expert Testimony Cases

- *Daubert v. Merrell Dow Pharmaceuticals, Inc.*, 509 U.S. 579 (1993).
- *Kumho Tire Co. v. Carmichael* (97–1709) 526 U.S. 137 (1999), 131 F.3d 1433, reversed.
- *Frye v. United States*, 293 F. 1013 (D.C., Cir 1923).

Daubert v. Merrell Dow Pharmaceuticals

It is generally recognized that the U.S. Supreme Court established with *Daubert* a gatekeeping function for the federal trial judge. The U.S. Supreme Court stated that "the trial judge must determine at the outset . . . whether the expert is proposing to testify to (1) scientific knowledge that (2) will assist the trier of fact to understand or determine a fact in issue. This entails a preliminary assessment of whether the reasoning or methodology properly can be applied to the facts in issue."[4]

In addition to a gatekeeping function, the U.S. Supreme Court opined on the requirements for the admissibility of scientific expert testimony as outlined following:

- The scientific theory or technique can be, or has been, tested.
- The scientific theory or technique has been subjected to peer review and publication.

- The known or potential error rate of the particular scientific technique.
- The existence and maintenance of standards controlling the technique's operation.
- The degree of acceptance within an explicit identified relevant scientific community.

Due to its significance, the actual relevant text of *Daubert* is captured below. The financial expert witness should read and be familiar with this opinion as it is frequently cited as the source for courts to evaluate the admissibility of expert testimony.

DAUBERT v. MERRELL DOW PHARMACEUTICALS, INC.

ON WRIT OF CERTIORARI TO THE UNITED STATES COURT OF APPEALS FOR THE NINTH CIRCUIT

No. 92–102. Argued March 30, 1993–Decided June 28, 1993

Ordinarily, a key question to be answered in determining whether a theory or technique is scientific knowledge that will assist the trier of fact will be whether it can be (and has been) tested.[5] "Scientific methodology today is based on generating hypotheses and testing them to see if they can be falsified; indeed, this methodology is what distinguishes science from other fields of human inquiry." Green, Expert Witnesses and Sufficiency of Evidence in Toxic Substances Litigation: The Legacy of *Agent Orange* and Bendectin Litigation, *86 Nw. U. L. Rev. 643*, at 645 (1992) (hereinafter Green). See also C. Hempel, Philosophy of Natural Science 49 (1966) ("[T]he statements constituting a scientific explanation must be capable of empirical test"); K. Popper, Conjectures and Refutations: The Growth of Scientific Knowledge 37 (5th ed. 1989) ("[T]he criterion of the scientific status of a theory is its falsifiability, or refutability, or testability") (emphasis deleted).

Another pertinent consideration is whether the theory or technique has been subjected to peer review and publication. Publication (which is but one element of peer review) is not a *sine qua non* of admissibility; it does not necessarily correlate with reliability, see S. Jasanoff, The Fifth Branch: Science Advisors as Policymakers 61–76 (1990), and in some instances well-grounded but innovative theories will not have been published, see Horrobin, The Philosophical Basis of Peer Review and the Suppression of Innovation, 263 JAMA 1438

(1990). Some propositions, moreover, are too particular, too new, or of too limited interest to be published. But submission to the scrutiny of the scientific community is a component of "good science," in part because it increases the likelihood that substantive flaws in methodology will be detected. See J. Ziman, Reliable Knowledge: An Exploration of the Grounds for Belief in Science 130–133 (1978); Relman & Angell, How Good Is Peer Review?, 321 New Eng. J. Med. 827 (1989). The fact of publication (or lack thereof) in a peer reviewed journal thus will be a relevant, though not dispositive, consideration in assessing the scientific validity of a particular technique or methodology on which an opinion is premised.

Additionally, in the case of a particular scientific technique, the court ordinarily should consider the known or potential rate of error, see, e. g., *United States v. Smith*, 869 F.2d 348, 353–354 (CA7 1989) (surveying studies of the error rate of spectrographic voice identification technique), and the existence and maintenance of standards controlling the technique's operation, see *United States v. Williams*, 583 F2d. 1194, 1198 (CA2 1978) (noting professional organization's standard governing spectrographic analysis), cert. denied, 439 U. S. 1117 (1979).

Finally, "general acceptance" can yet have a bearing on the inquiry. A "reliability assessment does not require, although it does permit, explicit identification of a relevant scientific community and an express determination of a particular degree of acceptance within that community." *United States v. Downing*, 753 F. 2d, at 1238. See also 3 J. Weinstein & M. Berger, Weinstein's Evidence, P 702[03], pp. 702–41 to 702–42. Widespread acceptance can be an important factor in ruling particular evidence admissible, and "a known technique which has been able to attract only minimal support within the community," *Downing*, 753 F. 2d, at 1238, may properly be viewed with skepticism.[6]

Today, the basic tenets of the U.S. Supreme Court *Daubert* opinion are largely encompassed in the FRE and have been broadened for applicability to all forms of expert testimony, not just scientific testimony, as confirmed in the *Kumho* opinion.

Kumho Tire Co. v. Carmichael

In the *Kumho* case, the U.S. Supreme Court held that the *Daubert* gatekeeping function applies to "all expert testimony."[7] In the *Kumho* opinion, the U.S. Supreme Court stated that "(FRE) Rules 702 and 703 grant all expert witnesses, not just 'scientific' ones, testimonial latitude unavailable to other witnesses on the assumption that the expert's opinion will have a reliable basis in the knowledge and experience of his discipline."[8] This legal precedent subjects the financial expert witness to the *Daubert* guidelines now reflected in the FRCP. Therefore, the financial expert witness should also be aware of the impact of the *Kumho* ruling on financial expert witness testimony.

Frye v. United States

Before *Daubert*, both federal and state courts widely applied the "general acceptance" standard set out by the Court of Appeals for the District of Columbia in the *Frye* case. There, the court explained that:

> [t]he rule is that the opinions of experts or skilled witnesses are admissible in evidence in those cases in which the matter of inquiry is such that inexperienced persons are unlikely to prove capable of forming a correct judgment upon it, for the reason that the subject-matter so far partakes of a science, art, or trade as to require a previous habit or experience or study in it, in order to acquire a knowledge of it. When the question involved does not lie within the range of common experience or common knowledge, but requires special experience or special knowledge, then the opinions of witnesses skilled in that particular science, art, or trade to which the question relates are admissible in evidence.
>
> Numerous cases are cited in support of this rule. Just when a scientific principle or discovery crosses the line between the experimental and demonstrable stages is difficult to define. Somewhere in this twilight zone the evidential force of the principle must be recognized, and while courts will go a long way in admitting expert testimony deduced from a well-recognized scientific principle or discovery, the thing from which the deduction is made must be sufficiently established to have gained general acceptance in the particular field in which it belongs.[9]

The generally accepted principles the Court of Appeals of the District of Columbia established in *Frye* provided a starting point for the more comprehensive and objective standards the U.S. Supreme Court later established in *Daubert* and *Kumho*. Ultimately, this directive made its way to the FRE to be applied to all cases.

The Impact of *Daubert* and *Kumho* on Financial Expert Testimony

PricewaterhouseCoopers LLP (PwC) conducted a study of *Daubert* and *Kumho* challenges to expert witnesses in federal and state courts from 2000 through 2012.[10] A portion of this study focused specifically on challenges to financial expert witnesses. In total, 12,553 cases studied by PwC cited *Daubert*, *Kumho*, or a combination of the two. The results of the PwC study show that *Daubert* attempts to exclude financial expert witness testimony increased in 2012 to a 13-year high of 192 challenges.[11] The success rate of these challenges was approximately 45 percent for both partial and complete exclusions of testimony, with previous-year exclusions ranging from 29 to 59 percent.[12] These are remarkably high numbers.

From 2000 through 2012, plaintiff's financial expert witnesses were more likely to be challenged than defendant's experts.[13] However, from 2004 to 2012, plaintiff's financial expert witnesses were slightly less likely to have testimony successfully limited or excluded. Further refining this observation, economists and accountants were most frequently challenged from 2000 through 2012.[14] Appraisers were the most likely to survive a challenge and economists excluded the most.

According to the PwC study, the reason financial expert witnesses had their testimony limited or excluded during the period 2000 through 2012 was reliability, relevance, and qualifications.[15] Of the three, relevance was the leading reason in 2012. However, PwC did note that a number of successful challenges were based on a combination of several deficiencies. The results of this study should forewarn financial expert witnesses of likely challenges and the areas to be watched.

Financial Expert Witness Immunity

In general, the financial expert witness is immune from civil claims regarding their testimony given during legal proceedings.[16] This makes sense, because the financial expert witness's testimony is designed to assist the trier of fact and that can only be faithfully done without the threat of lawsuits hanging over the experts' head. In 1983, the U.S. Supreme Court held that there is absolute expert witness immunity from claims raised by opposing parties related to trial testimony.[17]

However, as it relates to "friendly fire" (i.e., a client suing his own expert witness), there are questions about absolute financial expert witness immunity. There have been a few cases brought by clients against their own expert witnesses, commonly based on claims of professional negligence.[18] Only a handful of such suits have been successfully asserted so far. Regardless, the financial expert witness must be ever cautious to perform his work in a professionally responsible manner to avoid this type of liability.

 ## LEGAL PRECEDENT

Legal precedent is a judicial decision that may be used as a standard for other cases because it establishes a binding or persuasive rule or principle. The *Daubert, Kumho,* and *Frye* cases all are examples of legal precedent establishing rules or principles related to expert testimony admissibility. There are other rules and principles created by legal precedent that the financial expert witness should be familiar with, especially when engaged to provide testimony on damages. One such precedent is the notion of "Reasonable Certainty." This concept is further developed by the "Best Evidence," "Fact and Amount," and "Wrongdoer" case precedents.

Reasonable Certainty

Reasonable certainty sounds like an easy concept to grasp. In order for a harmed party to be awarded damages, those damages have to be proven with reasonable certainty. The courts, however, have taken differing perspectives on what reasonable certainty means under the law. For example, the following case excerpt reports that the court was averse to almost any element of risk in order for lost profits damages to be awarded.

> This does not mean, however, that the "reasonable certainty" test lacks clear parameters. Profits which are largely speculative, as from an activity dependent on uncertain or changing market conditions, or on chancy business opportunities, or on promotion of untested products or entry into unknown or unviable markets, or on the success of a new and unproven enterprise cannot be recovered. Factors like these and others which make a business venture risky in prospect preclude recovery of lost profits in retrospect.[19]

The portion of the case appeal presented below reflects the inadmissibility of a financial expert witness's testimony because it was far from reasonably certain, based instead on "guesswork, speculation and conjecture."

> Here, the economic expert's opinion is more closely analogous to economic testimony the Circuit Court of Appeals for the District of Columbia Circuit found to be "based solely on guesswork, speculation and conjecture" and therefore, properly excluded. *Joy v. Bell Helicopter*, 303 U.S. App. D.C. 1, 999 F.2d 549 (D.C. Cir. 1993).[20]

The concept of reasonable certainty is cloudy based on the documented case record. Some further guidance can be found by examining the Best Evidence and Fact and Amount rules established by precedent in other cases. In any event, the financial expert witness must keep in mind the reasonable certainty rule, consulting with the client legal counsel to ensure compliance.

Best Evidence Rule

There are a number of court opinions that support the contention that the plaintiff must prove damages using the best evidence available. This rule cuts both ways. On the one hand, the plaintiff's financial expert witness may justify the calculation of damages as reasonably certain because it is based on the best evidence made available by the defendant in discovery. For example, the courts have held "[i]f the best evidence of damage . . . is furnished, this is sufficient."[21] On the other hand, the court may deem that the plaintiff's financial expert witness failed to prove damages with reasonable certainty because the computations were not based on the best available evidence produced in the case.

Fact and Amount Rule

There is precedent stating that the fact of damages must be proven with reasonable certainty, but that the amount of damages is subject to a lower standard. The case excerpt below exemplifies this principle.

> The claimant must establish the fact of damages with reasonable certainty, but it is not always possible to establish the amount of damages with the same degree of certainty. In some cases, the evidence weighed in common experience demonstrates that a substantial pecuniary loss has occurred, but at the same time it is apparent that the loss is of a character which defies exact proof. In that situation, it is reasonable

to require a lesser degree of certainty as to the amount of loss, leaving a greater degree of discretion to the court or jury.[22]

The U.S. Supreme Court later affirmed this thinking, stating that "[c]ertainty in the fact of damages is essential. Certainty as to the amount goes no further than to require a basis for a reasoned conclusion."[23] With this knowledge, the financial expert witness should be conscientious of the need for strong evidence of the fact of damage before calculating the amount of damages. Failure to do so may subject the financial expert witness to exclusion. When computing damages, the financial expert witness can be comforted somewhat by the knowledge that the amount of damages may be held to a more relaxed standard, but the courts require more than "speculation and conjecture" and different judges will reach different conclusions about where that line is drawn.

Wrongdoer Rule

The Wrongdoer rule established by the U.S. Supreme Court also may provide some comfort to the financial expert witness in appropriate circumstances. The Wrongdoer rule states that when the uncertainty in the calculation of damages to an injured party is caused by the defendant's wrong actions, the defendant should bear the risk of such uncertainty. The following statement reflects this thinking.

> Where the tort itself is of such a nature as to preclude the ascertainment of the amount of damages with certainty, it would be a perversion of fundamental principles of justice to deny all relief to the injured person, and thereby relieve the wrongdoer from making any amend for his acts. In such case, while the damages may not be determined by mere speculation or guess, it will be enough if the evidence shows the extent of the damages as a matter of just and reasonable inference, although the result be only approximate. The wrongdoer is not entitled to complain that they cannot be measured with the exactness and precision that would be possible if the case, which he alone is responsible for making, were otherwise.
>
> . . . whatever . . . uncertainty there may be in mode of estimating damages, it is an uncertainty caused by the defendant's own wrong act; and justice and sound public policy alike require that he should bear the risk of the uncertainty thus produced.[24]

Financial expert witnesses should be cautious, however, about assuming that the Wrongdoer rule will apply to any particular case. The best practice is to discuss the issue with counsel and, regardless of any other considerations, prepare an analysis that is as clear, well-founded, and reliable as the available information will allow.

The Book of Wisdom

In *Sinclair Refining Co. v. Jenkins Petroleum Co.*,[25] the U.S. Supreme Court addressed whether the calculation of damages is strictly limited to things known or knowable at the date of injury (i.e., *ex ante*), or whether damages may be affected by facts discovered after the harmful act has occurred (i.e., *ex post*). In this case, the U.S. Supreme Court refers to a "book of wisdom" in connection with its opinion, giving this case its moniker.

> At times, the only evidence available may be that supplied by testimony of experts as to the state of the art, the character of the improvement, and the probable increase of efficiency or saving of expense. *Dowagiac Mfg. Co. v. Minnesota Moline Plow Co.*, 235 U.S. 641, 235 U. S. 648–649; *Suffolk Mfg. Co. v. Hayden*, 3 Wall. 315, 70 U. S. 320; *U.S. Frumentum Co. v. Lauhoff*, 216 Fed. 610. This will generally be the case if the trial follows quickly after the issue of the patent. But a different situation is presented if years have gone by before the evidence is offered. Experience is then available to correct uncertain prophecy. Here is a book of wisdom that courts may not neglect. We find no rule of law that sets a clasp upon its pages and forbids us to look within.

The opinion citing a "book of wisdom" accepts that the trier of fact may be entitled to refer to facts occurring after the date of injury to determine controverted facts and issues. This ruling is significant because the financial expert witness must consider *ex post* and *ex ante* factors when preparing damages. As these matters are subject to extreme judgment, the client legal counsel should be consulted when considering either factor.

Orders Affecting Financial Experts

- Protective/Confidentiality
- Scheduling/Calendaring
- Restraining
- Compel Disclosure or Discovery

ORDERS

An order is a legally enforceable written command or instruction to the disputing parties from the judge. Although there are a number of orders that may be issued in a litigated dispute, there are a few common ones that are of particular significance to the financial expert. These are protective orders, scheduling orders, restraining orders, and orders to compel. Failure to comply with a court order can result in sanctions and/or a finding of contempt of court.[26]

Protective Orders

Protective orders issued in connection with civil litigation, also known as confidentiality orders, are orders to restrict the disclosure and handling of sensitive confidential facts and data under specific conditions. Protective orders are provided for by the FRCP, Rule 26, which states:

> A party or any person from whom discovery is sought may move for a protective order in the court where the action is pending—or as an alternative on matters relating to a deposition, in the court for the district where the deposition will be taken. The motion must include a certification that the movant has in good faith conferred or attempted to confer with other affected parties in an effort to resolve the dispute without court action. The court may, for good cause, issue an order to protect a party or person from annoyance, embarrassment, oppression, or undue burden or expense, including one or more of the following:
>
> A. forbidding the disclosure or discovery;
> B. specifying terms, including time and place, for the disclosure or discovery;
> C. prescribing a discovery method other than the one selected by the party seeking discovery;
> D. forbidding inquiry into certain matters, or limiting the scope of disclosure or discovery to certain matters;
> E. designating the persons who may be present while the discovery is conducted;
> F. requiring that a deposition be sealed and opened only on court order;
> G. requiring that a trade secret or other confidential research, development, or commercial information not be revealed or be revealed only in a specified way; and

H. requiring that the parties simultaneously file specified documents or information in sealed envelopes, to be opened as the court directs.[27]

It is common for the financial expert witness to be asked to read and sign a protective order as evidence of understanding and pledged compliance. Some protective orders require the financial expert witness to return, or destroy, any protected materials soon after the dispute is resolved. Financial expert witnesses subject to professional standards or policies related to the retention of work product as substantiation for work performed should confirm that such practices are consistent with the court's directives. This can be done by confirming this fact with the client legal counsel.

Scheduling Orders

Scheduling orders, also commonly referred to as calendaring orders, are orders required by FRCP, Rule 16(b), to be issued by the presiding judge "as soon as practicable, but in any event within the earlier of 120 days after any defendant has been served with the complaint or 90 days after any defendant has appeared." The scheduling order must include limits on the time that parties can join the lawsuit, amend pleadings, complete discovery, and file motions. The scheduling order may also modify the timing of disclosures and the extent of discovery, including disclosure or discovery of electronically stored information. Further, it can include agreements entered into by the disputing parties regarding claims of privilege or protection after information is produced, set dates for pretrial conferences and for trial; and any other matters deemed appropriate by the judge. A scheduling order can be modified with the permission of the judge after a showing of good cause. It is commonplace for some portion of the scheduling order to be modified over the course of the litigation proceedings.

The scheduling order usually includes the timing of financial expert disclosures. Therefore, it is vital that the financial expert witness ask for the scheduling order promptly after engagement or issuance of the order. Financial expert witness disclosures must be made at the dates and times ordered by the court and in a specific sequence order. Under FRCP, Rule 26(a)(2)(D):

[a]bsent a stipulation or a court order, the disclosures must be made:

(i) at least 90 days before the date set for trial or for the case to be ready for trial; or

(ii) if the evidence is intended solely to contradict or rebut evidence on the same subject matter identified by another party . . . within 30 days after the other party's disclosure.

If the financial expert witness's report must be disclosed under FRCP, Rule 26(a)(2)(B), the financial expert witness's duty to supplement that expert report extends both to information included in the report and to information given during deposition based on FRCP, Rule 26(e)(2). Any additions or changes to this information must be disclosed by the time pretrial disclosures are due.

FRCP, Rule 26(f) states that prior to the issuance of the scheduling order, the disputing parties must ". . . confer as soon as practicable—and in any event at least 21 days before a scheduling conference is to be held or a scheduling order is due . . . ." This conference is designed to obtain the disputing parties "views and proposals" on the following matters:

A. what changes should be made in the timing, form, or requirement for disclosures under Rule 26(a), including a statement of when initial disclosures were made or will be made;

B. the subjects on which discovery may be needed, when discovery should be completed, and whether discovery should be conducted in phases or be limited to or focused on particular issues;

C. any issues about disclosure or discovery of electronically stored information, including the form or forms in which it should be produced;

D. any issues about claims of privilege or of protection as trial-preparation materials, including—if the parties agree on a procedure to assert these claims after production—whether to ask the court to include their agreement in an order;

E. what changes should be made in the limitations on discovery imposed under these rules or by local rule, and what other limitations should be imposed; and

F. any other orders that the court should issue under Rule 26(c) under Rule 16(b) and (c).

In certain cases, an expedited discovery plan can be requested. But in any case, it should be clear that the scheduling order is important to the financial expert witness as it directs the due dates for required activities and disclosures. Failure to strictly adhere to a scheduling order may result in the exclusion of materials with little chance for appeal. If the financial expert witness discovers that a deadline included in a scheduling order is impractical or unachievable, this should be brought to the attention of the client legal counsel immediately. In many situations, the opposing attorneys can reach an amicable agreement to extend due dates that are usually approved by the court.

Restraining Orders

Under FRCP Rule 65, a restraining order is a written and legally enforceable command issued by a judge, typically to the defendant, barring a party from doing something until a preliminary injunction hearing can be held to determine a proper outcome. Restraining orders are often granted because of irreparable harm that may occur to the other party. At times, the financial expert will be asked to assist the plaintiff by preparing support for an injunction requesting a restraining order. Such requests frequently entail a financial expert witness assessment of irreparable harm. Alternatively, the financial expert engaged by the defendant may be asked to prepare a rebuttal to financial expert witness written statements supporting a request for a restraining order. In either case, the financial expert may be called to testify in a hearing regarding the request.

Orders to Compel

Orders to compel frequently impact the financial expert in discovery. Such orders are specifically provided for by the FRCP, Rule 37, which states "[o]n notice to other parties and all affected persons, a party may move for an order compelling disclosure or discovery." If an opposing party fails to make a required disclosure, the judge may compel disclosure and dispense appropriate sanctions. In addition, the judge may issue an order compelling an opposing party to answer, designate, produce, or allow inspection if a deponent fails to answer a question, an entity fails to make a proper designation, or a party fails to answer an interrogatory or permit inspection.

The financial expert witness may be asked by the client to assist with a motion to compel discovery from an opposing party. If so, the financial expert witness will be tasked with the identification of key financial records needed from an opposing party, together with the reasons such documents are critical to the case. This assessment and reasoning may take the form of a written statement attached to the motion to compel production as support for the pleading.

COURT RULES AND POLICIES

Federal courts apply both federal rules, such as FRE and FRCP, as well as local rules specific to the jurisdiction or courtroom. Financial expert witnesses should be aware of all applicable rules for the specific case in which they are involved. Violations can lead to serious consequences, including admonishment from the judge, liability, and jeopardizing a client's case. The FRE and FRCP are examples of national federal rules. Local court rules are those practices and procedures required to be used in a specific jurisdiction or courtroom. The financial expert witness should ask the client's attorney for the applicable rules for each jurisdiction, court system, and presiding judge. Violating a local rule can be a serious matter potentially leading to admonishment from the judge.

 ## PRIVILEGED COMMUNICATIONS

Privileged communications are exchanges between an attorney and client that are legally protected from disclosure and discovery requirements under the federal rules. Legal privilege is an evidentiary right belonging to the client of the attorney, and sometimes to the attorney, but not to the financial expert. In general, there are two forms of legal privilege the financial expert will encounter during litigation: (1) Attorney-Client privilege; and (2) Attorney Work Product privilege. It is imperative that the financial expert consult with the client attorney often about legal privilege protections and protocols to avoid unintentional waiver of such privileges.

Attorney-Client privilege refers to protections afforded to a party in litigation wherein that party can refuse to disclose any private communications with legal counsel concerning professional legal advice. In most circumstances, the Attorney-Client privilege will not apply to communications with the financial expert, but privileged communications may be disclosed to the expert witness in the course of the expert's engagement. Attorney Work Product privilege protects work product prepared in anticipation of litigation by an attorney, or by another person acting under the attorney's direction, from disclosure and discovery by an opposing party. Under the FRCP, Rule 26(b)(3), "[o]rdinarily, a party may not discover documents and tangible things that are prepared in anticipation of litigation or for trial by or for another party or its representative (including the other party's attorney, consultant, surety, indemnitor, insurer, or agent)," except in limited circumstances. The Attorney Work Product privilege often will apply to work product created by the financial expert witness to assist counsel in preparation for trial, but not always.

PROFESSIONAL STANDARDS

Many financial experts belong to professional associations that require adherence to standards of conduct and performance to remain in good standing. The financial expert witness should be knowledgeable about such professional standards and their applicability to any work performed in litigation. Failure to adhere to applicable professional standards can be fatal to the credibility of the financial expert witness. In certain situations, it may even lead to the limitation or exclusion of the financial expert witness's testimony in trial.

COMING UP

In addition to the federal rules, laws, and case precedence, the financial expert must act and perform in an ethical manner. Chapter 9 covers professional ethics considerations for the financial expert.

NOTES

1. *Daubert v. Merrell Dow Pharmaceuticals*, 509 U.S. 579 (1993).
2. *Kumho Tire Co. Ltd. v. Carmichael*, 526 U.S. 137 (1999).
3. *Frye v. United States*, 293 F. 1013 (D.C., Cir 1923).
4. *Daubert*, 509 U.S. 579 at 593.
5. *Daubert*, 509 U.S. 579 at 593.
6. Ibid.
7. *Kumho*, 526 U.S. 137 at 147.
8. Ibid.
9. *Frye v. United States*, 293 F. 1013, 1014 (D.C., Cir 1923).
10. *Daubert* Challenges to Financial Experts: A Yearly Study of Trends and Outcomes, PricewaterhouseCoopers LLP, (2012), available at www.pwc.com/en_US/us/forensic-services/publications/assets/daubert-challenges.pdf.
11. Ibid. at 7.
12. Ibid.
13. Ibid. at 10.

14. Ibid. at 11.
15. Ibid. at 13.
16. W. Page Keeton, Dan B. Dobbs, Robert E. Keeton, and David G. Owen, *Prosser and Keeton on Torts*, 5th ed., § 114, 816–817 (St. Paul, MN: West Publishing, 1984).
17. *Briscoe v. LaHue*, 460 U.S. 325 (1983).
18. *See*, e.g., *Mattco Forge v. Arthur Young & Co.*, 52 Cal. App. 4th 820, 834 (1997) ("As experts, they are subject to liability if they perform the services negligently.").
19. *Texas Instruments v. Teletron Energy Management*, 877 S.W.2d 276, 279 (Tex. 1994).
20. *Conklin v. St. Lawrence Valley Educ. Television Council*, 93 CV 984 (TJM-DS), 1994 U.S. Dist. LEXIS 20188 (N.D.N.Y Oct. 28, 1994).
21. *Mid-America Tablewares v. Mogi Trading Co.*, 100 F.3d 1353, 1356 (7th Cir. 1996). *See also, Oral-X Corp. v. Farnam Cos.*, 931 F.2d 667, 671 (10th Cir. 1991).
22. *Ameristar Jet Charter, Inc. v. Dodson Int'l Parts, Inc.*, 155 S.W.3d 50, 55 (Mo. 2005).
23. *Palmer v. Connecticut R. & Lighting Co.*, 311 U.S. 544 (1941), superseded by statute on damage calculation grounds. *Taunton Mun. Lighting Plant v. Enron Corp. (In re Enron Corp.)*, 354 B.R. 652, 654 (S.D.N.Y. 2006).
24. *Story Parchment Co. v. Paterson Parchment Paper Co.*, 282 U.S. 555, 563-64 (U.S. 1931).
25. *Sinclair Refining Co. v. Jenkins Petroleum Process Co.*, 289 U.S. 689, 698 (1933).
26. FRCP, Rule 37(b), Failure to Comply with a Court Order.
27. FRCP, Rule 26(c), Protective Orders.

CHAPTER NINE

9

Professional Ethics Considerations

 ## PROFESSIONAL ETHICS

Financial experts must provide services in a professionally ethical manner. This is a widely recognized obligation of any profession. Professional ethics for the financial expert are derived from an instinct to do the right thing. They are an internal compass pointing to the true north of ethical behavior. The tenets of professional ethics can be reinforced with training and consultation with other professionals; however, a gut check must alert the financial expert when ethical situations are in play. This concept is demonstrated by the following comment made to staff by a managing partner of a law firm at an annual meeting: We don't have a lot of rules around here because we hire people that don't need them.

A large number of financial experts belong to professional organizations that bind them to conform to specified ethical requirements. Obviously, pro-scribed ethical mandates must be understood and followed when applicable. More broadly, the financial expert should know how to recognize and handle ethical issues related to conflicts of interest, objectivity, confidentiality, integrity, fees, and discovery. In addition to these issues, the financial expert in the role of an expert witness should be aware of ethical situations that may arise in the preparation for, or during, trial.

Professional Ethics for the Financial Expert

- Conflicts of interest
- Objectivity
- Confidentiality
- Integrity
- Fees
- Discovery
- Trial preparation
- Trial behavior

Conflicts of Interest

The financial expert must be free from conflicts of interest in order to provide services in litigation or alternative dispute resolution. In this context, a conflict of interest is the acceptance of a client engagement and the subsequent provision of services that is incompatible with the best interests of, and professional duties owed to, another client, former client, or third party. Conflicts of interest may be legal, personal, professional, or business-related.

Legal Conflicts

Legal conflicts are situations where the financial expert has an actual conflict with a disputing party that may reasonably cause an unfair disadvantage to that party. A legal conflict may be caused by the financial expert having knowledge gained from previous services. It may also stem from close relationships. Legal conflicts of interest preclude a financial expert from serving any party in a dispute.

Personal Conflicts

Personal conflicts of interest are situations where there is an opportunity for undue personal benefit to the financial expert in conflict with the professional responsibilities owed to a client. Professional standards also may impose restrictions on the provision of professional services where they are or may be contradictory to personal interests.

Professional Conflicts

Professional conflicts of interest are those defined by applicable professional standard, rule, or regulation. Professional conflicts of interest must be observed in order to remain in good standing with governing organizations ascribed to the financial expert. By way of example, generally accepted auditing standards in the United States prohibit the provision of expert witness services to an audit client because it is an independence conflict of interest. The financial expert must be familiar with applicable professional conflicts of interest to avoid ethical issues when providing dispute resolution services.

Business Conflicts

Business conflicts of interest involve the provision of financial expert services that may reasonably result in a business relationship issue with an existing client, referral source, or prospect. These types of conflicts of interest are typically avoided as a professional courtesy or to preserve a valuable relationship. Examples of avoided business conflicts are the refusal to act as a financial expert witness against an industry competitor; or the choice to decline an engagement because it will anger a large client with an interest in one of the disputing parties. Business conflicts of interest are subjective matters that may require consultation with others to reach a practical solution.

Waivers and Consents

Under certain circumstances, the financial expert may be able to serve a client when a conflict of interest exists. To do so, the financial expert must determine that he or she can reasonably provide the services with the requisite level of competence and diligence and disclose the conflict of interest to each and every conflicted party. In more limited situations, by law, rule, regulation, or standard, the financial expert may also need to obtain waivers of the conflict of interest from each and every conflicted party as an indication of informed consent. Due to the potential legal issues and adverse consequences that can attach to conflicts of interest, the financial expert should consult with others, possibly including his or her own personal attorneys, when clearing potential conflicts of interest that may involve requesting waivers and consents. In addition, the financial expert should advise the potential client's legal counsel, being cautious not to disclose confidential matters.

Irreconcilable Conflicts

If the financial expert determines that an irreconcilable conflict of interest exists, the potential client legal counsel should be informed promptly. When making such a disclosure, the financial expert should avoid disclosing the reasons for the conflict of interest, as this information may be contrary to duties owed related to client confidentiality. Simply put, the financial expert should state something along the lines of: "I am sorry to report that I have discovered a conflict of interest that will prevent me from serving in this matter." If pressed for a reason, the financial expert should be cognizant about the need for client confidentiality.

Objectivity

Objectivity is critical for the financial expert in both consulting and expert witness roles. The financial expert must not subject his judgment to others and remain steadfastly independent of mind and thought. The true value of a financial expert derives from this impartiality. It allows the client to get true professional advice that is free from bias. In a consulting role, the financial expert has more freedom to assist the client's legal counsel with advocacy activities. However, the financial expert must always keep in mind that the client's attorney is an advocate and the financial expert is an engaged objective financial expert. Serving as an expert witness, the financial expert must remain keenly focused on the Federal Rules of Evidence Rule 702 responsibility to "assist the trier of fact to understand the evidence or to determine a fact in issue." As such, the financial expert witness is professionally obligated to be unaffected by the client's litigation objectives and impartial to the outcome of the proceedings. The only advocacy demonstrated by the financial expert witness is advocacy for his own opinions.

Confidentiality

The concept of confidentiality is a well-established professional responsibility for the financial expert. From the moment of initial contact regarding possible retention and potentially forevermore, the financial expert may bear this responsibility. Accordingly, the financial expert must take reasonable steps to protect client confidences. Confidential information learned while being considered for retention and after engagement termination should never be used for personal gain or unlawful purposes.

Confidentiality is likely to come into play a number of times during the dispute resolution process. It may arise in the due diligence process to engage the financial expert. In addition, it may present concerns when the opposing legal counsel requests the financial expert witness's complete file during discovery. Finally, confidentiality may present issues in deposition or at trial. The financial expert must always remember that client confidentiality is protected in the following ways, among others:

- Professional ethical responsibility.
- Applicable public practice law, rule, and regulation.
- Applicable professional standards.
- Applicable court rule and orders.
- Applicable stipulations between the disputing parties.
- Applicable employer policies.
- Engagement letter contract agreement.

For these reasons, the financial expert should refuse to disclose any client confidential information, without expressed permission from the legally responsible parties. If the financial expert is asked to disclose or provide confidential information, whether it be during due diligence, by subpoena, in deposition, or trial, the response should be a refusal to comply to protect client confidentiality. Of course, if a judge issues an order compelling disclosure, the financial expert should comply, excepting any legally acceptable withholding.

Integrity

For the financial expert to have integrity, he or she must be honest and truthful, and act in an honorable way. This can prove to be difficult when the client's legal counsel is particularly passionate as an advocate and the financial expert is serving as an expert witness. In these cases, the financial expert witness may believe he or she is being asked to adopt disputed facts or assumptions, or stretch personal qualifications and opinions, to help the attorney's cause. Such requests are a normal part of the interaction between the financial expert and the client attorney. Suggestions and inquiries from the client attorney are fine and an important part of the process. However, it crosses the line if the financial expert witness knowingly discloses or testifies to fabricated facts, unreasonable assumptions, or states an opinion that he or she does not support and find personally convincing.

If you have integrity, nothing else matters. If you don't have integrity, nothing else matters.

—*Alan K. Simpson*

Fees

In general, the financial expert may arrange for service compensation using any legally permitted terms. In the vast majority of cases, fees are charged on a time-and-materials basis. However, some tasks may be accomplished on a fixed fee, or not to exceed limitation. The financial expert witness is not permitted to arrange for or accept the payment of fees on a contingent basis.

Fees to be paid contingent on the outcome of litigation are prohibited by most financial and legal professional standards. Although such contingent arrangements for consulting financial experts are not specifically barred by every profession, there are some that specifically forbid contingent fees by law, rule, regulation, or standard. The reason contingent fee arrangements are prohibited is obvious: Contingent fees present an appearance of bias that is incompatible with the professional objectivity that is appropriately expected. The financial expert witness to be paid a contingent fee based on the ultimate resolution of a case has an irrefutable incentive to shed objectivity in favor of the client's interests.

ETHICAL CONSIDERATIONS FOR THE FINANCIAL EXPERT WITNESS

Discovery

The financial expert has ethical obligations in discovery. Such obligations arise from the adversarial nature of dispute resolution. These obligations extend to interactions with opposing parties, the preparation of expert reports, the production of documents, and deposition preparation activities. Each of these matters is more fully discussed below.

Contact with Opposing Parties

In rare circumstances, an opposing legal counsel may attempt to contact the financial expert witness outside the norms of the rules. This may also be true for the consulting financial expert if his identity is discovered. It is improper for the financial expert to speak, or otherwise communicate, with any opposing party, including opposing legal counsel. The converse also applies; the financial expert must not initiate contact with an opposing party without the expressed permission of the client legal counsel. Any contact with an opposing party outside the prescribed federal rules provides too much risk that the financial expert will reveal client confidential information and, therefore, such communications should be avoided.

Expert Reports

It is unethical for the financial expert witness to subject his judgment to another. Furthermore, the financial expert witness has an obligation to be objective and act with integrity. Accordingly, the financial expert witness should not allow the client, client attorney, or any other person to write any portion of an expert report that the financial expert witness does not believe. The expert must be able to take complete ownership of the report as his or her own, as if he or she had written every word, regardless of any assistance provided by staff or others.

In order to state any opinion or conclusion in an expert report, the financial expert witness must have a reasonable basis for such a belief, including supporting facts, data, and evidence that have been independently analyzed by the financial expert witness. In addition, the financial expert witness should avoid undue influences from others to insert language in an expert report, especially if that language could be construed as untruthful, biased, or unsupported by the work performed and opinions reached.

Production of Expert's Documents

During the course of discovery, the financial expert witness may be asked by opposing legal counsel to produce work papers, notes, work product, e-mails, evidence sources, and other materials. The right to request these items is provided by the Federal Rules of Civil Procedure, Rule 26(b)(4)(C). It is unethical for the financial expert witness to knowingly withhold, conceal, or destroy any item requested in discovery by an opposing party. In some situations, such knowing acts may be subject to sanctions or criminal charges.

There may be, however, requested items that the financial expert witness believes are irrelevant, improper, or imprudent to produce. In these cases, the financial expert witness should work with the client legal counsel and his own professional and legal advisers to legally object to the production of such items. If a lawful subpoena was used to compel production, the financial expert witness can work with the client legal counsel and personal legal advisers to attempt to quash the subpoena, or at least the portions found to be objectionable.

Deposition and Coaching

It is improper for the client's legal counsel, or anyone else, to instruct the financial expert witness on what to say in response to deposition questions (or in any other testimony). Improperly telling the financial expert witness how to testify is commonly referred to as coaching the witness. Nonetheless, the financial expert witness will undoubtedly be exposed to communications that have the appearance of coaching. One of the times the financial expert witness is likely to encounter these efforts is when preparing for the deposition and while in attendance.

The preparation process for deposition should include at least one meeting with the client legal counsel to go over expected inquiries from opposing counsel. This may be reinforced by role playing, with the client legal counsel acting as the deposing legal counsel. The preparation process is designed, in part, to identify questions that are difficult for the financial expert witness to answer. As a rule, the more challenging the inquiry, the more practice is needed to answer clearly, concisely, and truthfully without creating confusion or inadvertently harming the client's case, or one's own career.

The nature of this preparatory activity will encourage the client legal counsel to suggest preferred answers to difficult questions. This is normal, expected, and encouraged. Suggested responses that clarify, provide alternative ways to communicate complex issues, or break answers down into more digestible parts are proper. However, the financial expert witness must not adopt recommended answers blindly. The financial expert witness must be able to stand by each response during deposition, or face disqualification or even potential perjury penalties.

The financial expert witness may also experience interventions by the client legal counsel during the deposition. For example, interruptions for valid and proper objections are normal. At times, however, the client legal counsel may ask to confer with the financial expert witness off the record during official breaks or unofficially during pauses in the proceedings. In addition, the client legal counsel may make a speaking objection during the deposition. In any case, the financial expert witness must resist the leads given by the client's legal counsel in these conferences and communications if they cross the line into coached responses. Responses during deposition must be exclusively those of the financial expert witness. The uncritical parroting of a coached answer is improper and, once again, may subject the expert witness to sanctions and perjury allegations.

Trial Preparation

The client's legal counsel similarly may not tell the financial expert witness how to testify in trial. Preparation for trial shares similar risks to deposition as there is the potential for improper coaching on the part of the client legal counsel. The financial expert witness must be wary of improper coaching during trial preparation and under no circumstances should the financial expert witness accept a request on how to testify in trial that is not completely consonant with the expert's own, independent opinions and analysis. Coaching is unethical and must not be tolerated by the financial expert witness.

To be clear, the client's legal counsel and the financial expert witness have a professional responsibility to be prepared for trial. That entails communication, meetings, back-and-forth exchange of ideas, and role play. The financial expert witness and the client legal counsel will typically work together closely to prepare the direct examination and practice the substance and flow of the expected testimony. In addition, the client attorney will anticipate cross-examination questions, especially tricky ones, and present them to the financial expert witness for study and response. Both direct and cross-examination may also become part of role play to ensure the financial expert witness's testimony is cogent and effective. These activities are appropriate and assist the financial expert witness to prepare for trial in a responsible and ethical manner.

TRIAL

Once a trial has started, the financial expert witness must be sensitive to situations that may present ethical challenges. Obviously, the financial expert witness must never intentionally lie under oath—that is clearly unethical and unlawful. The financial expert witness must also be careful not to testify about evidence that has been excluded or limited by the court. Lastly, the financial expert witness needs to be cognizant about communication restrictions while the trial is ongoing.

False Testimony

It is unethical, and potentially illegal, for the financial expert witness to intentionally provide sworn false testimony at trial. The provision of false testimony, whether by statement or omission, is a serious matter. It may result in professional censure, court fines, and sanctions, and charges of contempt and perjury. In total, giving false testimony has the strong potential to ruin a professional career and it must never be done.

Prohibited Testimony

Prior to and during trial, the financial expert witness's testimony may have been legally limited. Certain evidence or arguments may have been ruled inadmissible by the court. It is unethical for the financial expert witness to knowingly attempt to testify about facts, issues, and evidence previously ruled inadmissible. Therefore, the financial expert witness should consult with the client's legal counsel before trial and just before scheduled testimony to understand relevant facts, issues, and evidence deemed inadmissible by the court.

Communications

Outside of the ethical considerations regarding financial expert witness communications when testifying, there are other situations that may arise during the trial that require special attention. The financial expert witness should know how to handle possible contact and communications with others participating in, or affiliated with, the courtroom proceedings. These parties include the audience attending the proceeding, the judge, the jury, opposing parties and legal counsel, other witnesses, and potentially the media.

Gallery

If the financial expert is allowed to sit in the gallery of the courtroom during the trial, it is important to be still and silent and remain unreactive to the activities in the courtroom. Talking, making noise, or vocally responding to activities in the courtroom during the trial is strictly prohibited. Electronic, photographic, and recording devices, such as cell phones, computer tablets, and laptops are also typically not allowed in the courtroom while in session. Taking notes quietly is usually allowed, but the exchange of information by passing notes is strongly discouraged. In addition, emotional facial expressions and body movements should be avoided as they may be observed by the judge or jury, thereby potentially affecting perceptions about the objectivity of the financial expert witness.

Judge

As a rule, *ex parte* communications with the judge by either disputing party while a trial is in process is prohibited. The same rule applies to the financial expert witness. There is to be no *ex parte* communication with the judge during the pendency of the trial. Of course, common sense must also apply. The financial expert witness should exchange insignificant professional pleasantries with the judge where the situation calls for it, for example, in the elevator on the way to the courtroom or when approaching the witness stand. The financial expert witness must never, however, speak to the judge about the case and testimony at hand. On the outside chance that a judge requests a private conference permitted by the law, the financial expert witness should comply and report the meeting promptly to the client legal counsel.

Juror

The financial expert witness may not communicate with any sitting juror outside of the testimony given from the witness stand under oath during trial. That means that the financial expert witness must not have *ex parte* communication with any juror. It is permitted to professionally acknowledge a juror in the courtroom or a public area. However, the financial expert witness should never discuss the case with any juror during an active trial.

Opposing Parties and Legal Counsel

The financial expert witness should not have *ex parte* communications with opposing parties and legal counsel during an active trial. The financial expert witness has strict duties of client confidentiality and loyalty that would likely be compromised if such communications were to occur. Once again, chance encounters inside or outside the courtroom can acceptably be responded to with professional acknowledgment. In no circumstance should the financial expert witness communicate about any matter associated with the pending case.

Other Witnesses

In some cases, the judge may sequester the financial expert witness from the courtroom. This is done to prevent the financial expert witness from hearing other witnesses before taking the witness stand and testifying personally. This sequestration is not limited to the physical courtroom facilities. If such exclusions are required by the court, the financial expert witness may not be allowed to talk with other witnesses, read trial transcripts, or otherwise make efforts to learn about the trial proceedings. Therefore, it is important that the financial expert witness discuss the protocols for trial attendance with the client legal counsel before making an appearance in court.

Client's Legal Counsel

In certain courts, when the financial expert witness is sworn in to testify he or she is prohibited from having any contact with the client legal counsel outside the witness stand until the trial has concluded. That includes any contact on recess, during meal breaks, or by phone, text, or e-mail. The financial expert witness should consult with legal counsel regarding any applicable restrictions before trial. Unless given specific approval and direction by the client legal counsel, the cautious practice will be to avoid any substantive discussion of the case or the expert's testimony with the client legal counsel until after that testimony has been concluded.

Media

The financial expert witness has significant obligations of client confidentiality and professionalism that act as a bar against disclosure of case details to any member of the media. In some cases, this obligation is legally required by a gag order or other means. If contacted by the media, the financial expert witness should respond with no comment, citing client confidentiality, if desired. Any such contact should be reported to the client legal counsel, who may request that future inquiries be directed to their office.

> Ethics is knowing the difference between what you have a right to do and what is right to do.
>
> —*Potter Stewart*

 COMING UP

The next part of this book covers the reporting and testimony of the financial expert witness in litigation, beginning with the preparation of the expert report.

PART THREE

Financial Expert Witness Reports and Testimony

CHAPTER TEN

Preparing the Financial Expert Witness Report

 ## FEDERAL RULES ON FINANCIAL EXPERT WITNESS DISCLOSURE

Under the federal rules governing civil litigation, the Federal Rules of Civil Procedure (FRCP), Rule 26(a)(2)(B), requires that financial expert witnesses provide a signed written report containing specific disclosures. This federal rule states that financial expert witness written reports must include the following disclosures:

> Witnesses Who Must Provide a Written Report. Unless otherwise stipulated or ordered by the court, this disclosure must be accompanied by a written report—prepared and signed by the witness—if the witness is one retained or specially employed to provide expert testimony in the case or one whose duties as the party's employee regularly involve giving expert testimony. The report must contain:
>
> (i) a complete statement of all opinions the witness will express and the basis and reasons for them;
> (ii) the facts or data considered by the witness in forming them;
> (iii) any exhibits that will be used to summarize or support them;

(iv) the witness's qualifications, including a list of all publications authored in the previous 10 years;

(v) a list of all other cases in which, during the previous 4 years, the witness testified as an expert at trial or by deposition; and

(vi) a statement of the compensation to be paid for the study and testimony in the case.

Previously in this book, we discussed the meaning and significance of each of the required disclosures, so they will not be repeated here. Suffice it to say, the federal rules must be complied with fully by the financial expert witness if expert testimony is to be allowed as admissible in trial by the court.

 ## A PRACTICAL WAY TO PREPARE A FINANCIAL EXPERT REPORT

Beyond the technical compliance with federal rules, the preparation of an effective financial expert report is part art and part science. In the spirit of this book serving as a practical guide for practitioners, the art of financial expert witness reporting is described using the acronym PRACTICAL. The PRACTICAL method provides an easy-to-remember approach to ensure technical compliance with the federal rules and effective communication: The letters in the acronym stand for the critical elements needed to prepare an expert report subject to the federal rules. Each of these elements is described more fully below.

PRACTICAL Financial Expert Witness Report Writing

- Persuasive
- Relevant
- Accurate
- Complete
- Timely
- Impartial
- Clear
- Appropriate (opinions)
- Lucid

Persuasive

A persuasive financial expert witness report uses logic and reasoning under-pinned by reliable facts and reasonable assumptions to convince another to believe what the financial expert witness believes. Persuasiveness is built on eloquence, compelling thoughts and convincing relevant and reliable facts, data, and assumptions. Persuasiveness appeals to the trier of fact's logic and emotions. This is often one of the most difficult skills for a technical writer to master.

> In making a speech one must study three points: first, the means of persuasion; second, the language; third, the proper arrangement of the various parts of the speech.
>
> —*Aristotle*

Relevant

The financial expert witness report must demonstrate the use of relevant case facts and data. Relevance is shown by connecting actual case evidence and assumptions to the work performed, opinions offered, and facts and issues in dispute. To accomplish this end, the financial expert witness should consider referencing relevant evidence details in the expert report. This will aid the reader to link relevant facts and data to methods and principles used, work performed, key assumptions, and ultimate opinions formed by the financial expert witness.

Accurate

It is plainly obvious that the financial expert witness report must be accurate. An inaccurate written report undermines the credibility of the financial expert witness and may contribute to concerns that may be raised by opposing legal counsel about the suitability of the witness to testify and the reliability of opinions for use in the case. The financial expert witness report should be based on reliable facts and reasonable assumptions that have been appropriately veri-fied or corroborated. Therefore, the financial expert witness must employ con-siderable rigor with quality control to ensure avoidable mistakes are detected and corrected before issuance of the written report. Of course, minor mistakes like typographical issues may happen. If immaterial, these do not present any real problems for the financial expert witness. Once discovered, however, the financial expert witness should acknowledge mistakes and correct them as necessary. Quality control over reporting is discussed in more detail later in this chapter.

Complete

For a financial expert witness report to be complete, it must comply with the federal rules in all respects. To be considered complete, the written report must include all of the financial expert witness's (a) opinions and the reasons supporting them; (b) facts and data considered; (c) exhibits supporting or summarizing opinions; (d) qualifications, including publications authored in the last 10 years; (e) testimony in trial or deposition for the last 4 years; and (f) compensation. The report must also be properly dated and signed by the financial expert witness.

Timely

Financial expert witness reports must be prepared and delivered in timely fashion based on instructions provided by the court. Failure to meet deadlines set by the court may result in exclusion of the written report and the financial expert witness from the proceedings. Under FRCP Rule 26(a)(2)(D), the plaintiff's financial expert witness report must be filed at least 90 days before the trial is scheduled. Rebuttal reports from the defendant's financial expert witness are due 30 days after the delivery of the plaintiff's financial expert witness's report. Supplemental expert reports are due when pretrial disclosures are required by the court as provided by FRCP Rule 26(e). Of course, this timing may be adjusted by the court.

Impartial

The overarching responsibility of the financial expert witness is to be an impartial, objective expert participating in the proceedings to assist the trier of fact. As such, the financial expert witness's report should reflect an impartial approach and be unbiased in its conclusions. Statements indicating potential bias should be avoided, together with emotional commentaries and personal sentiments. Neutrality should permeate the financial expert witness's report.

Clear

Clear means that the financial expert witness's report is easily understood by the reader. For this to happen, the financial expert witness's report must be comprehensive but concise and avoid the use of technical jargon. In the ideal financial expert witness report, straight thinking is translated into straight reporting using an objective voice organized into simple, concise, coherent, persuasive, and easy-to-understand thoughts.

Appropriate (Opinions)

The financial expert witness's opinions must be reliable for use in court. Therefore, they must be believed by the financial expert witness based on sufficient work performed using relevant case facts and data. It is inappropriate for the financial expert witness to blindly adopt and report any other person's opinion without having a sufficient basis to do so personally. It is also not proper for the financial expert witness to express an opinion that is overreaching, based on speculation or guesswork, as an accommodation to another.

Lucid

A well-written financial expert witness report gets to the point, its purpose is identified, the intended use and audience is clearly documented, and the results are easily identified and understandable. In addition, it creates interest in the reader. One component of lucidity is the logical organization and presentation of the materials in the financial expert witness report. The report should include a title, reference to the pending dispute using the official caption and court docket number, include page numbers, be properly formatted, and the location of any exhibits used should be included. In some cases, numbering paragraphs and sentences may help the reader digest and recall content. Furthermore, the readability of larger, more complex reports may be enhanced using a table of contents and tabs.

ORGANIZATION OF THE FINANCIAL EXPERT WITNESS WRITTEN REPORT

There are many ways to organize the financial expert witness's report. Some are influenced by the client attorney's preferences or habit. Others are based on the financial expert witness's research of what other experts have done in the past. Following is a model for the organization of the financial expert witness report:

- **Title page**, including the official case caption, court case number, date of the report, and the name and contact information for the financial expert witness.

- **Table of contents**, listing report section headings and associated page numbers, exhibits, appendices, tabs, or other accompanying materials.
- **Expert report**, with each page numbered and including the official case caption, court case number, date of the report, and the name of the financial expert witness. Within the expert report, the major sections may be headed as follows:
  - **Background**, including a brief summary of the case, disputing parties, and the complaint.
  - **Qualifications**, including uniquely relevant reasons the financial expert witness is suitable to serve as an expert for the matter at hand. This section may refer to an accompanying curriculum vitae of the financial expert witness.
  - **Assignment**, including a brief summary of what the financial expert witness was engaged to do.
  - **Summary of opinions**, including a highly summarized version of ultimate opinions reached. Placing the summary of opinions closer to the front part of the report is stylistic and done to assist the reader in quickly finding this important information.
  - **Materials considered**, including all facts and data considered when forming opinions in compliance with the federal rules. It is also advisable to report the key assumptions used by the financial expert witness in this section, or another section of the report. This section may include a reference to an accompanying listing of the facts and data considered.
  - **Work performed**, including the methods and principles used and the procedures completed.
  - **Opinions and bases therefor**, including all opinions to be given at trial and the foundation for each.
  - **Compensation** to comply with federal rules.
  - **Signature and date**.
- **Attachments**, including exhibits required by federal rule. Attachments may include, but not be limited to, the financial expert witness's curriculum vitae, a listing of documents considered, exhibits, appendices, charts, graphs, and tabs.

Of course, this model format can be altered based on individual preference, court requirements, or the needs of the case.

Model Organization for the Financial Expert Witness Report

- Background
- Qualifications
- Assignment
- Summary of opinions
- Documents considered
- Work performed
- Opinions and reasons therefor
- Compensation
- Signature
- Date

WRITING THE FINANCIAL EXPERT WITNESS REPORT

Writing an effective financial expert witness report is a challenging task. Few financial expert witnesses ever truly master this challenge. Accordingly, most financial expert witnesses employ disciplined practice and study toward the goal of consistently improving report-writing skills over time. Rest assured, the more times you write an expert report, the more you will see growth. In the case of expert reports, practice does move the financial expert witness closer to perfect.

Writing the financial expert report requires careful attention to authorship and the basics of report writing. The financial expert witness should author the expert report, or be in a position to faithfully and truthfully assert ownership for the report. When it comes to the words to be used in the report, certain subjects should be handled with discretion. In addition, the report should be well-organized and plainly written in easy-to-understand language.

Authorship of the Financial Expert Witness Report

It is almost a given that the financial expert witness will be asked by opposing legal counsel to disclose who wrote the expert report. It is strongly recommended that the true answer be that the financial expert witness wrote the report personally. It is expected and necessary that others, such as the client legal counsel, staff engagement members, and quality control reviewers, will have input into the expert report. However, the financial expert witness should be keenly aware of the potentially serious issues that may arise if he or she allows others to write substantial portions of the expert report, edit it materially, or put words in the mouth of the financial expert witness.

There are a number of reasons why the financial expert witness should write his or her own expert report. Number one, by federal rule, the expert witness is required to sign and date the expert report. That means it is legally the report of the financial expert witness. Number two, the expert report will be subject to deposition inquiry by opposing legal counsel and it is easier to remember and defend a report that is in the financial expert witness's own voice and style. Number three, the discovery that material portions of the expert report were authored by another may raise serious admissibility issues. At the very least, it will give the opposing attorney the opportunity to attack the credibility and reliability of opinions in trial.

Now, that is not to say that qualified professional staff cannot draft an outline of the expert report at the direction of the financial expert witness. However, the financial expert witness must do enough work to truthfully explain the nature of the work done by others and take full responsibility for the expert report as his own. Legally and professionally, the financial expert witness must be in a position to take complete ownership and be personally accountable for the entire report and all of the opinions expressed therein.

Statements to Avoid

> My task, which I am trying to achieve is, by the power of the written word, to make you hear, to make you feel—it is, before all, to make you see.
>
> —*Joseph Conrad, from* Lord Jim

The financial expert witness should not lose sight of the fact that the expert report must be defended from attacks expected from opposing legal counsel during deposition and trial. As such, the words used by the financial expert witness in the expert report are important. Well-chosen words provide the financial expert witness a buttress of protection. Conversely, a poor choice of words can subject the financial expert witness to reproach and impeachment. Following are a few statements the financial expert witness should consider avoiding in the expert report.

Absolutes

Few things in life are absolute. Benjamin Franklin said: "In this world, nothing can be said to be certain, except death and taxes." This fact may also hold true for the financial expert witness. Therefore, the financial expert witness should carefully consider the need to make absolute statements in the expert report. Statements using the words "always" and "never," for example, create absolute certainty that may be unclear, unnecessary, and dangerous for the financial expert witness. Such statements leave no wiggle room for uncertainty and, if proven wrong or questionable, open the financial expert witness up to criticism and possible exclusion.

Ambiguities

The financial expert witness should steer clear of statements in the expert report that may be open to widely variable interpretation or ambiguity. Precise language should be used by the financial expert witness to reduce the risk of engendering uncertainty of meaning. The comedian Jay Leno often makes fun of ambiguous newspaper headlines. Here are a few to consider:

> Affordable housing too expensive . . .
> One-armed man applauds the kindness of strangers
> Federal Agents Raid Gun Shop, Find Weapons
> School board member suspected of honesty
> County to pay $250,000 to advertise lack of funds
> Fish need water, Feds say
> Most doctors believe that breathing regularly is good for you

Extraneous Words

Expert reports should not include extraneous words that dilute clarity and fail to add substance to meaning. Irrelevant, immaterial, and superfluous wording also exposes the financial expert to unnecessary scrutiny. For example, statements using the terms "certain" or "select" are often extraneous. The words "certain" and "select" imply that the financial expert witness has limited a comment to a specific item or matter. When a financial expert witness writes, "I found that *certain* invoices were incomplete," or "I tested *select* invoices," it raises the question of which specific ones the expert is referring to. A good opposing legal counsel will find these comments and ask the financial expert to explain the limitations and the reasons for the restrictions. Alternatively, the meaning of the sentence is not compromised by eliminating the extraneous words and stating, "I found that invoices were incomplete," or "I tested invoices."

Professional Jargon, Acronyms, and Complex Wording

> Don't use words too big for the subject. Don't say "infinitely" when you
> mean "very"; otherwise you'll have no word left when you want to talk
> about something really infinite.
>
> —C. S. Lewis

The expert report is not a research white paper intended for use by academics and scholars. It is a legally mandated form of discovery used to provide an opposing party with required disclosures. Many financial expert witnesses fail to fully embrace this concept because they are more comfortable in their world of complexity, professional jargon, and acronyms. The use of professional jargon, undefined acronyms, and unwieldy words impairs the reader's understanding of the expert report and should be avoided.

Reasonable Certainty in the Field

As we learned earlier in this book, the financial expert witness must express opinions with reasonable certainty in his chosen field of expertise. Therefore, it may be prudent to word opinions and conclusions using these terms. For example, the financial expert may add a statement like this to the expert report: "I hold my opinions with a reasonable certainty in the field." In this way, the financial expert recognizes in writing the legal obligation to state expert opinions with reasonable professional certainty. However, this matter should be discussed with the client legal counsel to make sure such language is proper and necessary.

Use of Legal Citations

A number of financial expert witnesses include references to the law or cases believed to set legal precedent relevant to work performed. This is especially common in intellectual property disputes where 35 U.S.C. § 284, *Panduit Corp. v. Stahlin Bros. Fibre Works, Inc.*[1] and *Georgia-Pacific Corp. v. United States Plywood Corp.*[2] are frequently cited. References and citations to law and legal precedent must be done carefully by the financial expert witness. The reasons why are simple. First, the financial expert witness is not an attorney and is, therefore, not qualified to reach an opinion on legal matters. Second, it is the court's exclusive purview to make determinations about legal issues. According, the financial expert witness should not reference or cite the law or legal precedent in the expert report without consultation and approval from the client legal counsel.

 ## CAVEATS TO CONSIDER

The financial expert witness should consider the inclusion of caveats into the expert report, if appropriate. Caveats ensure that the reader has a clear understanding about what is disclosed and how to interpret it. Caveats also provide the reader with any significant limitations that should be considered when reading the report. Caveats that are commonly used by the financial expert witness cover the use of supervised staff, use of the report and opinions, potential for the production of additional material evidence in discovery, use of confidential information, and missing facts and data. Each of these matters is explained more fully next.

Supervised Staff

In many cases, the financial expert witness uses qualified professional staff to perform work in connection with engagement assignments. This is perfectly acceptable, if the financial expert witness directs the staff on what is to be done and such staff perform the work under the direct supervision of the financial expert. In this way, the financial expert witness can truthfully assert responsibility and accountability for the work performed and the contents of the expert report. Following is a sample form for such a caveat:

> The work described in this expert report has been performed by me or professional staff under my direct supervision.

Use of Report and Opinions

Limitations on the use of the expert report and opinions may be appropriate under some circumstances. Therefore, the financial expert witness may want to tell the reader about any restrictions on the use of the report and the intended use for any opinions contained therein. This will help to ensure that the reader is fully prepared to read the report with the proper understanding. An example of such language is shown here:

> This expert report has been prepared for exclusive use in the pending litigation and is not to be used, referred to, quoted, reproduced, or distributed for any other purpose without my expressed written permission.

Ongoing Discovery

The financial expert witness's report will be prepared and delivered before the conclusion of discovery. As such, potentially relevant and material facts and data or testimonial evidence may be produced after the financial expert witness report is issued. That could impact the work and opinions disclosed in the previously released expert report. Accordingly, the financial expert witness may want to include something along the lines of the following language in the expert report:

> At this time, discovery is ongoing and facts, data, and evidence potentially relevant and material to my assignments and opinions may be produced after the date of this expert report. I may later consider these materials and, if deemed necessary, amend or supplement this expert report and the opinions contained herein.

Confidential Information

Many cases provide access to confidential information protected by court order, privacy laws, or other means. In these cases, the financial expert witness should consider conspicuously marking all pages of the expert report as confidential. If confidential by court order, it is advisable to include that fact in the disclosure. The financial expert witness may also be asked by the client legal counsel to redact certain personal and confidential information from the expert report and accompanying attachments. If so, the following language, or similar disclosure, may be prudent:

> Facts, data, and evidence cited herein or accompanying this report are confidential. To protect this material, it has been marked as "Confidential" and personal information has been redacted.

Missing or Incomplete Facts and Data

Rarely will the financial expert witness have a perfect set of facts and data to work with in forming opinions. That being the case, the financial expert witness may feel compelled to explain the extent of missing or incomplete facts and data and the impact on reported opinions. The following disclosure is intended to show a possible way to report this fact and the determination that it does not materially affect the opinions reached:

> Requested facts, data, and evidence have not yet been produced to me for analysis. Regardless, I believe the materials produced to me thus far provide a sufficient basis to support the opinions contained herein.

Alternatively, if missing or incomplete facts, data, and evidence are significant enough to potentially impact the financial expert witness's opinions, the following statement might be appropriate:

> Requested facts, data, and evidence have not yet been produced to me for analysis. Because of the potential significance of this missing information, my opinions are subject to change if and when such materials are produced in the future.

Basics for Writing in Plain English

Writing a financial expert witness report in plain English can be a daunting task. After all, this is a technical report authored by a financial expert for use by laypersons in a complex dispute. As such, the deck is stacked against the financial expert witness when it comes to writing an expert report for the average person to digest easily. Fortunately, Bryan A. Garner, the author of *Legal Writing in Plain English*, has tackled this problem.

Garner offers the following 50 points to help the financial expert witness write in plain English:[3]

1. Have something to say—and think it through.
2. For maximal efficiency, plan your writing projects. Try nonlinear outlining.
3. Order your material in a logical sequence. Use chronology when presenting facts. Keep related material together.
4. Divide the document into sections and divide sections into smaller parts as needed. Use informative headings for the sections and subsections.
5. Omit needless words.
6. Keep your average sentence length to about 20 words.
7. Keep the subject, the verb, and the object together—toward the beginning of the sentence.

8. Prefer the active voice over the passive.
9. Use parallel phrasing for parallel ideas.
10. Avoid multiple negatives.
11. End sentences emphatically.
12. Learn to detest simplified jargon.
13. Use strong precise verbs. Minimize *is, are, was,* and *were.*
14. Turn *-ion* words into verbs when you can.
15. Simplify wordy phrases. Watch out for *of.*
16. Avoid doublets and triplets.
17. Refer to people and companies by name.
18. Don't habitually use parenthetical shorthand names. Use them only when you really need them.
19. Shun newfangled acronyms.
20. Make everything you write speakable.
21. Plan all three parts: the beginning, the middle, and the end.
22. Use the deep issue to spill the beans on the first page.
23. Summarize. Don't overparticularize.
24. Introduce each paragraph with a topic sentence.
25. Bridge between paragraphs.
26. Vary the length of your paragraphs, but generally keep them short.
27. Provide signposts along the way.
28. Unclutter the text by moving citations into footnotes.
29. Weave quotations deftly into your narrative.
30. Be forthright in dealing with counterarguments.
31. Draft for an ordinary reader, not for a mythical judge who might someday review the document.
32. Organize provisions in order of descending importance.
33. Minimize definitions. If you have more than just a few, put them in a schedule at the end—not in the beginning.
34. Break down enumerations into parallel provisions. Put every list of subparts at the end of the sentence—never at the beginning or in the middle.
35. Delete every *shall.*
36. Don't use provisos.
37. Replace *and/or* wherever it appears.
38. Prefer the singular over the plural.
39. Prefer numerals, not words, to denote amounts. Avoid word-numeral doublets.
40. If you don't understand a form provision—or don't understand why it should be included in your document—try diligently to gain an understanding. If you still can't understand it, cut it.

41. Use a readable typeface.
42. Create ample white space—and use it meaningfully.
43. Highlight ideas with attention-getters such as bullets.
44. Don't use all capitals, and avoid initial capitals.
45. For a long document, make a table of contents.
46. Embrace constructive criticism.
47. Edit yourself systematically.
48. Learn how to find reliable answers to questions of grammar and usage.
49. Habitually gauge your own readerly likes and dislikes, as well as those of other readers.
50. Remember that good writing makes the reader's job easy; bad writing makes it hard.

EXHIBITS

The financial expert witness is required to disclose any exhibits that may be used at trial to summarize or support expert opinions. The most effective trial exhibits are those that summarize or support expert opinions using simple and easily remembered visual aids, like pictures, graphs, or powerful words. At a minimum, opinions should be reduced to short memorable phrases on a demonstrative, with any monetary damages clearly and succinctly reflected as a number.

In the following examples labeled as Exhibits 10.1, 10.2, and 10.3, the financial expert has several choices on how to show lost profits damages.

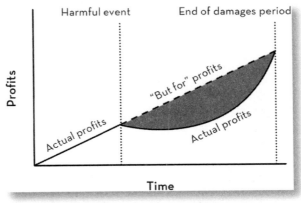

EXHIBIT 10.1 Lost Profits Exhibited as a Line Chart

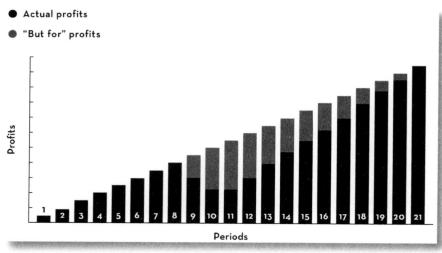

● Actual profits

● "But for" profits

EXHIBIT10.2 Lost Profits Exhibited as a Bar Chart

$$\frac{\text{Net revenue} - \text{Avoided costs}}{\text{Lost profits}}$$

EXHIBIT 10.3 Lost Profits Exhibited in Words and Figures

QUALITY CONTROL FOR FINANCIAL EXPERT WITNESS REPORTS

To have forensically acceptable opinions, the financial expert witness must have a robust quality-control process. Quality control ensures the financial expert witness that work and opinions are accurate and credible, making them reliable for use by the trier of fact. Following are some quality-control procedures the financial expert witness may want to consider when preparing an expert report:

- **Proofreading** is the process used to find errors or mistakes for the purpose of correcting them. Proofreading is designed to find and correct grammatical, clerical, spelling, and reference errors, and mistakes.
- **Independent review** employs an experienced practitioner with no direct involvement in the engagement to read the expert report and key documents to confirm, among other things, understandability, compliance with federal rules, propriety of methods and principles used, and appropriateness of opinions.
- **Calling** is the process of having an independent reader and listener read the expert report out loud to discover awkward wording, clumsy phrasing, and mistakes.
- **Footing** is the checking of mathematical calculations by recomputation.
- **Cross-referencing** has two prongs. The first prong verifies the *internal* consistency of the expert report between the table of contents, page numbers, calculations, dates, references, footnotes, citations, and quotes, among other items. The second prong, also called "cite-checking," confirms the accuracy and consistency of the expert report to *external* facts, data, and evidence cited, referenced, or footnoted.
- **Documents considered review** refers to the quality-control efforts regarding the receipt, inventory, and indexing of facts and data produced to the witness, or work product of the witness, to ensure these materials are properly disclosed in compliance with federal rules.
- **Editing** is the process used to prepare the expert report for issuance. It includes, without limitation, correcting errors and mistakes, reorganizing content, formatting the document, adjusting pagination, and amending the expert report to make it more readable and understandable for the reader.
- **Attorney review** is the editing, comments, questions, and suggestions provided prior to the issuance of the expert report by the client legal counsel. In many cases, counsel may review multiple drafts.
- **Printing review** ensures the quality of the printed, or electronically imaged, expert report and it may include, without limitation, pagination proofing, page number checking, layout, and printing quality.
- **Signature and dating** should be checked by the financial expert witness before signing the expert report.
- **Reference binder** is the final financial expert report tied out, or referenced, to source documents and evidence and placed in a summary binder.

The reference binder ensures all materials cited, referenced, noted, or called out in the expert report are accurately and completely disclosed. The reference binder is a handy source for answers to questions about the expert report and preparatory work for deposition or trial. Some financial experts may take the reference binder with them to deposition as a quick resource for recall.

 ## COMING UP

Now that we understand the considerations for preparing a compliant and effective financial expert witness report, in Chapter 11 we turn our attention to rebuttal of the financial expert witness report.

 ## NOTES

1. *Panduit Corp. v. Stahlin Bros. Fibre Works, Inc.,* 575 F.2d 1152 (6th Cir. 1978).
2. *Georgia-Pacific Corp. v. United States Plywood Corp.,* 318 F. Supp. 1116 (S.D.N.Y. 1970).
3. Bryan A. Garner, Legal *Writing in Plain English: A Text with Exercises* (Chicago: University of Chicago Press, 2001).

CHAPTER ELEVEN

Rebutting the Financial Expert Witness Report

 ## THE FINANCIAL EXPERT REBUTTAL

Under Federal Rules of Civil Procedure (FRCP), Rule 26(a)(2)(D), the defendant is allowed to rebut a plaintiff's opposing financial expert witness report. A rebuttal is an important part of discovery, exposing flaws and weaknesses in an opposing expert's work and opinions. Once shortcomings are exposed, and differences in facts and assumptions are identified, admissibility, reliability, and credibility can be challenged. The objective for the financial expert witness rebuttal is to assist the trier of fact to make an informed decision about the issues by exposing inadmissible or unreliable testimonial evidence. In many cases, a powerful rebuttal can lead to expedited settlement.

 ## STEPS FOR AN EFFECTIVE REBUTTAL

There are many ways to approach the preparation of a financial expert witness rebuttal report. Many financial expert witnesses prefer to attack the numbers, seeking to find errors in formulas, calculations, and summaries. Others use the conceptual approach, making arguments about the validity and reliability of the methods used by the opposing financial expert witness. The federal rules, together with case precedence regarding expert witness testimony admissibility, provide guidance toward some steps for effective rebuttal. These steps are presented below.

Steps for an Effective Rebuttal

1. Assess qualifications.
2. Determine the propriety of legal remedies.
3. Identify potentially improper legal conclusions.
4. Analyze the reliability of principles and methods.
5. Confirm the relevance and reliability of facts, data, and assumptions.
6. Double-check clerical accuracy.
7. The common sense test.

Qualifications

The Federal Rules of Evidence (FRE), Rule 702, precludes the testimony of any witness who is not qualified as an expert. Therefore, this is an obvious place to start when rebutting an opposing financial expert witness. To be sure, it is not the financial expert witness's job to rebut the appropriateness of the qualifications of an opposing expert. That responsibility lies with the client attorney. The financial expert witness, however, is uniquely qualified to analyze an opposing financial expert witness's qualifications. The results of that analysis can then be shared with the client's attorney, who will then decide what to do with this information.

In some cases, the response may be to file a motion *in limine* in an attempt to keep the opposing expert from being heard. In other cases, the suboptimal qualifications are saved for voir dire during trial. In any case, if the financial expert witness can assist in efforts to limit or exclude an opposing expert witness's testimony, the rebuttal effort may be worthwhile. Obviously, if the testimony is ultimately excluded by the court, there is no need to further rebut the remainder of the opposing financial expert witness's work and opinions.

The analysis of an opposing financial expert's qualifications typically starts with the opposing financial expert witness's curriculum vitae (CV) that normally accompanies the initial disclosure statement or expert report. Every entry on the CV should be read and viewed with a critical eye. Areas that are likely to receive attention include the following:

- Universities attended and degrees awarded
- Professional certifications, designations, and awards
- Professional licenses
- Professional association memberships
- Work history and job titles
- Community work
- Research
- Continuing education
- Publications
- Prior testimony
- Relevant case experience

University degrees awarded to the opposing financial expert witness, if suspect, should be verified. Professional certifications, designations, and awards should also be corroborated. Special attention should be paid to professional licenses and trade association memberships because licensees and members have to meet and maintain regulatory and organizational requirements to qualify for valid and active status. The identification of disciplinary proceedings, the lapse of an important license, or the failure to maintain minimum requirements may be of considerable significance when considering a financial expert witness's qualifications and credibility.

In addition to this analysis, the financial expert should examine the opposing financial expert witness's work history, including roles, responsibilities, and titles. Terminations of any kind may be interesting as they may lead to work failings relevant to qualifications. Community work may seem innocuous on its face, but sometimes it is inflated or hides issues related to the opposing financial expert witness's activities and contributions while serving on volunteer boards. Research projects should be looked at to determine relevance to the case and to determine if they represent third-party or self-initiated activities. Professional continuing education should be reviewed for relevance and compliance with licensing and trade organization requirements.

The last qualification areas to analyze relate to the required disclosures for financial expert witnesses under the FRCP—publications and prior testimony. Publications for the past 10 years disclosed by the opposing financial expert should be requested and read for relevance to the case at hand. Furthermore, publications may contain differing positions when compared to the opposing financial expert witness's filed expert report. This can be a key part of rebuttal, or alternatively, the client attorney may want to save this intelligence for deposition or trial in an effort to impeach the opposing expert. Similar to publications, prior testimony may reveal opinions taken in the past that vary from the positions taken by the opposing financial expert witness in the present case. In addition, research into prior testimony may lead to the discovery of excluded testimony. Any history of inadmissible testimony can impair an expert's qualifications and credibility.

After raking through the opposing financial expert witness's CV, it may be prudent to perform additional investigation into qualifications. This can be easily accomplished though Internet searches, contacting peers, or using subscriber search engines designed to track *Daubert*-like motions and expert testimony. Any additional efforts should be undertaken with the knowledge and approval of the client attorney to avoid duplication of effort and other concerns.

Improper Legal Remedies

The next step toward an effective rebuttal is to analyze the legal remedies relied upon by the opposing financial expert witness. There are an extraordinary number of cases wherein expert testimony was deemed inadmissible by the court because the expert relied upon a legal remedy that was not available under governing law. This mistake can easily be made by an inexperienced financial expert witness who fails to recognize that many legal remedies for damages are proscribed by statute and case precedence—not generally accepted professional principles guiding the financial expert witness in the normal course of business. Do not be fooled, though. Even the most experienced expert can be convinced by a talented attorney to embrace an unproven legal theory. Regardless, if the legal remedy is unavailable, the testimony will be barred, negating the need for any other rebuttal. Therefore, rebuttal should include an analysis of the legal theories relied upon by the opposing financial expert witness.

Improper Legal Conclusions

Much like exclusion for the use of an improper legal remedy, there are a remarkable number of instances when expert witness testimony was ruled inadmissible because an improper legal conclusion was offered by a financial expert witness. Legal issues are the exclusive domain of the court. The financial expert witness is not qualified to offer such opinions, and to do so would violate court rule and the general code of professionalism. It may also encroach on applicable licensing requirements related to the practice of law. Therefore, rebuttal should include a cooperative analysis with the client attorney to determine if the opposing financial expert witness has crossed the line and offered opinions on legal issues.

The case excerpt below clearly shows the demarcation between the appropriate and unallowable opinions a testifying expert may give in trial as a financial expert. Such opinions do not include legal opinions. The name of the financial expert has been redacted.

> . . . ORDERS that Defendants' Motion to Exclude Portions of the Expert Testimony of EXPERT WITNESS . . . is GRANTED with clarification. EXPERT WITNESS may testify as to his expert opinion relating to the fields of accounting, auditing, and financial reporting. Likewise, EXPERT WITNESS may testify as to his experience in the fields of accounting, auditing, and financial reporting as it relates to corporate governance. However, EXPERT WITNESS may not testify as to legal issues concerning the perfection and priority of security interests under Article 9 of the Uniform Commercial Code. Likewise, EXPERT WITNESS may not testify as to legal issues relating to corporate governance.[1]

Similar to this case, the partial case report below shows that a financial expert witness will not be allowed to testify about legal issues.

> Some other opinions, however, are inadmissible legal conclusions. Both parties' experts are at fault. This order will not attempt to identify each paragraph in each expert report that is improper. This will be done at trial one question at a time. A general guidance: both experts will be limited on direct examination to testimony about custom and practice in the software industry, and likely be precluded from testimony about the particular contracts and conduct at issue in this action.[2]

Principles and Methods

Under the FRE, Rule 702, the financial expert witness may only be heard at trial if the testimony "is the product of reliable principles and methods." The failure to sufficiently prove that the financial expert witness's opinions are based on reliable principles and methods will result in a ruling of inadmissibility by the court. That is why an analysis of the reliability of the principles and methods used by the opposing financial expert witness is an important next step in rebuttal.

This is best understood by looking at court responses to methods and principles deemed unreliable. In the partial case summarized below, reasonable royalties are challenged. The court ruled that the principles and methods used by the financial expert witness were not reliable and the testimony was excluded. Once again, the name of the financial expert has been obscured.

> Defendants contend that the report by O2 Micro's damages expert, EXPERT WITNESS, is not "the product of reliable principles and methods" and would not serve to "assist the trier of fact to understand the evidence or to determine a fact in issue," and, therefore, the Court should preclude O2 Micro from presenting any testimony from EXPERT WITNESS. Fed. R. Evid. 702; *Daubert v. Merrell Dow Pharm., Inc.*, 509 U.S. 579, 591–94, 113 S. Ct. 2786, 125 L. Ed. 2d 469 (1993). Because O2 Micro's damages case is based entirely upon EXPERT WITNESS'S report, Defendants argue that they are entitled to summary adjudication that O2 Micro has no evidence of damages.
>
> A reasonable royalty analysis, like the one EXPERT WITNESS provides, "necessarily involves an element of approximation and uncertainty." *Unisplay S.A. v. Am. Elec. Sign Co.*, 69 F.3d 512, 517 (Fed. Cir. 1995). An expert determines a reasonable royalty based upon hypothetical negotiations and numerous factors, some of which are prescribed in *Georgia-Pacific Corp. v. United States Plywood Corp.*, 318 F. Supp. 1116, 1120 (S.D.N.Y. 1970), modified and aff'd, 446 F.2d 295 (2d Cir. 1971). Nonetheless, an expert report on damages, including a reasonable royalty analysis, may not rely on unreasonable inferences or resort to "mere speculation or guess." *Central Soya Co. v. Geo. A. Hormel & Co.*, 723 F.2d 1573, 1576 (Fed. Cir. 1983). The patent owner bears the burden of proving the amount of its damages, whether a reasonable royalty or lost profits. *Oiness v. Walgreen Co.*, 88 F.3d 1025, 1029 (Fed. Cir. 1996).
>
> EXPERT WITNESS "report states that the appropriate reasonable royalty rate for MPS" alleged infringement is a percentage "of the average retail price of a notebook computer." Using this approach, EXPERT WITNESS found that the appropriate reasonable royalty is $149 million, even though MPS' total sales of accused products is

$77.9 million and not all of the accused products are used in notebook computers. This approach has several flaws.

First, as noted above, it ignores that not all of MPS' allegedly infringing chips are used in notebook computers; some are used in LCD monitors and others are used in handheld personal data assistants. O2 Micro responds that MPS has neither cited nor produced any records that would allow EXPERT WITNESS to calculate a reasonable royalty for non-notebook uses of the infringing chips. However, O2 Micro, as the patent holder, bears the burden of proving its damages. If MPS refused to produce information that EXPERT WITNESS required to determine the reasonable royalty, then O2 Micro needed to get that information, if necessary through a motion to compel. O2 Micro fails to show any effort it took to get all the information necessary for its expert to provide a reasonable royalty calculation that does not rely on unreasonable inferences or speculation.

Second, O2 Micro's reasonable royalty calculation is based on EXPERT WITNESS'S determination that $3.04, the premium that Dell allegedly paid for O2 Micro's OZ960A inverter controller in 1999, represents a starting point in determining the royalty rate. In his report, EXPERT WITNESS acknowledges that this controller did not utilize the patented technology. Defendants note that, under a reasonable royalty theory, the hypothetical licensee would pay only for the value of the patented invention. *Riles v. Shell Exploration and Prod. Co.*, 298 F.3d 1302, 1312 (Fed. Cir. 2002). O2 Micro responds that the alleged price paid for its OZ960A inverter controller is relevant because that inverter controller, like the patented technology, included open lamp protection. It explains that O2 Micro's other inverter controller, the OZ962 product, lacked the open lamp protection. Therefore, O2 Micro argues that the price paid for its OZ960A inverter controller reflects the value of the open lamp protection.

The cited evidence, however, in particular Dr. Yung-Lin Lin's deposition testimony does not support O2 Micro's response or EXPERT WITNESS'S report . . .

Third, as Defendants point out, EXPERT WITNESS'S report does not account for the law of supply and demand. EXPERT WITNESS hypothesizes a royalty that would triple the average selling price for MPS' accused products, but he makes no allowance for the impact that increased prices would have had on demand. The Federal Circuit states, "All markets must respect the law of demand. According to the law of demand, consumers will almost always purchase fewer units of a product at a higher price than at a lower price, possibly substituting other products." *Crystal Semiconductor Corp. v. TriTech Microelectronics Intern., Inc.*, 246 F.3d 1336, 1359 (Fed. Cir. 2001) (citing Paul A. Samuelson, Economics 53–55 (11th ed. 1980)). O2 Micro attempts to distinguish this case, noting that the plaintiff there sought lost profits, not a reasonable royalty. That difference, however, is inconsequential.

O2 Micro complains that Defendants' motion is a *Daubert* motion, couched as a motion for summary judgment. . . . Defendants' motion is a *Daubert* motion, but their motion is not unsupported, as were the *Daubert* challenges in *Sharp Corp.* and *Monster Cable Products.* Defendants have not offered evidence from an economist or other expert, but they do point to flaws in EXPERT WITNESS'S report that, when combined, are serious enough to render it unreliable and inadmissible. As a result, O2 Micro has not met its burden of proving damages. The Court grants summary judgment in favor of Defendants that O2 Micro has presented no evidence of damages.[3]

Learned Treatises

The FRE, Rule 803(18), provides an exception to the hearsay rule for the financial expert witness when it comes to learned treatises as follows:

Statements in Learned Treatises, Periodicals, or Pamphlets. A statement contained in a treatise, periodical, or pamphlet if:

(A) the statement is called to the attention of an expert witness on cross-examination or relied on by the expert on direct examination; and
(B) the publication is established as a reliable authority by the expert's admission or testimony, by another expert's testimony, or by judicial notice.

If admitted, the statement may be read into evidence but not received as an exhibit.

In the forensic context, a learned treatise is a publication or similar evidence that the court allows to be offered as evidence in trial because it is deemed to be authoritative in a specialized field. Judgment on the admissibility and authoritative substance of any learned treatise is subjective and may include peer review and an evaluation of the general acceptance and use by the field or profession. Attacking opinions by rebutting them with learned treatises that report contrary evidence, or by discrediting any such treatise relied upon by the opposing expert, can be an effective way to critique the opposing financial expert witness.

The following case provides an example of a learned treatise accepted by the courts as admissible evidence. The comments made by the federal U.S. District Court judge infers the acceptance of a practice aid, deemed non-authoritative by the American Institute of Certified Public Accountants as, in essence, a learned treatise on the computation of lost profits. The name of the financial expert has been removed.

> Porcelanite's Motion to Exclude Expert Testimony: Porcelanite moves to exclude the testimony of Plaintiff's damages expert, EXPERT WIT- NESS, on the grounds that his opinions are not sufficiently reliable under Federal Rule of Evidence 702 and *Daubert v. Merrell Dow Pharmaceuticals, Inc.*, 509 U.S. 579 (1993). Porcelanite argues that EXPERT WITNESS'S analysis of damages in California, the Texas area, and for direct sales to Lowe's are unreliable under the *Daubert* standard. Porcelanite requests that the Court exclude his testimony and strike his expert report. Federal Rule of Evidence 702 provides: If scientific, technical, or other specialized knowledge will assist the trier of fact to understand the evidence or to determine a fact in issue, a witness qualified as an expert by knowledge, skill, experience, training, or education, may testify thereto in the form of an opinion or otherwise, if (1) the testimony is based upon sufficient facts or data, (2) the testimony is the product of reliable principles and methods, and (3) the witness has applied the principles and methods reliably to the facts of the case.
>
> In *Daubert*, the Supreme Court held that Rule 702 imposes a "gatekeeping" responsibility on judges to "ensure that any and all scientific testimony or evidence admitted is not only relevant, but reliable." *Ibid.* 509 U.S. at 589. Under this standard, an expert opin- ion is reliable if it is based on proper methods and procedures rather than "subjective belief or unsupported speculation." Id. at 590. The test for reliability "'is not the correctness of the expert's conclusions but the soundness of his methodology.'" *Stilwell v. Smith & Nephew, Inc.*, 482 F.3d 1187, 1192 (9th Cir. 2007) (quoting *Daubert v. Merrell Dow Pharms., Inc.*, 43 F.3d 1311, 1318 (9th Cir. 1995)). Alternative or opposing opinions or tests do not "preclude the admission of the

expert's testimony—they go to the weight, not the admissibility." *Kennedy v. Collagen Corp.*, 161 F.3d 1226, 1231 (9th Cir. 1998) (emphasis in original). "'Disputes as to the strength of [an expert's] credentials, faults in his use of [a particular] methodology, or lack of textual authority for his opinion, go to the weight, not the admissibility, of his testimony.'" *Ibid.* (quoting *McCullock v. H.B. Fuller Co.*, 61 F.3d 1038, 1044 (2d Cir. 1995)).

Porcelanite does not object to EXPERT WITNESS'S qualifications or the relevance of his opinions, but argues that his conclusions are unreliable . . .

. . . Atlas argues that Mr. Preber used an accepted methodology for calculating Atlas's damages based on consideration of Atlas's prior sales performance, analysis of costs, and potential market factors and forecasts. Atlas suggests that to the extent Porcelanite disagrees with EXPERT WITNESS'S conclusions, it will have the opportunity to cross-examine EXPERT WITNESS or to have OPPOS-ING EXPERT WITNESS, Porcelanite's rebuttal expert, explain why EXPERT WITNESS'S opinions should not be given much weight. Atlas asserts that EXPERT WITNESS used a professionally recognized methodology for calculating lost profits based on historical sales data and calculations to account for various alternatives and potential market changes. Atlas argues that his analysis is consistent with the "before and after method" of calculating lost profits included in the American Institute of Certified Public Accountants (AICPA) Practice Aid . . .

. . . The AICPA Practice Guide gives examples of appropriate benchmarks to use in determining lost profits in a given area, including a plaintiff's sales performance at a different location . . . The methodology used by EXPERT WITNESS is not unreliable . . .

With respect to EXPERT WITNESS'S calculation of lost profits for Porcelanite's sales to Lowe's for the Surface Source line, Atlas argues that the AICPA Practice Guide and other authorities allow an accounting of the profits realized by the defendant to be used as a measure of the plaintiff's lost profits . . .

Porcelanite disagrees with EXPERT WITNESS'S conclusions regarding the amount of Atlas's lost profits damages but has not shown that his methodology is unsound or unreliable. Porcelanite will have the opportunity to offer the testimony of its rebuttal expert and to cross-examine EXPERT WITNESS to explore the limitations of his analysis. Any such limitations will go to the weight, not the admissibility, of his testimony. Porcelanite's Motion to Exclude Expert Testimony is denied . . .

IT IS ORDERED denying Porcelanite's Motion to Exclude Expert Testimony of EXPERT WITNESS . . .[4]

This decision was affirmed by the U.S. Court of Appeals, as reflected in the following ruling:

> Porcelanite challenges the admissibility of the testimony of Atlas's damages expert, EXPERT WITNESS, under *Daubert v. Merrell Dow Pharms., Inc.*, 43 F.3d 1311 (9th Cir. 1995). Porcelanite did not challenge EXPERT WITNESS'S testimony on the basis of his qualifications or the relevance of his opinions but on the basis that his conclusions were unreliable because he used an unsound methodology. EXPERT WITNESS, a CPA, used a professionally recognized method of calculating lost profits. The district court correctly determined that Porcelanite's complaints about EXPERT WITNESS'S testimony went to the weight, not the admissibility, of the expert testimony. *Stilwell v. Smith & Nephew, Inc.*, 482 F.3d 1187, 1192 (9th Cir. 1995). The district court's decision to admit the testimony of EXPERT WITNESS was not an abuse of discretion. *Humetrix, Inc. v. Gemplus S.C.A.*, 268 F.3d 910, 919 (9th Cir. 2001).[5]

Facts, Data, and Assumptions

The facts and data considered, ignored, and ultimately relied upon by the financial expert witness to form opinions is fertile ground for rebuttal. A careful analysis should be done on the listing of documents considered that is required to be disclosed by the opposing financial expert witness. This analysis may identify relevant facts and data produced in the case, but missing from the opposing expert witness's list and, therefore, not properly considered or relied upon in forming expert opinions. In addition to this analysis, the following procedures may prove to be fruitful for rebuttal of facts, data, and assumptions (not all inclusive):

- Ensure evidence has been interpreted correctly.
- Determine whether facts and data used are relevant to the disputed facts, issues, and assignments.
- Confirm that reliable facts, data, and assumptions have been applied to reliable principles and methods in the field.

- Evaluate whether all material pertinent evidence was used.
- Assess whether too much, or too little, weight was given to evidence.
- Identify any failure to verify, corroborate, or test material evidence relied upon, particularly facts, data, and assumptions provided by the client or client legal counsel.
- Consider whether the facts and data are of a type normally used by peers in the field.
- Research to find assumption inconsistencies in prior testimony.

Areas frequently subject to fact, data, and assumption rebuttal include causation, damages period start and end dates, growth and shrinkage rates, profit margins, overhead costs, discount rates, missing evidence, and nonstatistical results extrapolation, among many others.

> A fair trial is one in which the rules of evidence are honored, the accused has competent counsel, and the judge enforces the proper courtroom procedures—a trial in which every assumption can be challenged.
>
> —Harry Browne

Attorney-Provided Facts, Data, and Assumptions

In every case, the client attorney will provide the financial expert witness with facts, data, and assumptions. This is common and an accepted and necessary practice. A good example is the disputed fact of liability that is present in every civil claim. A financial expert witness engaged to prepare or rebut damages is often asked by the client attorney to assume the fact of liability. In other words, even though it is unproven, without an unlawful civil act of liability there can be no damage. No damage means no need for a financial expert witness on damages. Accordingly, plaintiff's and defendant's financial expert damage witnesses will both likely acknowledge the adoption of the assumed fact of liability.

There are very few other circumstances where the financial expert witness should accept facts, data, and assumptions from legal counsel without doing some work. The failure to assess the reasonableness, completeness, accuracy, and reliability of facts, data, and assumptions provided solely by the client attorney can present material weaknesses in an opposing financial expert witness's work and opinions. For that reason, the financial expert witness rebuttal should focus efforts in this area.

Unquestioned, Unsupported, and Unreasonable Assumptions

We have all heard the saying about what happens when you assume something (i.e., it can make an *ass* [out of] *u* [and] *me*). Well, the same holds true for assumptions used by the opposing financial expert witness that are unquestioned, unreasonable, or unsupported. If not adequately disclosed in the opposing financial expert witness's report, he or she will undoubtedly be asked at some point by the client attorney to disclose the major assumptions used to form opinions. If any major assumption underpinning an opinion is found to be unquestioned, unreasonable, or unsupported, the entire opinion may be invalid, or at least unreliable for use by the trier of fact.

Use of Public Information

Financial expert witnesses may identify and rely on facts and data found in the public domain or obtained through subscription or paid providers as part of the basis for key assumptions or opinions. Sources for such facts and data may be government websites, surveys, analyst reports, and financial websites. In some cases, these sources can be forensically reliable for facts and data. For example, the Securities and Exchange Commission's Electronic Data Gathering, Analysis, and Retrieval website is a reliable source for reports filed by public companies under the Securities Exchange Acts. However, some public sources for facts and data are not reliable for use in court. Internet blogs, public surveys, and website promotional materials, to name a few sources, should be relied upon by the financial expert witness with extreme caution. It is advisable to confirm these sources as truly reliable if they are to be used.

The lack of reliability for a significant portion of facts and data in the public domain results from many things. It may be unreliable because the qualifications of the preparers cannot be determined. Or, the source of the facts and data may not be available for the financial expert witness to verify. Alternatively, there may be no way to prove that generally accepted methods and principles were used to gather, compile and report the facts and data. In any case, the identification of the improper usage of such unreliable facts and data is an important step in the rebuttal of an opposing financial expert witness report.

Clerical Accuracy

The last step, but not last in importance, is to test the clerical accuracy of the opposing financial expert witness's report, schedules, and exhibits. The reason this step is last in order is because the previous steps are home-run swings. If you can exclude the opposing financial expert witness's testimony because he or she is not qualified, used an improper legal remedy, offered legal opinions, or used an unreliable method or principle, there is no need for further rebuttal—the expert is out. But, like a home-run swing, most of the time the financial expert witness is going to miss a few pitches and, therefore, must be prepared to go head-to-head against the opposing financial expert witness at the most detailed level.

Testing clerical accuracy involves more than just double-checking the math. The fact and data references and footnotes in the opposing expert report and supporting work papers should be traced to sources. Internal cross-references should be scrutinized for consistency. Formulas and spreadsheet macros should be understood and recomputed. Acronyms, grammar, and spelling should also be critiqued. Keep in mind that in the eyes of a judge or jury, errors, even small ones, may cause a perception of sloppiness and the failure to pay attention to details. That perception can potentially impair the credibility of the opposing financial expert witness with the trier of fact.

Common Sense Test

At times, the opposing financial expert fails to step back from the details to assess whether expert opinions meet the common sense test. The common sense test asks if a reasonable person would find the opinions sensible given the facts and circumstances of the case. The common sense test can be applied to things like causation, assumptions, or damages calculations. Most experienced financial expert witnesses will be able to recall at least one opposing expert report that failed to meet the common sense test.

In the following case excerpt, the court rules that financial expert witness's testimony is inadmissible because it fails to assist the trier of fact to determine an ultimate issue in the case, in part, because it defies common sense. The financial expert's name has been removed.

> In assessing the reliability of an expert opinion, a resort to common sense is not inappropriate. EXPERT WITNESS'S opinion, despite its dazzling sheen of erudition and meticulous methodology, reaches a result which any average person could readily recognize as preposterous.
>
> Consider these figures: The period for which Mabuchi can collect damages extended only nine months, from July 15, 1988 to March 1989. During those three quarters, Johnson's worldwide sales of both series 100 and series 200 micro-motors totaled less than 2 million

units . . . EXPERT WITNESS stated that 14% of the motors sold outside the United States were incorporated in products that were imported into the United States. . . . If that is correct, less than 280,000 of these Johnson micro-motors were used in the United States. . . . On the sale of these micro-motors, Johnson grossed less than $200,000. Even assuming that, but for Johnson's infringement, Mabuchi would have sold every one of these motors, and further assuming, as EXPERT WITNESS did, that Mabuchi could have sold them at prices 15% higher than the competitive market prices, it would have made less than $230,000 in additional sales. There is no evidence as to the profit Mabuchi would have made on those sales, but it seems safe to assume that its profit would have been substantially less than $100,000. It is hard to perceive how Johnson's sales during the damage period injured Mabuchi in an amount greater than the sum of those potential lost profits.

Yet, after a dauntingly complex process involving the seemingly unnecessary construction of obviously unrealistic market models incorporating many irrelevant factors, EXPERT WITNESS arrives at the startling conclusion that Johnson's infringement entitles Mabuchi to $5.2 million in damages plus $1.4 million in pre-judgment interest for a total of $6.6 million. Thus, for every dollar of profit that Mabuchi arguably lost because of Johnson's legally cognizable infringement, EXPERT WITNESS would award Mabuchi damages of over $50 plus interest. This would make Mabuchi not merely "whole," but at least $5 million dollars richer than it would have been if Johnson had neither made nor sold any infringing micro-motors during the damage period.

The Court has not the slightest difficulty in concluding that EXPERT WITNESS'S opinion fails to satisfy Rule 702's requirement that it assist the trier of fact in understanding the evidence or determining factual issues in the case.[6]

CASE STUDY: EXCLUSION OF THE FINANCIAL EXPERT WITNESS

To drive the point home about the steps for an effective rebuttal beginning with qualifications and ending with clerical accuracy, the following case excerpt clearly demonstrates a worst-case scenario for two financial expert witnesses.

In this example, everything goes wrong. The names of the financial experts have been removed.

> Plaintiff has offered the testimony of EXPERT WITNESS as a damages expert regarding lost profits, yet plaintiff has not shown the court that the most basic prerequisites for admission of such testimony have been met. Although EXPERT WITNESS anticipates testifying as an expert, he did not sign the report . . . upon which his opinion is based . . . is not a partner with the firm for which he is employed and does not know when or if he will become one . . . is not a CPA . . . has not provided his resume for the court's review, has never before been asked to value harm caused by use of a trade name or trademark . . . has never testified either by deposition or in trial . . . has never published any books or articles on valuation . . . and does not believe he has ever done a financial analysis of any institution in Kansas before . . .
>
> "A trial judge has broad discretion in determining the competency of an expert witness." *Kloepfer v. Honda Motor Co.*, 898 F.2d 1452, 1458 (10th Cir. 1990). In making this determination, two general conditions must be met.
>
> First, the subject matter must be closely related to a particular profession, business or science and not within the common knowledge of the average layman; second, the witness must have such skill, experience or knowledge in that particular field as to make it appear that his opinion would rest on substantial foundation and would tend to aid the trier of fact in his search for truth.
>
> The admonition noted by the Seventh Circuit in *Schiller & Schmidt, Inc. v. Nordisco Corp.*, 969 F.2d at 416, is equally applicable here:
>
> . . . people who want damages have to prove them, using methodologies that need not be intellectually sophisticated but must not insult the intelligence . . . Post hoc ergo propter hoc will not do; nor the enduing (sic) of simplistic extrapolation and childish arithmetic with the appearance of authority by hiring a professor to mouth damages theories that make a joke of the concept of expert knowledge.
>
> Moreover, the court concludes that the testimony should also be excluded on this basis under Rule 403 because its minimal probative value would be substantially outweighed by unfair prejudice and the confusion to the jury that would result from the authoritative rendering of such substantial damage estimates by a purported economic expert.
>
> Defendants next contend that the testimony of OTHER EXPERT WITNESS, plaintiff's expert regarding costs of conducting a corrective

advertising campaign, is inadmissible under *Daubert* and *Kumho*, because it is neither relevant nor reliable.

The report provided by OTHER EXPERT WITNESS lists media expenditures totaling $122,118.49, and production expenditures totaling $64,034.00. No narrative is included, but the purpose of the report, and OTHER EXPERT WITNESS'S proposed testimony, is apparently to establish that plaintiff has been or will be damaged in those amounts.

OTHER EXPERT WITNESS'S report . . . is unsigned. No resume, curriculum vitae, or other indicia of his qualifications have been provided to this court. His deposition . . . fails to establish where he works, what his job title or duties are, or his educational or work history. It does, however, establish that OTHER EXPERT WITNESS has never given a deposition before . . . and none of his work has been published . . . When asked whether he had ever had any involvement in any similar ad campaign, OTHER EXPERT WITNESS admitted that he did not feel as though he knew enough about the specifics of the situation that he could answer the question . . . Although OTHER EXPERT WITNESS'S testimony appears to be based upon his experience or training, as opposed to any particular methodology or technique, the court has no clue what his experience or training is. Based upon the law set forth in Section I above, no basis for permitting OTHER EXPERT WITNESS to testify as an expert has been shown.

Additionally, the substance of OTHER EXPERT WITNESS'S testimony is not sufficiently reliable to warrant its admission. OTHER EXPERT WITNESS testified that he has never heard anything about any specific harm to plaintiff . . . OTHER EXPERT WITNESS did not review OTHER EXPERT WITNESS'S proposed figures regarding lost profits, or any other documents demonstrating either the nature or extent of harm suffered by plaintiff because of any name confusion. He was unaware of the words and logo the defendants used to market its banking services in Kansas, and had no understanding of how those words or logo differed from those used by plaintiff. . . .

OTHER EXPERT WITNESS'S figures are an "example" to establish what it might cost to do a campaign that could rehabilitate plaintiff's name . . . He assumed the following facts: that for three years there had been two financial institutions in the same marketplace with the same name and that confusion had resulted . . . OTHER EXPERT WITNESS did not go so far as to determine what the concept or message would be in the advertising campaign . . . but admits that the message can have an effect on the costs . . .

Because OTHER EXPERT WITNESS'S testimony fails to take into account the specific facts of the case, it is too speculative to assist the jury in determining the amount plaintiff would be damaged by engaging in a remedial advertising campaign. Based upon the law stated in Section I, the court concludes that OTHER EXPERT WITNESS'S testimony and report are inadmissible under rules 702 and 403.[7]

RISKS OF HAVING ONLY REBUTTAL OPINIONS

Rebuttal reports are, by their nature, limited to responding to the opposing financial expert witness's report and associated opinions. However, if the financial expert witness doing the rebuttal fails to offer an affirmative opinion independent of rebuttal testimony, there are risks involved. The court may conclude that rebuttal testimony is unhelpful to the trier of fact because an expert is not needed to handle what can readily be done through cross-examination. Therefore, in close consultation with the client's attorney, the financial expert witness may be asked to perform the work necessary to form affirmative opinions to be included as part of a rebuttal report.

COMING UP

We will now move to one of the most feared parts of litigation and alternative dispute resolution for financial expert witnesses—the deposition.

NOTES

1. *Lehocky v. Tidel Techs., Inc.,* 2004 U.S. Dist. LEXIS 31020, 4 (S.D. Tex. June 10, 2004).
2. *Actuate Corp. v. Aon Corp.,* 2012 U.S. Dist. LEXIS 87185, 3-4 (N.D. Cal. June 18, 2012).
3. *Monolithic Power Sys. v. O2 Micro Int'l Ltd.,* 476 F. Supp. 2d 1143, 1156 (N.D. Cal. 2007).

4. *Atlas Flooring, LLC v. Porcelanite S.A. de C.V.*, Case No. CV-07-1741-PHX-SRB, Dkt 187, Motion to Exclude Expert Testimony (Dist. of Ariz. 2009), affirmed *Atlas Flooring, LLC v. Porcelanite S.A. de C.V.*, 425 Fed. Appx. 629, 632 (9th Cir. Ariz. 2011).

5. *Atlas Flooring, LLC v. Porcelanite S.A. de C.V.*, 425 Fed. Appx. 629, 632 (9th Cir. Ariz. 2011).

6. *Johnson Elec. N. Am. Inc. v. Mabuchi Motor Am. Corp.*, 103 F. Supp. 2d 268, 286-287 (S.D.N.Y. 2000).

7. *First Sav. Bank, FSB v. United States Bancorp*, 117 F. Supp. 2d 1078, 1086 (D. Kan. 2000).

CHAPTER TWELVE

Discovery Using Deposition

 ## WHAT IS A DEPOSITION?

It has been said that a financial expert witness cannot win a case in deposition. But, he or she can sure lose one. Depositions are generally recognized as one of the most challenging tasks the financial expert witness will undertake in a career. They are designed to be fishing expeditions performed by intelligent, trained, educated, and highly motivated adversarial attorneys. There are scores of stories about atypical behavior, unusual questioning techniques, and ambush tactics employed by opposing legal counsel conducting depositions. As such, the financial expert witness must be well-prepared and practiced in the art of the successful deposition.

Deposition is a discovery tool for opposing counsel. Discovery is designed to allow the disputing parties to attempt to find relevant evidence from an opposing party to prove, or disprove, disputed facts and issues. These efforts may narrow the disputed facts and issues, uncover evidence not otherwise available to the disputing parties, and expose legal issues to be decided by the court. A deposition is sworn pretrial testimony given by the financial expert witness in response to questions posed by opposing legal counsel. Inquiries made by opposing legal counsel during deposition are designed to discover what the financial expert witness may say in trial.

There is no judge present at a deposition. This creates an interesting dynamic, as there is no one present at the deposition to handle the inevitable disputes that will arise. Also, there is no one to instruct the financial expert witness on what to do when disputes remain unresolved, including the client attorney who is not legal counsel to the financial expert witness. This can cause the financial expert witness to feel uncomfortable during the deposition and uncertain as to what course of action should be taken.

In addition to being a discovery tool, depositions are used to craft trial strategy. In deposition, the deposing attorney can experiment with cross-examination questions based on the identification of information believed to be damaging to the financial expert witness. Deposition responses are also frequently used to impeach the financial expert witness at trial, or to support an opposing expert witness's testimony or positions. Therefore, a significant part of the planning for cross-examination of the financial expert witness is based on deposition testimony. Finally, deposition of the financial expert witness is frequently used for pretrial settlement negotiations.

Federal Rules for Deposition

The Federal Rules of Civil Procedure (FRCP), Rule 26(b)(4)(a), provides that "[a] party may depose any person who has been identified as an expert whose opinions may be presented at trial. If FRCP Rule 26(a)(2)(B) requires a report from the expert, the deposition may be conducted only after the report is provided." A deposition is the provision of pretrial sworn oral testimony given by the financial expert witness during the discovery phase of the dispute resolution process in response to legally permitted inquiries posed primarily by opposing legal counsel. Deposition testimony is considered to be evidence, and if deemed admissible by the court, has the same evidentiary standing as trial testimony.

Reasonable Notice to Take Deposition

A deposition can only be conducted after reasonable notice has been given to the financial expert witness. Under FRCP Rule 30, proper notice must include the following requirements:

(b) Notice of the Deposition; Other Formal Requirements.
(1) **Notice in General.** A party who wants to depose a person by oral questions must give reasonable written notice to every other party. The notice must state the time and place of the deposition and, if known, the deponent's name and address. If the name is unknown, the notice must provide a general description sufficient

to identify the person or the particular class or group to which the person belongs.

(2) **Producing Documents.** If a subpoena *duces tecum* is to be served on the deponent, the materials designated for production, as set out in the subpoena, must be listed in the notice or in an attachment. The notice to a party deponent may be accompanied by a request under Rule 34 to produce documents and tangible things at the deposition.

(3) **Method of Recording.**

(A) **Method Stated in the Notice.** The party who notices the deposition must state in the notice the method for recording the testimony. Unless the court orders otherwise, testimony may be recorded by audio, audiovisual, or stenographic means. The noticing party bears the recording costs. Any party may arrange to transcribe a deposition.

(B) **Additional Method.** With prior notice to the deponent and other parties, any party may designate another method for recording the testimony in addition to that specified in the original notice. That party bears the expense of the additional record or transcript unless the court orders otherwise.

(4) **By Remote Means.** The parties may stipulate—or the court may on motion order—that a deposition be taken by telephone or other remote means. For the purpose of this rule and Rules 28(a), 37(a)(2), and 37(b)(1), the deposition takes place where the deponent answers the questions.

Subpoena Usage and Response

In many cases, a deposition is noticed using a subpoena that is officially served to the financial expert witness, or the client legal counsel on behalf of the financial expert witness. A deposition subpoena is a court-ordered notice to appear for deposition. Professional courtesy provides that opposing legal counsel consult with the client attorney and the financial expert witness to schedule a deposition on a mutually convenient date and place for all parties. That date is used for purposes of the subpoena compelling appearance by the financial expert witness. The FRCP Rule 45 provides guidance on the use of, and responses to, a subpoena. This guidance follows:

Rule 45. Subpoena (effective Dec. 1, 2013)

(a) IN GENERAL.

(1) **Form and Contents.**

(A) **Requirements—In General.** Every subpoena must:

(i) state the court from which it issued;

     (ii) state the title of the action and its civil-action number;

     (iii) command each person to whom it is directed to do the following at a specified time and place: attend and testify; produce designated documents, electronically stored information, or tangible things in that person's possession, custody, or control; or permit the inspection of premises; and

     (iv) set out the text of Rule 45(d) and (e).

  (B) **Command to Attend a Deposition—Notice of the Recording Method.** A subpoena commanding attendance at a deposition must state the method for recording the testimony.

  (C) **Combining or Separating a Command to Produce or to Permit Inspection; Specifying the Form for Electronically Stored Information.** A command to produce documents, electronically stored information, or tangible things or to permit the inspection of premises may be included in a subpoena commanding attendance at a deposition, hearing, or trial, or may be set out in a separate subpoena. A subpoena may specify the form or forms in which electronically stored information is to be produced.

  (D) **Command to Produce; Included Obligations.** A command in a subpoena to produce documents, electronically stored information, or tangible things requires the responding person to permit inspection, copying, testing, or sampling of the materials.

• • •

(b) SERVICE.

. . . (2) **Service in the United States.** A subpoena may be served at any place within the United States.

(3) **Service in a Foreign Country.** 28 U.S.C. § 1783 governs issuing and serving a subpoena directed to a United States national or resident who is in a foreign country.

• • •

(d) PROTECTING A PERSON SUBJECT TO A SUBPOENA; ENFORCEMENT.

(1) **Avoiding Undue Burden or Expense; Sanctions.** A party or attorney responsible for issuing and serving a subpoena must take reasonable steps to avoid imposing undue burden or expense on a person subject to the subpoena. The court for the district where compliance is required must enforce this duty and impose an appropriate sanction—which may include lost earnings and reasonable attorney's fees—on a party or attorney who fails to comply.

(2) **Command to Produce Materials or Permit Inspection.**

(A) **Appearance Not Required.** A person commanded to produce documents, electronically stored information, or tangible things, or to permit the inspection of premises, need not appear in person at the place of production or inspection unless also commanded to appear for a deposition, hearing, or trial.

(B) **Objections.** A person commanded to produce documents or tangible things or to permit inspection may serve on the party or attorney designated in the subpoena a written objection to inspecting, copying, testing, or sampling any or all of the materials or to inspecting the premises—or to producing electronically stored information in the form or forms requested. The objection must be served before the earlier of the time specified for compliance or 14 days after the subpoena is served. If an objection is made, the following rules apply:

(i) At any time, on notice to the commanded person, the serving party may move the court for the district where compliance is required for an order compelling production or inspection.

(ii) These acts may be required only as directed in the order, and the order must protect a person who is neither a party nor a party's officer from significant expense resulting from compliance.

(3) **Quashing or Modifying a Subpoena.**

(A) When Required. On timely motion, the court for the district where compliance is required must quash or modify a subpoena that:

(i) fails to allow a reasonable time to comply;

(ii) requires a person to comply beyond the geographical limits specified in Rule 45(c);

(iii) requires disclosure of privileged or other protected matter, if no exception or waiver applies; or

(iv) subjects a person to undue burden.

(B) **When Permitted.** To protect a person subject to or affected by a subpoena, the court for the district where compliance is required may, on motion, quash or modify the subpoena if it requires:

(i) disclosing a trade secret or other confidential research, development, or commercial information; or

(ii) disclosing an unretained expert's opinion or information that does not describe specific occurrences in dispute and results from the expert's study that was not requested by a party.

(C) **Specifying Conditions as an Alternative.** In the circumstances described in Rule 45(d)(3)(B), the court may, instead of quashing or modifying a subpoena, order appearance or production under specified conditions if the serving party:

   (i) shows a substantial need for the testimony or material that cannot be otherwise met without undue hardship; and

   (ii) ensures that the subpoenaed person will be reasonably compensated.

(e) DUTIES IN RESPONDING TO A SUBPOENA.

(1) **Producing Documents or Electronically Stored Information.** These procedures apply to producing documents or electronically stored information:

(A) **Documents.** A person responding to a subpoena to produce documents must produce them as they are kept in the ordinary course of business or must organize and label them to correspond to the categories in the demand.

(B) **Form for Producing Electronically Stored Information Not Specified.** If a subpoena does not specify a form for producing electronically stored information, the person responding must produce it in a form or forms in which it is ordinarily maintained or in a reasonably usable form or forms.

(C) **Electronically Stored Information Produced in Only One Form.** The person responding need not produce the same electronically stored information in more than one form.

(D) **Inaccessible Electronically Stored Information.** The person responding need not provide discovery of electronically stored information from sources that the person identifies as not reasonably accessible because of undue burden or cost. On motion to compel discovery or for a protective order, the person responding must show that the information is not reasonably accessible because of undue burden or cost. If that showing is made, the court may nonetheless order discovery from such sources if the requesting party shows good cause, considering the limitations of Rule 26(b)(2)(C). The court may specify conditions for the discovery.

(2) **Claiming Privilege or Protection.**

(A) **Information Withheld.** A person withholding subpoenaed information under a claim that it is privileged or subject to protection as trial-preparation material must:

   (i) expressly make the claim; and

   (ii) describe the nature of the withheld documents, communications, or tangible things in a manner that, without revealing information itself privileged or protected, will enable the parties to assess the claim.

(B) **Information Produced.** If information produced in response to a subpoena is subject to a claim of privilege or of protection as trial-preparation material, the person making the claim may notify any party that received the information of the claim and the basis for it. After being notified, a party must promptly return, sequester, or destroy the specified information and any copies it has; must not use or disclose the information until the claim is resolved; must take reasonable steps to retrieve the information if the party disclosed it before being notified; and may promptly present the information under seal to the court for the district where compliance is required for a determination of the claim. The person who produced the information must preserve the information until the claim is resolved.

• • •

(g) CONTEMPT. The court for the district where compliance is required—and also, after a motion is transferred, the issuing court—may hold in contempt a person who, having been served, fails without adequate excuse to obey the subpoena or an order related to it.

Subpoena Duces Tecum

In some cases, a subpoena *duces tecum* will be served on the financial expert witness. A subpoena *duces tecum* compels appearance at the deposition and specifies documents identified by opposing legal counsel to be produced by the financial expert witness in connection with such an appearance. A subpoena *duces tecum* commonly includes requests for the following items, which may be in hard copy or electronic form:

- Work papers
- Work product
- Evidence, facts, and data relied upon to form opinions
- Engagement letter
- Timekeeping records
- Billing and payment records
- Notes
- Speeches
- Presentations
- Instructional materials
- Publications
- Professional education
- Prior matter expert reports
- Prior matter deposition testimony

- Prior matter trial testimony and exhibits
- Generally accepted guidance and treatises used
- Research results
- Policies and procedures

Subpoena Duces Tecum Protocols

The financial expert witness should have protocols in place to ensure proper and complete compliance with a subpoena *duces tecum.* Any questions about the identification and production of requested documents should be discussed with the client legal counsel who will provide instructions on handling. Once the population of responsive documents has been identified, they should be reproduced in a format prescribed by the client legal counsel. In most cases, documents will be produced in electronic format as images.

Objections to Subpoena Duces Tecum

It is possible that the financial expert witness may object to the production of some portion of the documents requested to be produced by opposing legal counsel. Objections may be raised for many reasons, including but not limited to, overly burdensome or overly broad requests, confidentiality, propriety, relevance, or availability from public sources. In these instances, the financial expert witness should work with the client legal counsel and potentially personal legal counsel as well to prepare and file the proper motions to quash the subpoena or limit the required production. If successfully quashed, the subpoena will be revoked and nullified by the court. In rare cases, the judge may require the production of documents for an in-camera inspection by the court.

Native Format Production

It is likely that the financial expert witness will be asked by opposing legal counsel to produce electronic spreadsheets and databases in native format. Native format is the form the document was stored and accessed by the applicable software used to prepare it. Common application software packages are Microsoft Word and Excel, among others. If this request is made, it is important for the financial expert witness to lock down and fossilize the original format and data. This may require read-only production or some other form of protection to readily identify potential changes to the original documentation after production.

Production of Requested Materials

Once the financial expert witness has prepared responsive documents for production to the opposing attorney, it is a best practice to produce these materials exclusively to the client legal counsel. Only in unusual situations based on the client legal counsel's request should the financial expert witness directly produce anything to the opposing attorney. This way, the client's legal counsel can make a legal determination about what is to be produced to the other side of the dispute, considering relevance, rules, and legal privilege. These decisions are legal in nature and the financial expert witness is not qualified to make them.

DEPOSITION OBJECTIVES

Client Legal Counsel

How does the client's attorney define success for the financial expert witness in deposition? That question is best posed to the client's attorney—and it should be asked by the financial expert witness prior to deposition. In some cases, the answer is to briefly answer the question that was asked. That means the financial expert witness is to keep responses truthful and complete, but brief. In other cases, the "wow" factor is desired to show off the financial expert witness's expertise and communication skills as a threat to the opponent. In those instances, the financial expert witness may be asked to talk up qualifications or expand on approaches believed to be superior. In other cases, the client's attorney wants to drive toward settlement, instructing the financial expert witness to provide responses that may serve this purpose. In any case, the client legal counsel's ultimate objective is to not have the financial expert witness lose the case in deposition.

One thing to remember, most large civil litigation is resolved by settlement before, during, or after trial. Settlement before trial is desirable for a number of reasons, including time and cost savings. In order for this to happen, the disputing parties must have a realistic picture of the damages and potential risk of testimony expected to be given by the financial expert witness at trial. Therefore, it is important for the financial expert witness to keep in mind that deposition testimony is commonly critical for a more speedy resolution through settlement.

There can be no settlement of a great cause without discussion, and people will not discuss a cause until their attention is drawn to it.

—*William Jennings Bryan*

Deposing Legal Counsel

Deposing legal counsel may have a number of objectives to accomplish when taking the deposition of the financial expert witness. Of course, true to the adversarial nature of the proceedings, none of them are designed to benefit the financial expert witness. The basic goal is to find out what opinions the financial expert witness plans to deliver at trial. Subsidiary, but also high in importance, is the discovery of a basis to deny the financial expert witness an opportunity to testify at trial. This can be done by exposing major weaknesses in qualifications or finding fatal flaws related to admissibility. Last, but certainly not least, opposing legal counsel will use the deposition to go fishing. Fishing for credibility issues, fishing for harmful information, and fishing to see what rattles the financial expert witness. The goal is no surprises at trial.

Financial Expert Witness

The basic deposition objectives of the financial expert witness are to listen carefully to each question and confidently answer that question—and only that question—truthfully, briefly, completely, and articulately. Deposition objectives for the financial expert witness can be likened to a basketball game. Deposing legal counsel is going to score some points on the financial expert witness—and

Objectives of Deposing Legal Counsel

- Obtain opinions.
- Explore admissibility issues.
- Understand qualifications.
- Expose credibility problems.
- Fossilize the financial expert witness.
- Confirm the known and undisputed.
- Learn key assumptions and use of disputed facts.
- Discover new information.
- Size up the financial expert witness.
- Refine trial strategy.
- No surprises at trial.

some may appear to be slam-dunks. The financial expert witness must stay in the game and remain focused on a win, even if it is a slight one. Complete wins for either opposing side are rare.

Success is survival.

— *Leonard Cohen*

 COMING UP

In Chapter 13, we continue to learn about financial expert witness depositions, moving on to deposition preparation and testimony.

CHAPTER THIRTEEN

Financial Expert Witness Deposition Preparation

 PREPARATION FOR DEPOSITION

Preparation for financial expert witness deposition is necessary to ensure testimony is relevant, clear, and understandable. It also helps reduce the financial expert witness's stress levels to enable better personal performance. There are a number of things the financial expert witness can do to prepare for deposition. Some things are quick and easy to complete, but others may take several sessions over a number of days. In any case, every financial expert witness, regardless of experience level, has a professional responsibility to prepare thoroughly for deposition.

In the weeks leading up to a deposition, the financial expert witness should obtain engagement information and study materials expected to be the subject of deposition inquiries. Obviously, the financial expert witness must master knowledge about case facts and the financial expert witness's work, reports, declarations, and opinions. In addition, the financial expert witness must have command of important dates and events. This is likened to a final examination in college; it's all about the cram studies before the big test.

Basic Preparation Steps

As each case has differing facts and circumstances, there is no one way to prepare for deposition. However, there are some basic things that should be considered, regardless of case specifics. The financial expert witness should reread case orders, pleadings, and filings, paying particular attention to issues, claims, and other matters relevant to the financial expert witness's assignments. The financial expert witness should also have a solid understanding about legal remedies, especially those used by the financial expert witness to form opinions or rebut opposing experts.

Go over timelines, data productions, and key evidence, including, but not limited to, documents, interviews, and sworn testimony transcripts. In instances where documents requested were not produced, the financial expert witness should be ready to explain how his assignments could be reliably accomplished in light of missing requested evidence. In most cases, alternative sources of facts, data, and evidence will suffice and should be explained. The financial expert witness must also have an awareness of the rules governing the admissibility of expert testimony as this is likely to be an area of inquiry and attack by deposing legal counsel.

Of course, it is essential that the financial expert witness know his own work and expert report inside-out. Identify strengths and weaknesses and be prepared to articulate both. While studying your own materials, do not be surprised to find insignificant typographical errors, grammar and punctuation problems, or incorrect references to source documents. Even the best quality control process has potential shortcomings when faced with impending deadlines, computer interfaces, and masses of data. If these types of mistakes are discovered and they are inconsequential to the substance of the financial expert witness's report, take note and be prepared during deposition, if asked, to explain any minor issues. If, however, the financial expert witness finds a material mistake or inaccuracy, it is critical that the matter be brought to the attention of client legal counsel immediately and corrected promptly, if possible before the deposition.

The financial expert witness should be prepared to thoroughly explain the work performed by any staff or others acting at the expert's direction, including the expert's role in directing, supervising, and confirming the results of that work. It is also critical to be able to identify any assumptions that are material to the expert's conclusions or analysis, explain the basis for those assumptions, and describe why the expert believes they are reasonable and appropriate assumptions under the circumstances of the particular case.

If the financial expert witness is a member of a professional organization that requires adherence to professional standards for the work performed, know the standards and be able to describe them. If the financial expert witness considered and relied upon others, publications, databases, websites, treatises, or other sources, understand and be able to explain the bases for use, relevance, reliability, and general acceptance of these materials by the financial expert witness's profession. It may also be important to know if these materials have been previously accepted by the courts as admissible evidence. Study opposing experts' reports and supporting materials and identify commonalities and criticisms. The financial expert witness should be able to communicate these matters during deposition.

One method of preparation that can be employed by the financial expert witness from the start of any assignment is the use of a replicable work flow process. A replicable work flow process has the financial expert do a standardized set of activities in a certain order for quality control purposes. It also helps the financial expert witness remember what has been done and the order of completion. This can be helpful in deposition and trial when inquiries are made about work performed. A model work flow process is described next.

Repeatable Work Flow Process

The financial expert witness may find it helpful to use a replicable process to complete assignments likely to be subjected to deposition inquiries or cross-examination at trial. Such a process provides additional quality control and aids in the recollection and description of project execution. Such a process may begin with client acceptance and engagement, move to familiarization with case facts and issues, leading to the identification of materials likely to assist with the completion of assignments, thereby allowing the analysis of produced materials in order to form expert opinions. Within this process, the financial expert witness should know, among other matters, when materials were produced, when key testing was performed, who was interviewed, and when the financial expert witness formed his opinions (see Exhibit 13.1).

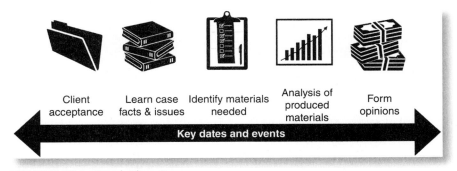

EXHIBIT 13.1 Work Flow Process

EXPECTED DEPOSITION QUESTIONS

Although it is impossible to anticipate every inquiry during the course of a deposition, there are a number of commonly asked questions that the financial expert witness should be prepared to answer. In general, they fall into the following categories:

- Opinions
- Relevance or "fit" to the issues in the case
- Qualifications
- Credibility
- Fossilize positions and opinions
- Facts, data, and assumptions
- Discover new information
- Business arrangements
- Assignment details and opinions
- Size up the financial expert witness
- Opposing experts

The financial expert witness should anticipate these questions and practice answers that are responsive, clear, and concise. Let's explore a few of these areas next.

Opinions

Central to any deposition taken by opposing legal counsel is the need to learn all of the financial expert witness's opinions to be expressed at trial. This need is met by posing a series of questions to the financial expert witness designed to elicit this information. In some situations, the deposing attorney will use the financial expert witness's report to identify opinions or statements that read like opinions. If so, the financial expert witness may be asked to confirm reported opinions based on statements made in the expert report.

Frequently, inquiries about financial expert witness opinions will begin with an open-ended question like this: "Can you tell me all the opinions you intend to give at trial?" After getting an answer from the financial expert witness, the opposing attorney may then ask: "Is that all of the opinions you intend to offer at trial?" If the financial expert witness answers "yes," the deposing attorney will move on to the next topic. This is often intentional because the deposing attorney believes she has locked the financial expert into those positions testified to in the deposition.

For that reason, the financial expert must be very careful about responding to this line of questions. If the answer from the financial expert witness about whether all opinions have been described is "no," the next question will likely be something like this: "What other opinions do you intend to express in trial?" This back-and-forth will continue until the deposing counsel is satisfied she has learned all opinions intended to be offered in trial by the financial expert witness.

In this line of questions, the opposing attorney is attempting to "close the door" on the expert witness so that opposing counsel can object to any testimony the expert might offer at trial that does not closely hew to the expert's testimony at deposition. Usually, the expert witness wants to keep that door open. Accordingly, the experienced expert often will answer along the lines of "those are all of the opinions I can think of right now, but there may be other points in my report that I am not remembering," or "I might develop additional opinions if I am asked by counsel to perform additional analysis or if significant new information is brought to my attention."

Relevance

Reflecting back on the discussion about the Federal Rules of Evidence (FRE), Rules 702 and 703, the *Daubert* case, and the requirements related to expert witnesses earlier in this book, opposing legal counsel will ask a number of questions designed to discover the witness's failure to comply with the rules. That means the financial expert witness should be prepared to answer the following types of questions:

- What relevant scientific, technical, or specialized knowledge qualifies the financial expert witness to testify in this case? Knowledge? Skills? Experience? Training? Education?
- How do the financial expert witness's opinions assist the trier of fact to: Understand evidence? Determine a fact in issue?
- What are the facts and data the financial expert witness used to form opinions? Why are those fact and data appropriate to the issues? Why are such facts and data sufficient?
- What principles and methods were used by the financial expert witness to form opinions?
- Why are the principles and methods chosen by the financial expert witness reliable? Are they widely accepted in the field? Have they been peer-reviewed? Are they testable? How are they relevant to the issues in the case? Is there a known or determinable error rate?
- What facts of the case have been applied using the financial expert witness's chosen principles and methods?

- Have the facts of the case been applied reliably by the financial expert witness using the chosen principles and methods?
- What facts or data were perceived or known to the financial expert witness at the time of the deposition?
- What facts or data perceived or known to the financial expert witness at the time of the deposition were considered in forming opinions?
- What facts or data perceived or known to the financial expert witness at the time of the deposition were relied upon to form opinions?
- What particular field is the financial expert witness an expert in? Why is that field of expertise appropriate to the issues in the case?
- Will the financial expert witness describe how the facts and data considered and ultimately relied upon to form opinions are reasonably relied upon by other experts in the field to form opinions or inferences on the subject?
- Has the expert performed the same or similar analyses in other engagements? Has the expert performed such analyses for business purposes, or only for litigation engagements?

In addition to these kinds of inquiries, the deposing attorney may dive deeper into the sources of facts and data used by the financial expert witness and the bases, or foundations, for opinions expressed. Furthermore, the deposing attorney may introduce sources for other, usually conflicting or contrary, sources for principles, methods, facts, and data commonly used in the field. Such sources are often referred to as learned treatises, periodicals, and pamphlets.

Learned treatises, periodicals, and pamphlets have a special place in litigated proceedings under the FRE, Rule 803(18):

Statements in Learned Treatises, Periodicals, or Pamphlets.
A statement contained in a treatise, periodical, or pamphlet if:
    (A) the statement is called to the attention of an expert witness on cross-examination or relied on by the expert on direct examination; and
    (B) the publication is established as a reliable authority by the expert's admission or testimony, by another expert's testimony, or by judicial notice.
If admitted, the statement may be read into evidence but not received as an exhibit.

In connection with questions used to determine the admissibility of opinions, deposing legal counsel will attempt to prepare a clean deposition record to support planned future motions to exclude or limit the financial expert witness's testimony. Many times, this effort is plainly obvious from the structure of the questions. Deposing counsel will frequently frame the question in a closed manner intended to drive the financial expert to a "yes" or "no" response.

For example, deposing legal counsel may ask: "Is the method you used to compute damages one that you came up with yourself?" This may be a bit of a trick question. The financial expert witness may be thinking that the method was applied to the unique facts and circumstances in the case using methods selected from many commonly used in the field. Therefore, the answer is "yes." However, if the financial expert answers "yes," it creates a clean record that appears to state that the method is not reasonably used by others in the field and was not subject to peer review—both grounds for exclusion.

A better response might be to explain the reasoning before the "yes" or "no" answer. The financial expert could state: "I chose the method as the proper one from a number of available methods in the field, yes." This clarifies the record and avoids a clear opening for criticism in future motions to be filed by opposing legal counsel. Rest assured, deposing legal counsel will ask the question in differing ways many more times during the deposition, trying to get that clean record. Therefore, the financial expert witness should be wary and resolute.

Qualifications

Expanding upon the commentary above related to the qualifications of the financial expert witness and admissibility, deposing counsel may also explore qualifications to reveal credibility issues or to learn the financial expert witness's weaknesses in comparison to an opposing expert. This can be done by testing the financial expert witness on the accuracy, relevance, and completeness of his curriculum vitae (CV). Among other things, the deposing attorney is seeking to find out if the financial expert witness's CV contains errors, overreaches, or omits key information like prior rejections of expert testimony. Furthermore, the deposing attorney will be searching for shortcomings in qualifications in comparison to the opposing financial expert witness.

In cases where the financial expert witness is aware of prior excluded testimony or potentially conflicting prior testimony or published information, be prepared to explain the unique facts and circumstances that make the matter at hand different and, therefore, not comparable to previous cases or published content. Remember, the point of many of these questions is to prove the financial expert is not qualified and should not be heard by the trier of fact at trial. As such, the financial expert witness should be prepared to defend his or her qualifications during deposition.

Credibility

In addition to potential credibility issues that may be discovered related to understanding the financial expert witness's qualifications, the deposing attorney will ask questions far afield in an attempt to find a lack of professional acceptance or limitations on the work performed. Of course, attempts will be made to uncover bias, in fact or appearance. Any or all perceived weaknesses discovered can be used to impeach the financial expert witness's credibility during trial.

The deposing attorney may want to know who in the field agrees, or disagrees, with the financial expert witness's approach, principles, methods, analysis, and conclusions. In some cases, comparisons are drawn between the financial expert witness's work and conclusions and the opposing expert witness. Material discrepancies will usually be confirmed during deposition. Alternatively, similarities will be identified to bolster the credibility of the opposing financial expert witness.

Many deposing attorneys are also curious about what facts, data, and evidence the financial expert witness considered and relied upon to form opinions. The deposing attorney will want to know what facts, data, and evidence was asked for, who asked for it, and who produced it. This often leads to questions about what was requested and not produced, why it was not produced, and what the financial expert witness did in response to these issues. For facts, data, and evidence relied upon by the financial expert witness, deposing counsel may be interested in why such information was deemed reliable. Conversely, deposing counsel may focus on any facts, data, and evidence ignored, or found to be unreliable, by the financial expert witness.

It is also common for the deposing attorney to ask who did the work supporting the financial expert witness's opinions. The deposing attorney recognizes that most financial expert witnesses use professional staff to assist with the work performed to reach opinions. Regardless, the deposing attorney will ask questions to bring forth potential arguments at trial that the work was poorly supervised, done in large part by others, or completed by unqualified personnel. These are all attempts to impugn the credibility of the financial expert witness.

Fossilize the Positions and Opinions

Deposing legal counsel understands the financial expert witness is required to state all opinions expected to be given at trial in the expert report. Such opinions are usually confirmed by deposing legal counsel during deposition using questions designed to narrow and limit the financial expert witness's opinions. This technique is intended to lock the financial expert witness down to finite opinions, thus fossilizing the opinions of the financial expert witness for use at trial. The theory is that any additional opinions or expansions of stated opinions given by the financial expert witness later will be excluded as inadmissible at trial under the federal rules.

Facts, Data, and Assumptions

Oftentimes, when the financial expert witness has a deposition taken, the universe of disputed facts at issue has not been fully vetted. As such, the deposing attorney can use the deposition of the financial expert witness to identify undisputed known facts, thereby potentially limiting the facts to fight over. This can be accomplished by feeding the financial expert witness questions about facts believed to be undisputed and asking for confirmation. Facts acknowledged as undisputed by the financial expert witness can then be used by the opposing legal counsel to limit the financial expert witness's testimony in trial.

The Federal Rules of Civil Procedure (FRCP), Rule 26(b)(4)(C), provides that the financial expert witness must reveal, if properly asked by opposing legal counsel, the facts, data, and assumptions provided by the client legal counsel and relied upon by the financial expert witness to form opinions. The federal rule is recited next.

(C) **Trial-Preparation Protection for Communications Between a Party's Attorney and Expert Witnesses.** Rules 26(b)(3)(A) and (B) protect communications between the party's attorney and any witness required to provide a report under Rule 26(a)(2)(B), regardless of the form of the communications, except to the extent that the communications:
  (i) relate to compensation for the expert's study or testimony;
  (ii) identify facts or data that the party's attorney provided and that the expert considered in forming the opinions to be expressed; or
  (iii) identify assumptions that the party's attorney provided and that the expert relied on in forming the opinions to be expressed.

Accordingly, deposing legal counsel will be inclined to ask the financial expert witness what facts, data, and assumptions were provided by the client legal counsel that were ultimately used by the financial expert witness. However, deposing counsel is not limited to just learning about facts, data, and assumptions provided to the financial expert witness by the client legal counsel. They will want to know all the material facts and data considered and relied upon by the financial expert witness, particularly disputed facts and data. The basis for reliance on any disputed facts and data will be queried. Assumptions will be investigated to determine source, significance, and the foundation for reliance. In some cases, facts, data, and assumptions that vary from adversarial positions may be pursued in deposition.

Discover New Information

The essence of financial expert witness deposition is to discover the unknown. Much like any venture for discovery, it is based on a readiness, willingness, and ability for the deposing legal counsel to ask questions about things unknown, but discoverable. This is often referred to as a fishing expedition—put on some bait, cast a line, and see what has taken the bait.

Common baited questions for the financial expert witness fall into the classic journalism set of queries of "Who?," "What?," "Where?," "When?," "How?," and "Why?" The deposing attorney may ask who did the work, why the work was done, or why work was not performed. There may be inquiries about how the work was done and supervised. Results can be challenged, with alternatives and hypotheticals used to confirm with the financial expert witness the possibilities for differing outcomes.

> Man can learn nothing except by going from the known to the unknown.
>
> —*Claude Bernard*

Business Arrangement Inquiries

Business arrangements are also often of interest to deposing legal counsel. They are interested in how you got engaged, whom you know, how much you are getting paid, and whether you are owed money. Many of these inquiries are designed to discover potential bias in fact or appearance in order to impair the credibility of the financial expert witness. The effectiveness of this argument is debatable, as most current-day judges and juries understand that the financial expert witness has been retained and is being paid by one of the disputing parties to give expert opinions.

Furthermore, the American Institute of Certified Public Accountants, the world's largest professional accounting trade association, and the Securities and Exchange Commission both consider expert witness services to be advocacy services in defined situations. Regardless, the financial expert witness should take precautions to avoid the perception of bias when accepting and performing financial expert witness services. For example, each engagement should be memorialized with a fully executed engagement letter. In addition, it is important to timely bill and collect for work performed, preferably collecting all outstanding billed amounts before deposition.

Assignment Inquiries

The majority of the deposition is usually saved for inquiries about the assignment and associated results. Deposing legal counsel will want to know what you were asked to do, who worked on the engagement, what materials you used and who gave them to you, work performed (and not performed), bases for opinions and, of course, any opinions the financial expert witness intends to offer at trial. Therefore, the financial expert witness should be able to explain the initial and final assignment scopes and the reasons for any changes. The financial expert witness will also need to be prepared to describe the relevant qualifications of every person on the project. In addition, the financial expert witness will be asked whether any requested documents were not produced and, if so, the effects on the work performed and resulting conclusions. Concluding questions in this area typically cover any work anticipated to be performed by the financial expert witness after the deposition and any conclusions expected thereon.

Size Up the Financial Expert Witness

The deposing attorney understands that the perception of the trier of fact about the financial expert witness as a personality is critical for credibility. Accordingly, the deposing attorney will use techniques designed to test the demeanor of the financial expert witness. These range from being a friend to outright intimidation. Regardless of the technique used, the purpose is the same—to find out the hot buttons driving behaviors such as fear, anger, defensiveness, and evasiveness so that they can be used during trial against the financial expert witness.

> Nobody ever defended anything successfully, there is only attack and attack and attack some more.
>
> —*George S. Patton*

Opposing Expert

Most of the time, the deposing attorney will be curious about the financial expert witness's views about his opposing expert witness and opinions. Therefore, the financial expert witness may be asked if he knows the opposing expert witness and, if so, his opinion on the professional character and work of this expert. In an abundance of caution, such questions should be answered professionally and concisely. The deposition is not the time for the financial expert witness to attack an opponent. In addition, the deposing attorney may ask the financial expert witness to identify areas of agreement and disparity between the two opposing expert witnesses related to facts, data, and assumptions used; the work performed; and the opinions reached.

 ## CONFER WITH CLIENT LEGAL COUNSEL

The preparatory process for deposition also includes meeting with legal counsel that engaged the financial expert witness. This meeting is critical for setting expectations and communicating important information before formal testimony is recorded. Ideally, the meeting with client legal counsel should take place a few days prior to the scheduled deposition. The meeting agenda may include, but not be limited to, logistics, intelligence exchange, deposition formalities, sharing practical advice, and role-play.

Logistics

Among other matters, logistics includes location, parking, start times, expected duration, dress code, parties participating, video or audio transcript recording, and compensation for deposition preparation, travel, and attendance. For expert witness depositions taken under the FRCP, Rule 30(d)(1), the standard time limit is seven hours, unless modified with the consent of the parties. Expansion of the seven-hour deposition time limit for experts is common, so the financial expert witness should check with client legal counsel to confirm duration expectations. Attire for a deposition is courtroom dress. A suit and tie for men and equivalent professional wear for women. Under FRCP, Rule 26(b)(4)(E), the financial expert witness is to be compensated for preparation, travel, and attendance at the deposition by the legal counsel requesting the deposition. However, in practice, the disputing parties may not demand compensation from the deposing party, perhaps believing that this is an administrative burden and that it will be a wash if experts are to be deposed for each party.

Intelligence Sharing

The exchange of intelligence between the financial expert witness and legal counsel often involves a discussion about the possible objectives of deposing legal counsel and potential areas to be examined. It may also be helpful to talk about the personality, style, and demeanor of deposing legal counsel and any questioning tactics observed in previous encounters. Because deposing legal counsel has significant latitude about the scope of questioning, it is prudent for the financial expert witness to explore a wide range of topics and subject matters in anticipation of deposition.

Deposition Formalities

Reminders about the legal formalities of a deposition should also be discussed with legal counsel, including compliance with any subpoena requiring attendance at the deposition, the role of the court reporter, the process to swear in the witness, penalties for perjury, objection handling, and the right to read and sign the written transcript after deposition. It is important for the financial expert witness to remember that client legal counsel is not your personal legal counsel, but instead legal counsel to the underlying client. Therefore, knowledge about the admissibility of expert testimony is critical. Financial experts who are not experienced in the process may wish to consult separately with a personal attorney not otherwise involved in the case.

Objections

Objections are timely, legally proper notices made by legal counsel representing the disputing parties to the court about beliefs that evidence is inadmissible under the federal rules. Objections during deposition are typically made orally by the client's attorney defending the deposition for the client. In most cases, the financial expert witness must answer a pending question from opposing legal counsel. Once recorded in the deposition transcript, formal motions for the court to rule on deposition objections may be requested. However, even if this step is not taken, objections in the deposition transcript can be helpful guideposts to the financial expert witness for testimony needing attention before trial.

Objections, although limited for depositions, are for the benefit of the underlying client—even though they may feel like they are for the testifying financial expert witness's protection. That is not to say that objections are not helpful at times to the financial expert witness. Carefully listening to an objection may offer the financial expert witness important information about the question and the type of response required from the financial expert witness in the circumstances. For example, the statement, "objection, form" may indicate to the financial expert witness that the pending deposition question is compound, with more than one question included, complex, or containing an undefined qualifier or improper premise.

There are several objections that the financial expert witness must know before deposition in order to understand the reason for the concern about admissibility. Following are some of these objections, together with brief explanations about what the legal bases for inadmissibility are intended to be:

- **Argumentative**—the question is a legal argument for a trier of fact that the witness is improperly asked to acquiesce.
- **Asked and answered**—the question calls for an answer to a question already asked and answered; the question is repetitive.
- **Compound**—the question contains more than one fact and to answer would be misleading.
- **Confusing/ambiguous/vague**—the question is unclear or confusing and to answer would be misleading.
- **Document speaks for itself**—the question can best be answered by referring to the original document.
- **Immaterial**—the question calls for an answer that has no reasonable bearing on the case.
- **Improper characterization**—the question improperly characterizes a fact, person, or event.
- **Legal conclusion**—the question calls for an answer that would be a prohibited legal conclusion.
- **Misleading**—the question is misleading and to answer would be misleading.
- **Misquoted or mistakes evidence**—the question improperly misquotes testimony given by the witness.
- **Privileged**—the question calls for an answer that will contain legally privileged information (this is rare for the financial expert witness).
- **Relevance**—the question calls for an answer that will be irrelevant to the disputed issues at hand.
- **Speculation**—the question calls for an answer that is speculative.
- **Unresponsive**—the answer to the question is unresponsive (usually objected to by deposing legal counsel).

Practical Tips and Advice

It is also helpful in preparation for deposition to share practical advice gained from experience. After all, the only real mistake is not to learn from your prior mistakes. Fundamentals such as clearly speaking all answers, telling the truth, listening actively to each question, pausing before answering to allow objections, answering only the question asked, and admitting you do not recall or know the answer to a question are good examples of valuable practical advice every financial expert witness can use. It is also good advice to ask for a recess if the financial expert witness is tired, losing concentration, or would benefit from a personal break for any reason.

Role-Playing

One of the most effective deposition preparation techniques is to role-play. Role-play has the financial expert witness practice listening to and answering anticipated deposition questions in a mock deposition environment. It is recommended that this activity include obvious questions about the financial expert witness report and opinions, as well as challenge questions about bad facts and hard issues. If the financial expert witness has no one to role-play with, he should practice answering questions out loud to himself.

 ## LEADING UP TO DEPOSITION

Similar to any important event, the financial expert should allow enough time the night before a scheduled deposition to get a good night's rest. Depositions are taxing and having the energy to last several hours of adversarial inquiries is critical. The financial expert witness should confirm transportation and meeting details, but heavy lifting in the form of studies should be avoided before retiring for the night. One activity that might be helpful the night before deposition is self-actualization. The financial expert witness clears the mind and mentally reviews the upcoming deposition performance in a quiet setting, free from distractions. Self-actualization is used by professional athletes to visualize a performance in an athletic event yet to be competed.

The day of the deposition should be reserved for last-minute preparations and provide for a stress-free commute to the deposition with plenty of time to assess the surroundings and acclimate to the situation. The financial expert witness should follow a normal routine of eating before the deposition, remembering to hydrate well. A complete breakfast is highly recommended, among other reasons because there is no guarantee of a timely lunch break. In the moments before the deposition, the financial expert witness should consider finding a solemn place to clear the mind and focus on the task at hand. Some financial expert witnesses find meditation, contemplation, or prayer to be helpful for this purpose.

 ## COMING UP

After preparation for the deposition, the financial expert witness attends the deposition and provides testimony under oath. Chapter 14 describes financial expert witness testimony in deposition.

CHAPTER FOURTEEN

Financial Expert Witness Deposition Testimony

 DEPOSITION TESTIMONY

Let's set the stage. The financial expert witness arrives early to the deposition location accompanied by client legal counsel, or perhaps you meet legal counsel there. Typically, the deposition is scheduled to take place in the office of the deposing legal counsel. You walk into the conference room designated for the deposition, noting the court reporter setting up recording and transcription equipment, and if there is a videographer, a backdrop screen is set up opposite the video and audio equipment. The financial expert witness seating is arranged around a table alongside the court reporter. Client legal counsel seating is next to the financial expert witness on the same side of the table as the financial expert witness. Directly opposite from the financial expert witness is the seating for deposing legal counsel and others invited by deposing counsel.

In some situations, deposing counsel may be accompanied by her client and an opposing expert witness. The opposing expert witness is in attendance to assist deposing legal counsel with questioning and the interpretation of technical answers. It is common for an attending opposing expert to take notes and pass them to deposing counsel during the deposition to suggest follow-up questions immediately relevant to the financial expert witness's testimony. The financial expert witness should ignore this activity as it may be distracting and is not relevant to the witness's job of clearly, carefully, and truthfully answering each question.

The financial expert witness takes a seat and deposing legal counsel asks for the financial expert witness to be sworn in. The court reporter asks the financial expert witness to raise his right hand and answer affirmatively to commands to testify truthfully to the best of personal abilities. The financial expert witness responds to the court reporter's commands with a "yes," "I do," or "I will," as appropriate.

Depending on the preferences of the deposing legal counsel and the experience level of the financial expert witness, the financial expert witness may be given opening instructions by deposing legal counsel. The financial expert witness may be asked to confirm the following types of matters, in no particular order:

- The name of the financial expert witness.
- The financial expert has been deposed before in other matters.
- Answers must be spoken out loud for the record.
- Speak slowly and clearly for the benefit of the court reporter.
- Only one person may speak at a time.
- If a question is not understood, ask for it to be repeated or rephrased.
- If a break is needed, please request one.
- Any reason the financial expert witness cannot testify truthfully, fully, and completely.
- The financial expert witness is not impaired (i.e., on drugs, illness, injury).

Once these opening formalities are out of the way, deposing legal counsel begins questioning about other matters. This is the time when the financial expert witness's preparation and professionalism come into play, combined with personal experience. The combination of preparation and experience often leads financial expert witnesses to the realization that there are a number of "do's and don'ts" related to performing well during a deposition. Following are a few pointers that may be helpful to remember.

Mental State and Behavior

The mindset and demeanor of the financial expert witness play a significant role in deposition success. Mindset is the mental state of the financial expert witness leading up to, and during, the deposition proceeding. Demeanor refers to the behavior of the financial expert witness during the deposition. A proper mindset and appropriate demeanor will help to make the deposition more effective for the financial expert witness.

Mindset

The financial expert witness mindset going into the deposition is about being your honest self. The financial expert witness should avoid pretending to be someone else, or putting on a false pretense to appear more comfortable and knowledgeable to opposing legal counsel. Acting is tough to disguise for very long and it dilutes focus. So don't do it.

Next, the financial expert witness must be clear in the conviction to be truthful and intellectually honest. This mindset, combined with a solemn respect for the deposition process, will set the stage for a successful deposition for all parties. At the end of the day, the financial expert witness has to be comfortable knowing that he has acted with integrity to assist the trier of fact.

Demeanor

The demeanor of the financial expert witness should be professional at all times. That means the financial expert witness's behavior should be calm, collected, and confident. In addition, the financial expert witness should demonstrate the behaviors indicative of cooperation, objectivity, likability, credibility, and reliability during deposition. Under no circumstances should the financial expert witness allow himself to behave in an angry, arrogant, biased, combative, fearful, obstructive, or evasive manner.

Attire

The dress for the financial expert witness attending deposition should be business professional. Business suit or sports coat and tie for men and conservative business attire for women are appropriate. Shoes should be conservative and business professional. There are studies that support the contention that certain colors are better suited for specific types of skin tone. Other studies claim that color schemes and fabric patterns may affect perceptions about trustworthiness, power, or status. The financial expert witness should consider these studies, but can rarely go wrong with dark colors—black, navy blue, gray, or dark brown. However, if black is worn, the financial expert witness should be wary about resembling a religious figure.

Extravagant jewelry and flashy neckwear generally should be avoided. In addition, unkempt hair and eyeglasses that obstruct eye contact with the trier of fact should be addressed before deposition. Also, take special care when dressing for videotaped depositions. The camera may "wash out" the financial expert witness wearing white or record strange effects with stripes, plaids, or other strong patterns. The key to remember for attire is that when it comes to deposition, dress for success.

Nonverbal Communication

A significant part of communication by the financial expert witness in deposition is nonverbal. Posture, body position, facial expressions, hand gestures, and silent pauses all contribute to what is communicated. If a deposition is transcribed, but not videotaped, the transcript will be void of these nonverbal communications. However, the financial expert witness must understand that the deposing attorney will, nonetheless, be looking for nonverbal communications as cues for attack or surrender. If the deposition is videotaped, all nonverbal communications will be recorded for all to see, including the trier of fact. Therefore, extra precautions must be taken for videotaped depositions.

> The most important thing in communication is hearing what isn't said.
>
> —Peter Drucker

Videotaped Depositions

Most of the tips related to nonverbal communications apply to both transcribed and videotaped depositions. However, there are some differences, so the items unique to videotaped depositions are covered here. The majority of financial expert witness nonverbal communications that will occur during deposition involves the body, eyes, face, arms, hands, and breathing. Body movement, eye contact, facial expressions, arm positions, hand gestures, and breathing will all be amplified on camera and can be frozen or replayed for a trier of fact in court. Following are a few pointers related to each of these matters:

- **Body**—Sit up straight with seat centered in the chair and the body leaning slightly forward. Leaning with a large amount of weight on the on the table in front is bad form. Shifting excessively can be interpreted as nervousness or fear. The feet can be crossed or separated comfortably about shoulder length apart on the ground. Leg-crossing should be avoided, but is acceptable. Think of this as a quasi-meditation position, designed for long periods of seated rest.

- **Eyes**—In a deposition that is not videotaped, comfortable eye contact with the deposing attorney should be maintained throughout the deposition. Staring, squinting, and excessive blinking should be avoided. When the deposition is videotaped, however, it will appear unnatural to keep consistent eye contact with the deposing attorney, who will be off-camera. Therefore, the financial expert witness should train to give answers while looking directly at the camera. Occasionally, the financial expert witness should feel free to look elsewhere, as long as it is natural and not evasive in appearance.

- **Face**—Facial expressions can be telltale signs of peacefulness or panic. As any financial forensics specialist will agree, there is an art to reading faces to detect deception. Many deposing attorneys have studied this art and a few are masters. As such, facial expressions, such as brow-raising, smiling, and head-nodding can be effectively used to indicate understanding, disagreement, or the emphasis of a point. Conversely, frowns, smirks, and looks of anger or fear will likely make the financial expert witness look bad on videotape, as well as set up the witness for aggressive questioning by a deposing attorney.

- **Arms**—Arms should rest comfortably at the side of the financial expert witness. Raising the arms behind the head or crossing them over the chest may be taken as indications of nonchalance, lack of interest, or anger. In addition, shoulder shrugs may show a lack of knowledge or disrespect for the questioner. Therefore, these arm positions are seldom appropriate during a deposition.

- **Hands**—For most of the deposition, the financial expert witness's hands should be on the table in front, either folded or a comfortable distance apart. Small hand gestures are encouraged, but should not be larger than the chest area or done incessantly. Of course, there is no place for obscene gestures in a deposition.

- **Breathing**—Breathing should be maintained at a comfortable resting rate. Panting, sighs, and yawns all send a nonverbal message and should be controlled, if possible. It is useful to remind oneself regularly to take full, deep breaths. Surprisingly often, witnesses fall into shallow or nervous breathing patterns that cause them to become uncomfortable and fatigued. A sophisticated questioner may identify this tendency and take full advantage.

The financial expert witness will increase the odds of conveying strength and confidence if these recommendations are followed. The alternative is an uncomfortable, slouching, and potentially weak-looking expert witness, the kind of financial expert witness that seasoned adversarial attorneys like to eat for lunch.

Intonation and Pauses

Inflection, deflection, and pauses in speech are each important communication tools for the financial expert witness. However, used improperly, intonation and pauses can be the downfall for a financial expert witness. Changes in the voice pattern, especially raising and lowering tone, quickening or slowing speeds of delivery, and pausing are ways for the financial expert witness to effectively and convincingly respond to questions in deposition.

Intonation and the appropriate use of pauses are even more important when the deposition is videotaped. One caution on pauses: They cannot be easily detected when the deposition is transcribed and not videotaped. However, if the deposition is videotaped, pauses at the wrong time, or pauses that are painfully long, can be interpreted as evasiveness, ignorance, fear, or advocacy, among many other awful things. Accordingly, the financial expert witness may want to say out loud on the record something like this: "Excuse me while I take a moment to pause and think about the question." Once the thoughts are gathered, the financial expert witness can answer the question with comfort that the audience expected a short break for contemplation.

Response Methods

There are a few techniques that the financial expert witness may consider using to assist with responses during a deposition. One method uses a process to absorb questions and form effective answers. Another is a technique that funnels questions from broad general responses to more detailed ones. Of course, the financial expert witness must also read anything provided by deposing legal counsel before responding to questions about that item. By following these methods, the financial expert witness can improve the effectiveness of responses given in deposition.

Response Process

The financial expert witness should consider adopting a practical process to field and respond to deposition questions. Using such a process serves as a safeguard for the financial expert witness under pressure. It will help the financial expert witness form an accurate and concise response, without revealing more than necessary. Being a process, it is repeatable with minimal effort.

One such process is for the financial expert witness to internally contemplate a series of questions after listening carefully to the question:

- Did I hear the question accurately?
- Do I understand the question?
- Do I know or remember the answer?
- How do I answer truthfully, completely, and briefly in an articulate fashion?

Once contemplated, the financial expert witness can respond confidently to the pending question.

Inverse Funnel Technique

In order to keep responses concise and to the point, the financial expert may want to consider using an inverse funnel technique. An inverse funnel technique answers questions broadly at first and then provides more detailed information only when specifically asked to do so by deposing legal counsel. An example of this technique might play out as follows:

Question: Did anyone assist you in doing your work?
Answer: Yes.

Question: Who assisted you?
Answer: My staff.

Question: What are the names of your staff?
Answer: Ms. Jones, Ms. Smith, and Ms. Thomas.

Question: What are Ms. Jones', Ms. Smith's, and Ms. Thomas's titles?
Answer: Manager, senior, and staff.

Question: How did Ms. Jones assist you?
Answer: She performed analysis and project oversight.

Question: What kind of analysis did she do?
Answer: Financial analysis.

Question: Can you describe the financial analysis she did?
Answer: Yes.

Question: Would you describe the financial analysis Ms. Jones performed?
Answer: She did a comparative financial statement analysis and an analysis of financial evidence.

The inverse funnel technique can be effective to assist the financial expert witness to answer only the question asked in a concise and controlled fashion. The inverse funnel technique is reflected in Exhibit 14.1.

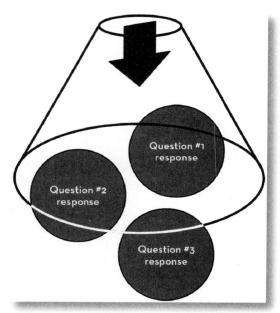

EXHIBIT 14.1 Inverse Funnel Technique

Read Items Provided

All documents used in the deposition will be marked as exhibits that may potentially be used in trial. If the financial expert witness is asked a question about a document, he should ask to see the document. Once given the document the financial expert witness should scrutinize it to determine it is a complete version of the right document. If a multipage document, the financial expert witness should look at every page, stopping to read as deemed necessary, before answering any question about the document.

Best Answers to Deposition Questions

There is a short list of model answers that can be given by the financial expert witness in deposition. The list was developed by David M. Malone and Paul J. Zwier in the book entitled *Effective Expert Testimony*.[1] Malone and Zwier assert that the best answers are as follows:

- Yes.
- No.

- Green.
- I don't know.
- I don't remember.
- I don't understand.
- I need a break.

"Yes" and "no" are the proper response when the question can be answered exclusively with these words. "Green" is a reference to a single-fact answer. Malone and Zwier give the example using this question: "What color is your car?" The response of the financial expert witness should not be: "My car is a green Buick." Instead, the response should be "Green."[2] The financial expert witness answers "I don't know" if he does not know a fact and "I don't remember" or "I don't recall" if he cannot remember a fact. The response "I don't understand" is designed for questions that are unclear, misleading, compound, or generally confusing. This response may also be appropriate if the question contains an improper premise or qualifier. In these cases, the financial expert witness may want to follow this response with: "Can you repeat the question?" or "Can you rephrase the question?" "I need a break" is reserved for any recess deemed necessary by the financial expert witness. Just remember, it is bad form to request a break when a question has been asked, but not yet answered. Only in rare circumstances will a break be allowed when a question is pending. However, it is a best practice to request a break at least every two to three hours.

When it comes to questions of fact that can initially be answered with "green," like the example above, the financial expert witness should be aware that deposing legal counsel will seldom stop asking topical questions after a short factual response from the financial expert witness. Instead, open-ended questions requiring explanation and description will be asked in the hopes that the financial expert witness will elaborate. In these instances, the financial expert witness should consider employing the answering process described above and the funnel technique to control responses. As a rule of thumb, the financial expert witness should strive to keep any answer provided in deposition to 25 words or less.

The following example paraphrased from an actual deposition transcript shows the dialogue between a deposing attorney and a financial expert witness after a confusing question is asked:

Question: Oh, I see. You are using the executed contract to compare—as a way to compare—to show how the—you explain it better than I do. Can you tell me what I'm thinking?

Answer: I have no way of knowing what you are thinking.

Key Parties, Events, and Dates to Know

In deposition, and trial, for that matter, there are key parties, dates, and events that the financial expert witness should try to commit to memory. Although deposition is like an open-book test wherein notes, work papers and documents can be used, the financial expert witness can bolster credibility by being able to instantly recall key parties, dates, and events. Key parties, dates, and events to know include, but are not limited to, the following:

- Names of the parties to the dispute (i.e., plaintiff and defendant);
- Allegations and claims for relief;
- Case timeline;
- Damages period (i.e., start date and end date);
- Date first contacted for retention;
- Name of the person who first contacted financial expert witness for retention;
- Date of retention (this is usually the engagement letter date);
- Assignment;
- Facts and data requested, dates requested, and facts and data received and from whom;
- Facts, data, and assumptions provided by client's legal counsel;
- Assumptions relied upon to form opinions;
- Work performed and dates performed;
- Hours worked and fees incurred by financial expert witness and others (this is usually reflected on invoices and billing statements);
- Applicable profession standards governing work performed;
- Information on the financial expert witness's curriculum vitae;
- Date opinions formed;
- Author(s) of the financial expert witness expert report and dates drafted and completed; and
- Additional work performed, or to be performed, after the date of expert report.

Handling Common Deposition Questions

The financial expert witness will be asked questions during deposition that are commonly expected. Therefore, the financial expert witness should anticipate these questions and prepare on how to handle them. By doing this, the financial expert will reduce personal stress levels and perform in a more effective manner. The handling of some common inquiries expected during deposition are described next.

Opinions

You will recall from a previous chapter in this book that financial expert witnesses must state their opinions with a reasonable degree of certainty in the particular field. The courts have expressed differing opinions on the exact meaning of reasonable certainty, but suffice it to say, the courts are looking for the financial expert witness to express opinions with reasonable certainty. Opinions from experts that are deemed by the courts to be speculative, guesswork, or conjecture are regularly rejected.[3] With that in mind, the financial expert witness should consider stating opinions in deposition with the predicate that such opinion was formed with reasonable certainty in the field. For example, the financial expert witness may respond to an inquiry about an opinion in this way: "In my opinion, which I express with reasonable certainty in my field of expertise, damages are $1,000,000."

Retention Process

The circumstances surrounding the financial expert witness's retention is frequently the subject of inquiry for deposing counsel. This should be remembered when considering the acceptance of any client engagement assignment. Deposing counsel will likely have questions about how the financial expert witness was initially contacted and by whom. That may lead to questions about the financial expert witness's relationship with the contacting attorney and law firm. In addition, any preretention discussions about the assignments, including parties, allegations and claims, opinions sought, fees, and engagement terms, may be questioned. More importantly, the financial expert witness may be asked to recall any doubts, concerns, or reservations expressed about client and assignment acceptance.

In these situations, the financial expert witness should fall back on the processes, protocols, and policies used for client engagement acceptance. Ideally, the responses should be factual and consistent with existing processes, protocols, and policies. In other words, normal course of business retention is the desired mantra for these lines of questions. For example, a response to this line of questioning might be as follows:

> Question: When you were initially contacted about this case, did you ask any questions of Mr. Jones, the attorney who reached out to you?
>
> Answer: Yes.

Question: What did you ask?

Answer: I asked for the names of the parties and a description of the dispute.

Question: Why did you ask those questions?

Answer: Those are the questions I normally ask when considering the acceptance of new work.

The back-and-forth can go on from there, but the point is that any exchange between the prospective client and the financial expert witness was in the due course of completing normal business activities similar to every case considered for acceptance. This provides context for the exchanges and reduces the opportunity for the deposing legal counsel to later use these communications as evidence of potential bias.

Preparation for Deposition

Deposition preparation often piques the interest of deposing counsel. That is because such activities may have included discussions about the financial expert witness's weaknesses or exposure areas. In addition, the financial expert witness would have studied documents and work papers in advance of the deposition to ensure these materials are more easily recalled. For these and other reasons, the financial expert witness should be prepared to answer questions about deposition preparation.

Questions about what was done by the financial expert witness to prepare for the deposition can easily be handled. In addition, inquiries about work papers and documents reviewed can usually be responded to without any significant downside risk. In many cases, these facts and data have already been produced to the opposing party in discovery. Questions delving into conversations with the client legal counsel are a bit more troubling and must be handled with care.

When asked a precise question by the deposing attorney, the financial expert witness typically must respond to inquiries about conversations. Conversation with the client legal counsel in preparation for the deposition may not be protected by applicable legal privileges. Accordingly, the financial expert witness's responses to such questions should be discussed with the client legal counsel during preparation for the deposition. In this way, the financial expert can find a comfortable and appropriate way to answer.

Technical Terms and Jargon

The financial expert witness's expertise and work naturally leads to the usage of technical terms and jargon. This is particularly true for complex matters. The use of techno-speak, however, potentially impairs a layperson's understanding of the financial expert witness's testimony and should be avoided. There are a number of ways to address this issue. Identify and use simple and commonly recognized words to replace technical terms. Alternatively, use metaphors and analogies to explain complex technical matters. For example, a "discount rate" can be described as: "An adjustment to account for the risk that you will not get your money back from an investment, including a reasonable return."

Hypotheticals

Without doubt, the financial expert witness will be asked questions by deposing legal counsel using hypothetical situations and supposed facts. In these instances, the deposing attorney attempts to get the financial expert witness to entertain, or agree with, suppositions buried inside a question. The suppositions vary from the facts used by the financial expert witness to reach opinions. Oftentimes hypothetical questions include the words: "assume"; "wouldn't you agree"; "if these facts are true"; or "is it fair to say." An example of a hypothetical exchange follows.

> *Question: Does your damages calculation consider mitigation?*
>
> Answer: No.
>
> *Question: Why not?*
>
> Answer: I found no reasonable basis to support mitigation.
>
> *Question: If the plaintiff had sold assets at a discount to mitigate losses, how would that have affected your calculation of damages?*
>
> Answer: If those were the facts in this case, which I do not believe they are, damages would be reduced.

Hypothetical questions get hypothetical answers.

—*Joan Baez*

In every case, there will be a wide range of potential hypothetical questions. Some will be appropriate to the case and require thoughtful answers; others may stray far afield. In the latter situation, it may be appropriate for the expert witness to answer simply that he or she does not know or has not considered how his or her conclusions or analysis would be affected. The financial expert witness's deposition preparation with the client's legal counsel generally will include anticipating potential hypothetical questions and considering how to answer them.

Level of Effort and Fees

Deposing attorneys may try to expose potential credibility and bias issues surrounding the financial expert witness by exploring hours worked, fees incurred and unpaid billings. Each of these areas has the potential to create undesirable perceptions with the trier of fact. Fortunately, each can be easily handled if addressed *before the deposition.* Ways to deal with these matters are briefly discussed below.

Hours Worked

Inquiries about hours worked are likely to be focused on the number of hours worked by the financial expert witness on the case in comparison to other staff. This information can be gleaned from time-keeping records or elicited from the financial expert witness during deposition. If the financial expert witness has few hours logged on the engagement in comparison to others, that fact can be used by opposing legal counsel to create the perception that the financial expert witness is not credible or believable—he simply has not done enough work to form a reliable opinion. Therefore, the financial expert witness must ensure that sufficient personal time has been given to the case to reduce this risk to acceptable levels.

Fees Incurred

Fees and expenses incurred on a case by the financial expert witness and his staff can be a double-edged sword. On one hand, high billing rates and large billed fees may allow the opposing legal counsel to create the perception that the financial expert witness is a greedy hired gun. On the other hand, low billing rates and small fees could help opposing legal counsel show that the financial expert witness failed to do enough work to reach a reliable opinion. If the financial expert witness is questioned on billing rates, he should confidently respond that such rates are the normal amounts charged for services in similar types of matters. Importantly, the financial expert witness is paid for his time and *not* his opinions. Regardless, when it comes to fees, the financial expert witness should remain aware of the potential risks for criticism and be prepared to give reasonable (and succinct) explanations in defense of rates and fees.

Unpaid Billings

Large amounts of unpaid billings owed to the financial expert witness may provide opposing legal counsel with the opportunity to present the financial expert witness as biased. This is especially true if invoiced amounts are overdue. Opposing legal counsel may attempt to paint the picture that the financial expert witness will get paid only if his client gets the opinion wanted. Of course, this is preposterous. To avoid this possibility, the financial expert witness should have a policy that requires unpaid billings be paid in full prior to the release of the expert report, deposition, and trial. Realistically, this can be difficult at times. So, the financial expert witness should in the normal course enter into enforceable arrangements for client payment before releasing deliverables or testifying.

Mistakes and Errors

Sometimes, regardless of the quality-control efforts employed by the financial expert witness, there will be mistakes and errors in the expert report. The financial expert witness may also make mistakes during deposition testimony. Although uncommon, mistakes and errors are part of being human. If a mistake or error is brought to the attention of the financial expert witness during the deposition, it should be calmly acknowledged. Arguing or becoming defensive about an obvious mistake or error looks stubborn and unprofessional to a trier of fact, which will adversely impact credibility. The financial expert witness must remember any mistake or error brought to attention in deposition is one that can be corrected before trial.

> A man must be big enough to admit his mistakes, smart enough to profit from them, and strong enough to correct them.
>
> —*John C. Maxwell*

Responses to Avoid

During the course of a deposition, there are a handful of responses that the financial expert witness should avoid. Some of these responses involve absolute statements, overly broad answers, client advocacy, long-winded commentaries, talking during silent pauses, and answering questions after testifying to a lack of recall or knowledge. The reasons to avoid these responses are many. They may provide a basis for opposing legal counsel to exclude testimony or impair the credibility and reliability of the financial expert witness.

Deposition Responses to Avoid

- Absolutes
- Universal truths
- Client advocacy
- Lengthy speeches
- Filling a void
- Answering questions with no recall or knowledge

Absolutes

The financial expert witness is cautioned to avoid using words and statements that may irrevocably lock him in to a fact or position. Even if such testimony could be rehabilitated later, it will likely raise serious issues about the credibility and reliability of the financial expert witness. The words "always," "never," "must," and "shall" are examples of absolutes. Instead, the financial expert witness should consider terms that provide a bit more flexibility to deal with potential unknowns.

Overly Broad Statements

Overly broad statements are ones that have the financial expert witness testify to broad generalities. These types of statements often contain ambiguous judgments about quality or reliability that will be difficult for the financial expert witness to retreat from in trial. Examples are statements that include the words "best," "authoritative," "foremost," "gold standard," "greatest," "most recognized," "most appropriate," and "ultimate source." There are a few situations where such statements are appropriate, but they should be used only when the expert genuinely intends such a broad or sweeping characterization. The general approach should be extreme caution in using these types of broad statements in deposition.

Client Advocacy

As stated elsewhere in this book, it is the attorney's job to be an advocate for his client. The financial expert witness is an objective assistant to the trier of fact who must remain objective. The financial expert witness may advocate for his opinions, but not for the client. Client advocacy reflects poorly on the expert, creates an appearance of bias, and undercuts the expert's credibility and professionalism. Client advocacy can be reflected in deposition testimony. This is done when the financial expert witness, instead of responding exclusively to the questions posed, intentionally makes comments that sound like the client's arguments about the case. A perception of advocacy also can be created if the financial expert witness allows the deposing attorney to refer to the financial expert witness as "my witness," the "client's witness," or the "law firm's witness." Any such references should be corrected promptly, but gently, to avoid any perception of improper association.

In a similar vein, the financial expert witness should avoid identifying himself with the underlying client. Thus, the financial expert witness should not refer to the client or the client's attorney as the expert's client. A more appropriate phrasing would be to say that the attorney has retained the expert to assist in the attorney's representation of the attorney's client. Similarly, the financial expert witness should avoid statements that use the words "our" or "we" to refer to the financial expert witness together with the client, as though they were all members of a team. For example, the financial expert may respond in deposition: "Our position is that there are few alternative sources." The financial expert witness should avoid making such client advocacy statements, in fact or appearance, as they may be perceived as improper bias.

Lengthy Speeches

Rarely will a lengthy commentary made by a financial expert witness on the record yield benefits. Such speeches are usually in some way nonresponsive. In addition, long-winded answers play into opposing legal counsel's hands, providing unearned discovery and insights into the witness's strengths and weaknesses at trial. Long answers also invite follow-up questions and longer depositions. Therefore, lengthy responses should be avoided.

Filling a Void

Inevitably, during the course of a deposition there will be silent pauses between questions and answers. Some of these can be quite long and a few of them are intentional on the part of deposing legal counsel. The deposing attorney knows that long periods of silence can cause anxiety in some people. The response to this uncomfortable silence is to fill the void with talking. That's just what the deposing attorney wants—the financial expert witness to talk. As such, the financial expert witness should avoid talking during silent pauses.

Instead, the financial expert witness should use silent pauses as part of a time-management strategy. The deposing counsel has a finite amount of time to conduct the deposition. If he wants to use it sitting in silence, that's his prerogative. No harm can come to the financial expert witness in silence. So, the financial expert witness should sit back, relax, and enjoy the quiet time.

Answering without a Basis

If the financial expert witness answers a question with the response "I don't know" or "I don't recall," nothing else should be said. Unfortunately, many a financial expert witness inappropriately follows an acknowledgment of no knowledge or recollection with additional commentary. For example, the financial expert witness answers by saying, "I don't know, but . . . ." If the financial expert witness doesn't know or remember the answer, that's it—stop talking. Any further response has no basis.

This rule is frequently hard to follow for an expert who is accustomed to being consulted for his or her opinions and judgment, or whose informed speculation or "educated guesses" often may be welcomed in other contexts. Depositions are different and require a more careful and more guarded mindset. Speculation or guesswork, no matter how well-intentioned or well-informed, are not appropriate.

Handling Objections

Objections can be made during deposition, hearings, or trial. Objections made during deposition are timely, legally proper notices made by legal counsel to the court about beliefs that evidence is inadmissible or not discoverable under the federal rules. Deposition objections are typically made orally on the record by the client's attorney defending the deposition for the client. Once recorded in the deposition transcript, formal motions for the court to rule on deposition objections may be requested. In rare cases, the deposition may be stayed until the court can rule on a pending objection.

Deposition objections are usually made right after a question has been posed by deposing legal counsel. As such, the financial expert witness should pause slightly before answering any question in anticipation of an objection. If an objection is offered, the financial expert witness should sit silently while the opposing attorneys decide how to proceed. In some instances, the client's legal counsel may make an objection and then immediately direct the financial expert witness to answer. If this happens, the financial expert witness should answer the pending question, if possible. If the pending question is forgotten, the financial expert witness can ask for the question to be repeated or read back from the record by the court reporter.

In some cases, opposing legal counsel may not agree about whether the financial expert witness should answer after an objection. If this happens, the financial expert witness should patiently wait for the opposing attorneys to resolve the dispute. This can be uncomfortable at times as the opposing attorneys argue (sometimes aggressively) about what the financial expert witness should do. Under no circumstances should the financial expert witness answer a pending question with a standing objection without express permission from the client legal counsel. In addition, the financial expert witness should never participate in the debate between the attorneys about a disputed objection. Objections are legal matters for counsel to resolve, or, if they cannot, for the court to decide.

Instructions from the Client's Attorney

Occasionally, the client legal counsel defending the deposition will give the financial expert witness instructions on the record. Instructions are not objections. They are an alternative to prevent the financial expert witness from disclosing information during deposition. The information sought to be protected can be confidential, proprietary, or sensitive in nature.

There is no clear guidance on when it is legally permitted for the defending attorney to give instructions to the financial expert witness. Remember, the client attorney defending the deposition is not the financial expert witness's personal legal counsel. Therefore, he has no client–attorney standing to support such instructions. That being the case, the financial expert witness should follow the instructions given by the defending attorney with the understanding that the opposing attorneys have a legal dispute that the financial expert witness cannot decide.

Off-the-Record Discussions

An off-the-record discussion is any conversation that takes place when the court reporter has officially stopped recording the deposition. Off-the-record periods will occur just before the deposition starts and during breaks agreed upon by the opposing attorneys. Off-the-record discussions may happen between the financial expert witness and the client attorney, deposing attorney, or any other party. Although technically off the record, the rule of thumb is that all off-the-record conversations are fair game for the deposing attorney. That means the deposing attorney can, and often will, ask the financial expert witness about off-the-record discussions once back on the record. For this reason, the financial expert witness should avoid having substantive off-the-record case or testimony discussions with any party.

Curiosity is lying in wait for every secret.

—*Ralph Waldo Emerson*

Use of Files and Notes in Deposition

The financial expert witness is allowed to bring and refer to notes and other materials during the deposition. Typically, these notes and other materials consist of the financial expert witness's work files or referenced tie-out binders containing the expert report and supporting documents. This can be particularly helpful to the financial expert witness in cases that are document-intensive and complex. However, the financial expert witness must remember that deposing counsel is entitled to copies of anything the financial expert witness brings to the deposition to assist with recollection.

There are two schools of thought about this practice. One school believes that it is inadvisable for the financial expert witness to bring anything to the deposition, except items required by a valid and legally enforceable subpoena. It is believed that any materials brought to the deposition by the financial expert witness may provide lengthy and potentially harmful inquiries. Alternatively, the other school believes that professionally referenced materials organized in a fashion to allow ready access to key facts and work product may expedite the deposition and show deposing counsel that the financial expert witness is prepared and ready for business. Either way, the financial expert witness should get permission from client legal counsel before voluntarily bringing anything to a deposition. Taking into account both schools of thought, the financial expert witness should take care to ensure that any notes or other materials prepared and brought to the deposition contain only the bare essentials.

Responding to Deposing Counsel Behavior

Remember, one of the deposing attorney objectives for the deposition is to test the mettle of the financial expert witness. To do this, deposing legal counsel may behave in odd and socially unacceptable ways to get a rise out of the financial expert witness. In some instances, deposing legal counsel gets frustrated with the financial expert witness, and may explode in either real or mock anger. Following are a few of the behaviors the financial expert witness may encounter from deposing legal counsel during a deposition:

- Breaking pens or pencils
- Criticism
- Intimidation
- Pounding on the table
- Sarcasm
- Disparaging remarks
- Scribbling
- Shaking the head in disgust
- Shouting
- Standing
- Threatening with sanctions, standards violations, or to call a judge
- Throwing documents

- Wagging a finger in the face
- Whispering under the breath

In cases where this happens, the financial expert witness should remain calm, cool, and collected. Never respond in kind. However, it may be useful for the financial expert witness to mention the bad behavior on the record to show the duress experienced. For example, an expert might politely request the questioning attorney to lower his or her voice, or state that the expert finds it distracting for the attorney to be standing or moving around the room. Of course, if deposing legal counsel crosses the line too far, the client attorney may terminate the deposition and request court action. In that situation, hopefully unusual, the expert should follow the lead of the client's attorney, say nothing, and discuss the next steps in private.

Closing Questions

After deposing counsel has completed her deposition, it is possible that the defending attorney will want to close the deposition with a few questions to be answered by the financial expert witness on the record. These questions are usually asked to clarify an earlier answer, expand on a response, or rehabilitate the financial expert witness. These closing questions should be welcomed by the financial expert witness as they are designed to help clean up the record. However, don't be surprised if the deposing attorney gets the last word by asking additional questions after the defending attorney is done.

 ## POST-DEPOSITION ACTIVITIES

The deposition is required to be administered and recorded by an officer of the court. The court reporter typically serves this role in deposition. Under the Federal Rules of Civil Procedure (FRCP), Rule 30(b)(5), the officer of the court's obligations related to a deposition are as follows:

Officer's Duties

(A) **Before the Deposition.** Unless the parties stipulate otherwise, a deposition must be conducted before an officer appointed or designated under Rule 28. The officer must begin the deposition with an on-the-record statement that includes:
   (i) the officer's name and business address;

    (ii) the date, time, and place of the deposition;

    (iii) the deponent's name;

    (iv) the officer's administration of the oath or affirmation to the deponent; and

    (v) the identity of all persons present.

(B) **Conducting the Deposition; Avoiding Distortion.** If the deposition is recorded nonstenographically, the officer must repeat the items in Rule 30(b)(5)(A)(i)–(iii) at the beginning of each unit of the recording medium. The deponent's and attorneys' appearance or demeanor must not be distorted through recording techniques.

(C) **After the Deposition.** At the end of a deposition, the officer must state on the record that the deposition is complete and must set out any stipulations made by the attorneys about custody of the transcript or recording and of the exhibits, or about any other pertinent matters.

At the conclusion of the deposition proceedings, the financial expert witness will be asked by the court reporter whether he will allow the transcript to be finalized, or prefers to read and sign the transcript before finalizing the record. Except in rare and unusual situations, the financial expert witness should exercise the right to read and sign the transcript before allowing it to become an official record. The process of reading and signing gives the financial expert witness a chance to carefully peruse the unofficial record to correct errors or incorrect testimony.

Clerical and grammatical errors can be corrected within a specified time limit, usually 30 days, using an errata sheet provided by the court reporter under the provisions of the FRCP, Rule 30(e). The financial expert witness notes changes on the errata sheet, signs it, and forwards the recommended corrections to the client's legal counsel for submission to the opposing party and the court reporter. Substantive changes in testimony may require judicial review and in certain circumstances may provide the opposing attorney an opportunity to clarify the testimony through continued deposition.

While reading the deposition transcript, the financial expert witness should take note of poorly worded answers, areas of weakness or vulnerability, and things that may require additional work. These insights will be useful in preparing for later testimony at trial. Once identified, these matters should be discussed with the client's legal counsel and agreement reached on any remedial actions that might be taken by the financial expert witness, such as searching for more evidence, performing more work, or crafting more effective responses to difficult questions.

COMING UP

It is common for the financial expert witness to assist with motions and hearings leading up to trial. In Chapter 15, the financial expert witness's involvement in motions and hearings is explained.

 NOTES

1. David M. Malone and Paul J. Zwier, *Effective Expert Testimony*, 2nd ed. (Boulder, CO: NITA, 2006), 81–83. (Reprinted with permission from *Effective Expert Testimony*, 2nd ed. by David M. Malone and Paul J. Zwier. Copyright owned by the National Institute for Trial Advocacy. A full copy of this publication may be purchased at www.lexisnexis.com/nita/product.aspx?prodid=prod-US-NITA-FBA0959#table-of-contents.)
2. Ibid.
3. *See Texas Instruments v. Teletron Energy Management*, 877 S.W.2d 276, 279 (Tex. 1994) and *Conklin v. St. Lawrence Valley Educ. Television Council*, 1994 U.S. Dist. LEXIS 20188 (N.D.N.Y Oct. 28, 1994).

CHAPTER FIFTEEN

The Financial Expert Witness and Motions and Hearings

 MOTIONS

Motions are used by a disputing party to request that the court issue a favorable ruling or order for something to be done in a pending dispute. Motions can be made orally or in writing. Oral motions are most common during hearings, deposition, or trial. Often, written motions are accompanied by supporting documents and witness statements. There are a few motions that commonly use statements, such as declarations and affidavits, prepared by the financial expert witness. These motions are described more fully below.

Exhibit 15.1 is a sample motion form prepared by the Sixth Judicial Circuit Court of Florida.

Injunction

An injunction is a court order for a party to stop doing something harmful to another party. Alternatively, an injunction can require a party to do something in order to prevent injury to another party. Injunctions may be either temporary or permanent, depending on the specific case facts and circumstances.

IN THE CIRCUIT COURT OF THE _____ JUDICIAL CIRCUIT, IN AND FOR _____COUNTY, FLORIDA

REF:_____
UCN:_____
Division:_____

_____,
Petitioner,

and

_____,
Respondent.
_____/

MOTION TO/FOR:

_____, respectfully moves this Honorable Court to grant this Motion to/for _____, and as grounds therefore would show:

1. _____

2. _____

3. _____

4. _____

CERTIFICATE OF SERVICE

I HEREBY CERTIFY that a copy hereof has been furnished by mail/hand delivery/personal service to the persons listed below this _____ day of _____, 20___.

Party or their attorney(if represented)   Other
Name_____   Name_____
Address_____   Address_____

City   State   Zip   City   State   Zip

Telephone No._____   Telephone No._____
Telefax No._____   Telefax No._____
DATED:_____

Signature of party signing certificate and pleading
Printed name _____
Address _____

City   State   Zip

Telephone (area code and number)

Telefax (area code and number)

EXHIBIT 15.1 Motion Form

Source: Sixth Judicial Circuit Local Form, Motion to/for 12–2002, www.jud6.org.

Injunctions are covered by the Federal Rules of Civil Procedure (FRCP), Rule 65. At the heart of an injunction is the premise that irreparable damage will be done if an injunction is not ordered by the court.

That's where the financial expert witness comes in. In many cases, the moving party will ask for the assistance of the financial expert witness to objectively identify acts, events, and damaging effects giving rise to the request for injunction. The financial expert witness may be requested to investigate and identify facts and data needed to prove irreparable harm, or to perform analyses in support of the claim of irreparable harm. For example, an expert might be requested to opine on how a plaintiff company is likely to be injured if the court does not enjoin the defendant from infringing the plaintiff's patent or from soliciting the plaintiff's customers or employees in violation of a noncompete agreement. This work and the resultant findings are then written up and presented to the court in a signed or sworn disclosure statement accompanying the motion for injunction filed with the court.

Quash

A motion to quash asks the court to rule that an opposing party's request be deemed null and void so that it can be disregarded. Motions to quash a subpoena are included in the FRCP, Rule 45. A motion to quash can be used in a number of circumstances; however, if the financial expert witness gets involved, it frequently is in connection with production requests. If the client legal counsel believes that opposing legal counsel's requests for production are overly broad or burdensome, or otherwise unreasonable, he may ask the financial expert witness to assist by estimating the level of effort, timing, and cost to comply, or explaining why the information sought is not necessary for the kind of analysis being performed in the case. The financial expert witness's efforts are primarily focused on financial records and data, but are increasingly likely also to include broad ranges of electronically stored information, such as e-mail, databases, or spreadsheets. The expert's statement or analysis is either incorporated into the motion directly or prepared as a signed or sworn statement to accompany the motion when filed.

Compelling Production

The financial expert witness has experience and expertise to determine the likely sources and uses of financial records and data related to claims in a dispute. Therefore, the financial expert witness may be asked by the client attorney to describe the types of records needed and the potential value in the dispute resolution proceedings. This is typically done by having the objective financial expert witness analyze the production received to date and prepare a written statement on what is missing and why it is essential to be produced. This statement is signed and included with the paperwork supporting a motion to compel production. It is critical for the financial expert not to overstate the importance of the information being sought; he or she might not obtain it and then have no choice but to prepare an analysis without it.

Guidance for motions to compel is included in the FRCP, Rule 37. A portion of the federal rule is repeated below.

Failure to Make Disclosures or to Cooperate in Discovery; Sanctions

(a) Motion for an Order Compelling Disclosure or Discovery.

(1) **In General**. On notice to other parties and all affected persons, a party may move for an order compelling disclosure or discovery. The motion must include a certification that the movant has in good faith conferred or attempted to confer with the person or party failing to make disclosure or discovery in an effort to obtain it without court action.

(2) **Appropriate Court.** A motion for an order to a party must be made in the court where the action is pending. A motion for an order to a nonparty must be made in the court where the discovery is or will be taken.

(3) **Specific Motions.**

    (A) **To Compel Disclosure.** If a party fails to make a disclosure required by Rule 26(a), any other party may move to compel disclosure and for appropriate sanctions.

    (B) **To Compel a Discovery Response.** A party seeking discovery may move for an order compelling an answer, designation, production, or inspection. This motion may be made if:

        (i) a deponent fails to answer a question asked under Rule 30 or 31;

        (ii) a corporation or other entity fails to make a designation under Rule 30(b)(6) or 31(a)(4);

        (iii) a party fails to answer an interrogatory submitted under Rule 33; or

        (iv) a party fails to respond that inspection will be permitted—or fails to permit inspection—as requested under Rule 34.

    (C) **Related to a Deposition.** When taking an oral deposition, the party asking a question may complete or adjourn the examination before moving for an order.

In Limine

A motion *in limine* requests that the court rule evidence inadmissible for use at trial. Unfortunately for the financial expert witness, exposure to this motion is usually because opposing legal counsel has filed a motion *in limine* to limit or totally exclude the testimonial evidence of the financial expert witness. This is serious business for the financial expert witness. Opinions ruled inadmissible, for any reason, will preclude the financial expert witness from testifying about these matters in trial. In addition, any finding of inadmissibility will provide future opposing attorneys an opportunity to impugn the credibility of the financial expert witness.

That is why the financial expert witness must actively participate in the defensive response to the motion *in limine.* Quite frankly, it is personal for the financial expert witness. Acknowledging that financial expert witnesses are not attorneys, they can still play a critical role working with the client legal counsel in rebutting motion arguments. This is so important to some financial expert witnesses that they may hire their own personal legal counsel to protect their interests. Some financial expert witnesses go so far as to include defense participation as a specific right in the language of the engagement letter with the client.

Following is an excerpt from a case wherein the court granted a motion *in limine* regarding a financial expert witness. The name of the financial expert witness has been disguised.

> As an alternative, Plaintiffs seek to exclude EXPERT WITNESS'S testimony because it is not reliable. It is unnecessary for the court to analyze this testimony under the *Daubert* standard because the court has excluded the testimony on alternative grounds. However, it is worth noting that parts of the report seem very unscientific. EXPERT WITNESS states he simply assumed all increases in Plaintiffs' income were directly due to their infringing activity. Without any evidence or figures to rely upon, this assumption is made regarding Plaintiffs' income. The court must act as a gate-keeper when it comes to expert testimony. This analysis by EXPERT WITNESS, while draped as expert, seems extremely superficial. Similarly, the court notes EXPERT WITNESS again shunned hard numbers when he assumed Mercado enjoyed a 9% increase of income for 2009 and 2010 . . . EXPERT WITNESS may not have had the relevant information necessary to make his calculations and EXPERT WITNESS may have done the best with the limited information available, but the court cannot allow assumptions and guesses to form the basis of expert testimony to then be

delivered to the jury. As such, even if the report was not excluded for other reasons, the court would be inclined to exclude this testimony pursuant to Federal Rule of Evidence 702.

. . . For the foregoing reasons the court GRANTS . . . Plaintiffs' motion to exclude EXPERT WITNESS'S testimony . . .[1]

Dismissal

A motion to dismiss asks the court to remove claims from the complaint or throw out the lawsuit altogether. The financial expert witness is seldom directly involved with this kind of motion, which is based largely on legal grounds. However, the financial expert witness is often affected by a motion to dismiss. Motions to dismiss may impact the scope, timing, and extent of work to be performed. In many cases, a filed motion to dismiss can put the financial expert witness on hold pending a decision by the court. Motions for dismissal are governed by the FRCP, Rule 12(b).

Summary Judgment

Motions for summary judgment are defined by the FRCP, Rule 56, as described below:

> (a) MOTION FOR SUMMARY JUDGMENT OR PARTIAL SUMMARY JUDGMENT. A party may move for summary judgment, identifying each claim or defense— or the part of each claim or defense—on which summary judgment is sought. The court shall grant summary judgment if the movant shows that there is no genuine dispute as to any material fact and the movant is entitled to judgment as a matter of law. The court should state on the record the reasons for granting or denying the motion.[2]

Motions for summary judgment ask the court for a favorable decision on the outcome of a dispute before trial using the evidence produced thus far. Summary judgment motions are usually due 30 days after the close of discovery, unless changed by the parties with the approval of the court. Motions for summary judgment are normally accompanied by legal arguments supported by briefs. In some cases, the financial expert witness may be asked by the client legal counsel to prepare supporting statements to be filed with the motion for summary judgment. Granting a motion for summary judgment happens infrequently. As such, a pending motion for summary judgment may not significantly affect the financial expert witness's preparations leading up to trial.

Motions Commonly Using a Financial Expert Witness

- Injunction
- Quash
- Compelling production
- *In limine*
- Dismissal
- Summary judgment

 HEARINGS

Judicial hearings are forums wherein the disputing parties are asked to present evidence or oral arguments to assist the court in case management, ruling on motions, and other pretrial matters. Hearings can range from a few minutes for an informal report by counsel on the status of the case to formal, multiday proceedings with live witness examinations. There may be instances when the financial expert witness is asked to assist with the preparations for a hearing. Occasionally, the financial expert witness will be asked to attend a hearing to provide oral testimonial evidence under oath to the judge. As a testifying witness, the financial expert witness may be asked a variety of questions from the opposing attorneys in attendance and the judge. Hearings are typically less formal in decorum but have all the other trappings of official trial proceedings.

> Judges are like umpires. Umpires don't make the rules. They apply them.
> The role of an umpire and a judge is critical. They make sure everybody
> plays by the rules. But it is a limited role. Nobody ever went to a ballgame
> to see the umpire.
>
> —*John Roberts*

Hearing Preparation

A hearing is an important event and should be taken as seriously as deposition or trial by the financial expert witness. Accordingly, preparation for a hearing, especially one where it is expected the financial expert witness will testify, should resemble the preparation process for deposition or trial. Among other tasks, key documents and work product should be studied, meetings are to be held with the client attorney, and role-play is recommended. The financial expert witness should not prepare a hearing report or demonstratives unless directed to do so by the client legal counsel.

Hearing Participation

The financial expert witness should dress, behave, and communicate in the courtroom the same as if it is a trial. When it comes to sworn testimony given at a hearing to a judge, the financial expert witness must be truthful, reliable, and objective. The testimony will be most effective if the financial expert witness comes across as likable and he teaches the judge in a helpful way. Challenges to the financial expert witness's testimony from opposing legal counsel should be responded to with a firm consistent conviction for opinions held.

 ## COMING UP

We have been leading up to it—trial testimony. Trial testimony and the financial expert witness are discussed in Chapter 16.

 ## NOTES

1. *Mercado-Salinas v. Bart Enters. Int'l, LTD.*, 2012 U.S. Dist. LEXIS 182749, 26-27 (D.P.R. Dec. 24, 2012).
2. FRCP Rule 56(a).

CHAPTER SIXTEEN

Financial Expert Witness Trial Testimony

 ## TYPES OF TRIALS

Civil dispute trials can be conducted with a judge or with a judge and jury. A trial heard exclusively by a judge is called a bench trial. A jury trial is a federal right memorialized in the Seventh Amendment of the U.S. Constitution and covered by the Federal Rules of Civil Procedure (FRCP), Rule 38. A jury trial is commenced after a proper demand and notice has been timely filed. Bench and jury trials have differences and a few of these are described next.

Bench

Bench trials have the judge as the sole trier of fact. As such, some of the formalities built into a jury trial proceeding may be relaxed. The judge is more likely to ask the financial expert witness questions directly during direct and cross-examinations. In addition, the admission of the financial expert witness's testimonial evidence may be more liberal. That is because the judge's experience and knowledge is better-suited to determine the relevance, weight, and reliability, if any, of such testimony as compared to a jury. All in all, these actions are intended to expedite the trial proceedings in a fair, just, and efficient manner. That is part of the draw for bench trials for some disputing parties.

There is no reason for the financial expert witness to testify differently in a bench trial than he or she would in a jury trial. The judge will likely be capable of understanding complex technical matters and professional jargon better than an average juror; but making that assumption is dangerous. Well-articulated, simple, and to-the-point communication is appreciated by judges and juries alike.

Jury

Jury trials are governed by federal rules that govern the number of jurors, the selection process (also called voir dire), and verdict requirements. Jury selection is governed by the FRCP, Rule 47, which is recited in part here:

> (a) **Examining Jurors.** The court may permit the parties or their attorneys to examine prospective jurors or may do so itself. If the court examines the jurors, it must permit the parties or their attorneys to make any further inquiry it considers proper, or must itself ask any of their additional questions it considers proper.

A jury trial will be conducted with the utmost formality and jurisprudence. The financial expert witness must know, understand, and adhere to potentially unique jurisdictional procedures and courtroom rules and preferences. These can be obtained by asking the client legal counsel, or by looking up these things on websites, where they exist. Juries add the dynamic of differing personalities, education levels, values, and viewpoints to the trier of fact. This adds considerable risk to dispute resolution for both disputing parties. It also should remind the financial expert witness to prepare and testify with this wide range of variables in mind.

> A fair trial is one in which the rules of evidence are honored, the accused has competent counsel, and the judge enforces the proper courtroom procedures—a trial in which every assumption can be challenged.
>
> —*Harry Browne*

 ## COMPONENTS OF TRIAL EXAMINATION

The testimonial evidence to be given by the financial expert witness at trial has several components. Just prior to being called to testify, the financial expert witness will typically be asked to sit in the courtroom audience gallery until called. In some instances, the financial expert witness may be asked to wait outside the courtroom. This can happen based on the client's legal counsel's preference or because the financial expert witness has been sequestered by the judge.

Sequestration usually happens at the request of one of the disputing parties. If the financial expert witness is sequestered from the courtroom proceedings, he or she is not allowed to hear (or otherwise discover and know) the courtroom testimony of other witnesses in the trial. The intent is to avoid tainting or supplementing the planned testimony of the financial expert witness at trial by undue influence of another's testimony.

After the financial expert witness is called to testify, he or she approaches the witness stand, passing through the bar between the gallery seating and the court. The financial witness will be met by an officer of the court who will ask the financial expert witness to raise his or her right hand and be sworn in by affirming an oath. The financial expert witness may already be seated or may affirm the oath standing before the judge. Testimony is now ready to begin.

The examination of the financial expert witness begins with the direct examination conducted by the client's attorney. Direct examination is followed by cross-examination led by the opposing legal counsel. Thereafter, the financial expert witness would be further examined through re-direct and re-cross-examinations. Once the testimony is completed, the financial expert witness is released as a witness.

 ## PREPARATION FOR TRIAL TESTIMONY

The financial expert witness's preparation for trial is very similar to the preparation for deposition. Preparation for deposition testimony was covered in the chapters devoted to depositions in this book. In addition to basic preparation steps, this material discussed the financial expert witness's mental state and behavior, attire, and nonverbal communication. The use of intonation and pauses was also introduced. Finally, a model response process was described to assist the financial expert witness with the handling of questions posed. This information is also applicable to trial testimony and should be reviewed. However, there are a few preparatory items specific to trials that the financial expert witness should know.

First of all, recognize that the client attorney will need the financial expert witness to help prepare the direct examination outline, especially as it pertains to complex technical matters. Together, the client attorney and the financial expert witness will agree upon the areas to be covered in direct examination. These areas will be the primary focus for pretrial preparation for the financial expert witness. They must be remembered and practiced with an eye toward the linkage between the financial expert witness's testimony and the case theory.

In addition, the financial expert witness and the client legal counsel must identify, in advance, the evidence to be used during direct examination. This will consist of trial exhibits and any testimonial evidence that must be established before the financial expert witness is called to the witness stand. This evidence will serve as foundational materials for the financial expert witness's testimony. The key evidence usually boils down to a handful of critical documents that the financial expert witness must know cold.

Lastly, the financial expert witness and the client legal counsel will discuss vulnerabilities likely to be exposed in cross-examination. Typically, one area of exposure is the risk of impeachment stemming from inconsistent statements made by the financial expert witness in the course of the proceedings. To avoid impeachment, the financial expert witness should study his deposition transcript and collaborate with the client attorney on strategies for handling tough questions. In some cases, this may result in the preparation of a defensive direct examination as a preemptive measure.

Next, we will more closely examine the special preparation for trial testimony. In particular, we will look at:

- Trial logistics
- Role-play
- Communication with a jury
- Last-minute preparations

Trial Logistics

Planning logistics in preparation for trial is one of the best ways to reduce stress for the financial expert witness. Logistics are the times and places the financial expert witness needs to be for trial. The financial expert witness should determine the amount of time needed to commute to the courtroom, locate a parking spot, deal with security protocols, and walk to the location of the courtroom. One of the best ways to do this is for the financial expert witness to visit the courtroom before being called to testify. If possible, enter the courtroom and sit in the witness chair when court is out of session, with the permission of the judge, to get a feel for the line of sight to the trier of fact. It is also wise to be familiar with courtroom technology, which can vary greatly from one jurisdiction to another. In most cases, the client legal counsel will control the technology during the trial; however, some basic knowledge will come in handy.

The financial expert witness should not plan on bringing anything to trial, except what a subpoena or summons requires. If the financial expert witness believes materials must be brought to the witness stand to assist with testimony, he or she should clear this with the client attorney in advance. Opposing attorneys may have a right to these materials before trial, if they were not produced previously. Furthermore, the financial expert witness and client attorney should practice how such material might be referenced in trial and have a system to keep the materials well-organized during the testimony. There is nothing worse than a fumbling expert who can't find something on the witness stand.

Role-Play

Much like deposition preparation, the financial expert witness should prepare for trial using role-play. Role-play places the financial expert witness in an imaginary live trial situation, wherein anticipated trial questions are posed by an actor and answers are provided the financial expert witness. Role-play can be accomplished using staff and peers, but the most effective role-play will be with the client attorney. By the time the trial date arrives, the client attorney has mastered the case theory and evidence and is best prepared to ask hard questions or recommend adjustments to answers to make them clearer, more concise, and accurate.

The direct and cross-examinations should both be practiced using role-play. Among a number of things, the rehearsal of the direct examination will refine testimony themes, evidentiary support, and the effectiveness of presentation. Performing role-play for cross-examination prepares the financial expert witness for the worst. It is better to be grilled by friendlies in practice than to go up against an adversarial opposing attorney untrained.

Jury Communications

On the whole, jurors are anxious about the job they have to do. Jurors don't want to make a mistake and hold someone wrongfully accountable for a claim made against them. One way they protect themselves from making a bad decision is cynicism. They are cynical about the financial expert witness, in particular. The jury understands that the financial expert witness is engaged and paid by one side of the dispute, which makes what is said by that expert suspect.

The financial expert has to find a way get the jury to listen and believe. This can be accomplished by addressing these matters:

- Give the jury a reason to listen.
- Give the jury a reason to believe.
- Give the jury a reason to care.
- With these tactics, you will give the jury a reason to adopt your opinions.

The financial expert also has to find ways to reduce juror stress. Stress builders result from fighting with the opposing attorney, attacking an opposing expert witness, talking down to or with arrogance, or openly advocating positions. So, don't do these things. Instead try things that reduce stress levels. Use process, structure, guidance, and evidence to support testimony. The vast majority of learners are visual, so use visual aids. The financial expert witness should be a dynamic and engaging presenter seeking to earn trust through objective and reasonable viewpoints.

It is also advisable not to become a pet peeve to a juror. There is no quicker way to shut down jurors than to irritate them. Avoid over-rehearsing responses and incessant, rambling answers. Don't behave oddly or inconsistently. Match behaviors with oral speech. There is nothing more disturbing than a witness nodding yes and answering, "no." If you happen to have an uncontrollable tic, tell the jury so that it is expected. Don't get overly technical with professional jargon or vocabulary. Admit mistakes when appropriate and don't be stubbornly unreasonable. Finally, be conscious about filling voids with sounds like "uhm" or using gratuitous verbiage such as "like." Like, you know what I mean?

For the financial expert witness, communicating with a jury is a lot like teaching a class with students that range in experience and education from middle school to PhD. The content and delivery of the educational material must be tailored to each student (or juror), but delivered to the entire class (jury). As a result, the disparity between jurors impacts the way the financial expert witness approaches his job to assist the trier of fact to decide complex disputed facts and issues. To be most effective, the financial expert witness should consider how elements such as anxiety, appearance, delivery, presentation of demonstratives, nonverbal communication, and numbers will affect jurors considering the wide range of perspectives on a jury.

Speech Anxiety

The financial expert witness speaks under oath in front of total strangers. This can contribute to speech anxiety. According to the National Institute of

Mental Health (NIMH), speech anxiety is a social phobia. The NIMH states that "[s]ocial phobia is a strong fear of being judged by others and of being embarrassed. This fear can be so strong that it gets in the way of going to work or school or doing other everyday things."[1] The example of social phobia given by the NIMH is as follows:

> Everyone has felt anxious or embarrassed at one time or another. For example, meeting new people or giving a public speech can make anyone nervous. But people with social phobia worry about these and other things for weeks before they happen.[2]

The fear of public speaking is common, in some casual polls often listed as the number-one fear for adults. One consulting company drilled down into the reasons for the adult fear of public speaking and the results track closely to the risks the financial expert witness faces in a courtroom when testifying. The top things the average adult dreads about public speaking are:[3]

- Making embarrassing mistakes
- Damaging career or reputation
- Forgetting/freezing

The financial expert witness should be aware of speech anxiety and recognize the need to take measures to avoid having an attack. This can be done by attending classes to practice testimony, participating in live role-play, and joining professional speaking organizations. The key is to be comfortable as a teacher in a public setting.

Appearance

The dress and attire of the financial expert witness was discussed earlier in this book in the section devoted to depositions. The basic rule is to wear appropriately conservative professional business attire. The same recommendations hold true for trial. Therefore, that material should be referenced for pointers on dress and attire for the financial expert witness in trial.

There is one other point to make about appearance and the financial expert witness in trial. Many jurors will have a preconceived notion about what a financial expert looks like, especially an accountant. For those jurors with thoughts on this topic, they will likely expect a conservatively dressed, spectacled, green-eyeshade-wearing, soft-spoken professional who does taxes. Well, perhaps the eye shades are a bit of an exaggeration, but the rest may not be that far off.

If the financial expert witness enters the courtroom inconsistent with this stereotype in any significant way, a juror may be hard-pressed to listen to anything said. Instead of listening to the testimony, the juror tries to reconcile any deviations from their "norm." Questions will be formed such as: "Why does he look like that?" This contemplation distracts the juror from paying attention and may even cause feelings of distrust.

The financial expert witness only gets one chance to make a good impression with the jury. So, he or she must be cognizant that such bias exists and be careful not to create unnecessary distraction by wearing loud clothing, acting wildly, or saying controversial things. The financial expert witness should attempt to use the embedded perception of what a financial expert witness "should" look like to advantage. Be that credible, conservative financial expert that many jurors expect. That way testimony will be more readily adopted as credible by a skeptical jury.

> Beware, so long as you live, of judging men by their outward appearance.
>
> —*Jean de La Fontaine*

Age of Technology

The courtroom trial is based on the ancient practice of fact-telling through oral testimony. However, in today's high-tech world of smartphones, instant messaging, and social networks, verbal communication is quickly becoming a lost art. This fact must be considered by the financial expert witness to ensure testimony is heard and understood. Getting your message across today needs to be quicker, to the point, and multifaceted.

This point is driven home by an article on the potential effects of technology on the average learner. Quoting Dr. Carina Paine Schofield, coauthor of the 2009 report entitled, "Generation Y: Inside Out":

> . . . there is still "a big question about how technology is impacting on the way we behave." She studied the behaviours of people born between 1982 and 2002—particularly how they learn and work—and found "mixed results" in terms of attention spans.
>
> While young people are "undoubtedly capable of long periods of concentration," those who spend a lot of time alone using technology "tend to have less in the way of communication skills, self-awareness, and emotional intelligence." [4]

Live Demonstrations

There are times when the financial expert witness may be inclined to supplement expert testimony during trial with a demonstrative crafted on a flipchart or overhead projection. Alternatively, it is possible that the client attorney or opposing legal counsel may ask the financial expert witness to perform an act, such as calculating a number, on the spot in the courtroom. These can be effective ways to educate the trier of fact, but such actions are fraught with risk.

The financial expert may not leave the witness chair during trial proceedings without the express permission of the judge presiding over the courtroom. Permission can be requested by the financial expert witness asking the judge for leave to exit the witness stand and approach the visual aid for the purpose of explaining testimony. Once granted permission, the financial expert witness may go to the flipchart or overhead projection equipment and prepare the demonstrative.

It is extremely dangerous to prepare a demonstrative on the spot in the courtroom, unless it has been rehearsed in advance with the knowledge and permission of the client legal counsel. It is simply too easy to make a mistake on the fly. If a mistake is made, it will instantly impugn the credibility of the financial expert witness and, rest assured, the opposing attorney will place the demonstrative front and center during cross-examination. It may even be referenced in the closing arguments.

If the financial expert witness decides to prepare a live demonstrative using a flipchart, there are a couple of warnings to heed. Make sure the flipchart stand is stable before writing on it. A toppled flipchart stand will not help your case. When writing on the flipchart, do not talk. Instead, write the content and then turn and talk to the trier of fact when done. Make sure that all writing is large and legible. Spelling and grammatical errors will be noticed and amplified in the courtroom.

If the financial expert witness is asked to perform an act while on the stand, the request should be reasonably resisted by the financial expert witness. It is possible, but extremely rare, that the client attorney built something like a live calculation into the direct examination. Such plans should be practiced in advance of the trial, especially if they require the use of a calculator. The financial expert witness should only agree to do live mathematics in his head under very limited circumstances. The risk of error under duress during the trial is too great. The same advice holds true for requests from opposing legal counsel to perform acts on the witness stand live in front of the trier of fact.

Unless the request is extremely simple, the financial expert witness should explain to the trier of fact the risk of error involved in doing such an act on the spot and that, therefore, the request is unreasonable. Of course, if pressed by the opposing attorney and assuming no valid objection is raised, the financial expert witness must try to comply.

Nonverbal Communication

In addition to the tips shared earlier in this book about nonverbal communication, the financial expert witness should consider the following matters:

- Approaching the witness stand
- Posture
- Drinking
- Eyes
- Hands and gestures

When asked to approach the witness stand, the financial expert witness should move quickly and confidently to the appointed rendezvous with the court officer to be sworn in. Once under oath, the financial expert witness should take a seat in the witness chair, positioning the chair so that it faces the jury. This may not be possible in all courtrooms, as many have fixed chair positions. Regardless, sit up straight, with weight slightly forward in the chair. The chest should be angled to face the jury comfortably and legs should rest about shoulder-width apart. Be conscious of fidgeting, such as leg bouncing or hand-wringing. The idea is to have a confident, attentive, and relaxed posture directed at the jury.

It is advisable to fill the available water glass immediately after seating. Take care not to spill or show obvious signs of the shakes due to nerves. The financial expert witness should sip water occasionally to hydrate and stay alert and energized. However, juries don't trust a witness who drinks excessively or lacks manners.

As for the eyes, the financial expert witness should make comfortable eye contact with the jury. It is best to focus on one juror at a time when speaking, moving to another after the completion of each thought. Of course, the financial expert witness will at times look at a questioning attorney or at the judge when addressed. That is natural and encouraged. However, quick glances at the client attorney, especially during cross-examination, can be perceived as suspicious and should be avoided. The financial expert witness will observe jurors taking notes, others nodding in agreement or denial, and yet others asleep. This is normal and expected. If the attention of the jury is drifting, eye contact can be a helpful tool to re-engage.

As for the hands and hand gestures, the financial expert witness must play in the middle, somewhere between rigidity and a motivational speaker. If the financial expert witness is too stiff and inflexible, for example, with his hands clenched and frozen in position, he or she will be perceived as unapproachable, scared, or uncooperative. These are all traits that may impair the effectiveness of testimony. On the other end of the spectrum, if the financial expert witness flails his arms or makes extravagant hand gestures, it can look like he or she is trying to sell the Brooklyn Bridge.

Therefore, the financial expert witness must play in the middle. Arms should rest comfortably at the sides of the torso, with hands on the lap or table in front if one is provided. If a table is provided, having the hands under the table can look deceptive. Hand gestures should be used to emphasize key testimony and must be timely and usually limited to the chest area in scope.

Numbers

All financial expert witnesses know this to be true—the average juror is likely to have anxiety about numbers and math. This often extends to taxes and accounting, believed by many a layperson to be closely linked to math. This phenomenon is well-documented. The research group PLoS ONE supported Ian M. Lyons and Sian L. Beilock with research into math anxiety. The result was a research paper entitled, *When Math Hurts: Math Anxiety Predicts Pain Network Activation in Anticipation of Doing Math*. The research reported that:

> Math can be difficult, and for those with high levels of mathematics-anxiety (HMAs), math is associated with tension, apprehension, and fear. . . . We show that, when anticipating an upcoming math-task, the higher one's math anxiety, the more one increases activity in regions associated with visceral threat detection, and often the experience of pain itself. . . . Interestingly, this relation was not seen during math performance, suggesting that it is not that math itself hurts; rather, the anticipation of math is painful. Our data suggest that pain network activation underlies the intuition that simply anticipating a dreaded event can feel painful. These results may also provide a potential neural mechanism to explain why HMAs tend to avoid math and

math-related situations, which in turn can bias HMAs away from taking math classes or even entire math-related career paths.[5]

As such, the financial expert witness must use knowledge about math anxiety to deliver testimony designed to reduce stress in the jury. This can be done by simplifying calculations, avoiding the details of complex formulas, and not asking the jury to perform personal math work. Most important, the financial expert witness should avoid talking to the jury with an "ivory tower" attitude that may be interpreted by the trier of fact as arrogant.

 OBJECTIONS

Objections are generally described in a previous chapter devoted to deposition testimony. Accordingly, only the unique matters related to financial expert witness trial testimony are discussed here. Unlike deposition objections, however, trial objections are made directly to the judge, who usually will rule immediately on the admissibility of the evidence at the time it is presented. Most relevant to the financial expert witness, that includes objections to testimonial evidence given at trial.

Commonplace Objections in Trial

The financial expert witness should expect objections from opposing legal counsel during direct examination. Conversely, the client's legal counsel may object to questions asked during cross-examination. The most common objection the financial expert witness may hear from opposing legal counsel during direct testimony will be "leading." Leading questions generally are prohibited during direct examination. On the flipside, the financial expert witness may hear the client's attorney object during cross-examination to questions that ask for responses beyond the scope of direct examination. In this event, the opposing attorney is limited to inquiries about subject matter testified to in direct examination when conducting cross-examination.

In addition to these objections, either side's attorneys may assert objections on the grounds of:

▪ Absence of foundation to present evidence—insufficient, or no, facts have been introduced and proven to allow an exhibit to be admitted into evidence.

- Argumentative—the question is simply a statement of advocacy with which the witness is asked to agree, or to which an answer would be inherently ambiguous or misleading.
- Assuming facts not in evidence—the question refers to disputed facts or facts not yet admitted into evidence.
- Authentication of evidence—written and oral communications and documents have not been proven as authentic.
- Best-evidence rule—the question is best answered by looking at an original document instead of hearing testimony.
- Compound—the question contains more than one fact for which a single answer is not possible.
- Confusion—the question is unclear or misleading.
- Cumulative testimony—the question has already been asked to other witnesses and a response would add no new evidence.
- Hearsay—the answer would be inadmissible hearsay under the federal rules.
- Inadmissible material—an exhibit includes an inadmissible disclosure, reference, image, or marking.
- Improper characterization—the question or answer improperly characterizes prior evidence in the case.
- Improper impeachment—the question improperly attempts to impeach the witness contrary to the federal rules.
- Improper legal conclusion—the question or answer calls for, or gives, an improper legal conclusion.
- Mistaken evidence—the question misstates the evidence or prior testimony.
- Narrative—the question calls for, or the answer is, unduly verbose.
- Prejudicial evidence—the evidence would have a prejudicial effect that outweighs any probative value.
- Relevance—the question or answer is irrelevant.
- Repetitive—the question has already been asked and answered.
- Speculation—the question calls for, or the answer is based on, speculation or conjecture.

After an objection has been made, the financial expert witness must remain silent and not answer any pending question until the judge has ruled whether the question, answer, or evidence will be admitted. The judge may ask the objecting attorney to comment on the legal basis for the objection. In addition, the opposing legal counsel may offer legal arguments in rebuttal. After consideration, the judge will orally communicate a decision that the objection was sustained or denied. Depending on whether the evidentiary objection was related to a question, answer, or an exhibit, if sustained, the question will be withdrawn, the answer stricken, or the exhibit deemed inadmissible. If denied, the evidence will be admitted.

Last-Minute Preparation

It is important that the financial expert witness touch base with the client's legal counsel immediately prior to appearing to testify. This will allow the client's attorney to tell the financial expert witness, within legal limitations, the following kinds of information:

- How the case is going
- Prior testimony to be considered
- Relevant rulings or comments by the judge
- Judge demeanor and preferences
- Which jurors are leaders or to be watched
- Areas to be added or removed from direct examination
- Areas to focus on for cross-examination

In addition, the client's legal counsel can advise the financial expert witness on when the financial expert witness is expected to be called to testify and the anticipated length of the direct and cross-examinations. However, the financial expert witness should remember that scheduled testimony is always subject to last-minute change and, therefore, he or she may be called later or earlier than expected.

 COMING UP

The financial expert witness is first questioned in trial by the client attorney using direct examination. Direct examination is discussed in Chapter 17.

 NOTES

1. National Institutes of Mental Health, U.S. Department of Health and Human Services, accessed January 29, 2014, www.nimh.nih.gov/health/topics/social-phobia-social-anxiety-disorder/index.shtml.

2. Ibid.
3. "FVS: Sales Presentation Skills," The Rainmaker Academy, 2013.
4. Duncan Jeffries, "Is Technology and the Internet Reducing Pupils' Attention Spans?," *The Guardian* (March 11, 2013), available at www.theguardian .com/teacher-network/teacher-blog/2013/mar/11/technology-internet-pupil-attention-teaching. For the complete *Generation Y: Inside Out* report, visit www .ashridge.org.uk and search: GenerationYInsideOut.pdf.
5. Ian M. Lyons and Sian L. Beilock, *When Math Hurts: Math Anxiety Predicts Pain Network Activation in Anticipation of Doing Math*, PLoS ONE, accessed October 31, 2012, www.plosone.org/article/info:doi/10.1371/journal.pone.0048076.

CHAPTER SEVENTEEN

Financial Expert Witness Direct Examination

 DIRECT EXAMINATION

Direct examination is like an orchestra (i.e., the financial expert witness) conducted by a talented conductor (i.e., the client's attorney). The questions posed by the conductor allow the financial expert witness to play musical harmony through testimony. During direct examination, the client's legal counsel has an opportunity to solicit answers from the financial expert witness to questions designed to present the expert's opinions as reliable for use by the trier of fact. However, the client's attorney may not ask leading questions in the direct examination.

To be leading, a question must propose the desired answer to the witness. For example, the question: "You did calculate damages using mitigation, right?" is leading. A question on the same topic that is not leading might be: "Did you use mitigation in your damages calculation?" Leading questions are used by opposing legal counsel to limit the financial expert witness's testimony, hopefully to "yes" or "no" responses, and prevent any opportunity for explanation. Leading questions are not permitted for direct examination because they create the risk that the financial expert witness may be improperly coached by the examining attorney on what to say.

The principal task of a conductor is not to put himself in evidence but to disappear behind his functions as much as possible. We are pilots, not servants.

—*Franz Liszt*

Objectives of Direct Examination

The client attorney, opposing attorney, and the financial expert witness each have differing objectives for direct examination. The client attorney seeks to tell the trier of fact her story through the financial expert witness in a convincing, credible, and reliable fashion. Limited in the ability to do anything substantive to the financial expert witness in direct examination, the opposing legal counsel attempts to keep inadmissible testimony and other evidence out of the proceedings using objections. Of course, the opposing attorney is also listening carefully for opportunities to cross-examine the financial expert witness successfully when her turn comes next. The financial expert witness strives to convincingly, objectively, and truthfully teach the jury about opinions held in the hopes that they will be believed by the trier of fact.

Client Attorney

The client attorney has one main objective: Get the trier of fact to agree with the facts and issues in favor of the underlying client. With respect to a financial expert witness, the attorney furthers this goal by eliciting oral testimony about the expert's opinions and the bases for them. In addition, the client attorney may seek to do the following things in direct examination:

- Establish the financial expert witness's qualifications.
- Prove the credibility of the financial expert witness.
- Prove the reliability of the financial expert witness's work and opinions.
- Critique opposing financial expert witness qualifications, work, and opinions.
- Establish and introduce as evidence undisputed facts tending to prove case theory.
- Prove disputed facts and issues.
- Provide the foundation to introduce evidentiary exhibits.
- Avoid long narratives to enhance understanding and retention.
- Minimize or insulate against bad facts, mistakes, and vulnerabilities likely to be the subject of cross-examination.

The client attorney strives to achieve these objectives by presenting the case consistent with case theory, which has been woven into a storyline designed to be clear and persuasive to the trier of fact. To be absorbed, the client attorney knows that the story must be told in an attention-getting and interesting way. As such, the client attorney may spend considerable time with the financial expert witness developing helpful analogies, metaphors, and visual aids to explain complex matters.

Opposing Attorney

The opposing attorney has two main objectives for direct examination. First, the opposing attorney must be alert for inadmissible testimony and evidence that is objectionable. Timely objections are critical for the opposing legal counsel. Second, opposing legal counsel is listening for additional content to use in the cross-examination. Although the majority of cross-examination has been prepared in advance of trial, there is always new material introduced in direct examination that may be useful in cross-examination. In addition to these two things, opposing counsel may also exercise the right to request voir dire of the financial expert witness's qualifications. However, this is not an overly common practice.

Financial Expert Witness

The financial expert witness's objective is to convince the trier of fact to adopt his or her opinions as credible and reliable. Secondary to this, the financial expert witness attempts to express testimony in a way that is complementary to the client's case theory and the client attorney's storyline. Be careful, though, this is not advocacy. Instead, it is the dovetailing of the presentation with case strategy to make the oral testimony more understandable to the trier of fact because it will be in context.

> Stories are the creative conversion of life itself into a more powerful, clearer, more meaningful experience. They are the currency of human contact.
>
> —Robert McKee

Components of Direct Examination

Although there are almost limitless ways to conduct direct examination, most follow a common, structured pattern. This pattern has proven to be effective in presenting financial expert witness testimony to a trier of fact in order to enhance comprehension and recall. The order of the items in the pattern will vary and the items may be combined together in practice. Following are the typical items included in this pattern, together with brief explanations.

- **Introduction of the financial expert witness**. The financial expert witness is introduced to the jury by asking for name, place of employment, position, and title, among other things. In addition, the client attorney may attempt to build rapport between the financial expert witness and the trier of fact. This is done by making inquiries designed to introduce the financial expert witness as a unique personality. The client attorney may also flavor the introduction with a teaser of what exciting testimony is to come later and why it is important to the case at hand. Following is one way a financial expert witness was introduced while building rapport.

Question: Mr. John Q. Public, what do you do?

Answer: I am a forensic accountant.

Question: What does a forensic accountant do?

Answer: Have you ever seen the television show called *CSI: Crime Scene Investigation?*

Question: Yes, but how is that relevant?

Answer: On that show, the detectives can find out what happened by looking at dead bodies. I can tell what happened in the accounting world by looking at the numbers.

- **Qualifications of the financial expert witness**. The skills, knowledge, education, experience, and training of the financial expert witness are solicited and explained. Technical competencies are revealed, with skills uniquely suited to the case at hand particularly stressed. In many cases, the conclusion of the presentation of qualifications is followed by a tendering of the financial expert witness for the presiding judge to confirm. The tendering of a financial expert witness may go something like this: Your honor, I would like to tender John Q. Public as an expert in accounting, financial forensics, and economic damages.
- **Summary of financial expert witness opinions**. Although it may seem backward, the financial expert witness is usually asked to give his opinions before providing the reasons for them. This is permitted by Rule 705 of the

Federal Rules of Evidence. It is also a technique that will assist the trier of fact to understand where the financial expert witness will be going with the testimony. Of course, the repetition aids with recall, as well.

- **Methods and principles used by the financial expert witness**. This allows the financial expert witness to explain what was done, how it was done, and why it was done. This is also the portion of the testimony wherein the general acceptance in the field is confirmed and inferior alternative methods and principles are explained.

- **Facts, data, and assumptions used by the witness**. After explaining the reliability of the methods and principles used by the financial expert witness, it must be demonstrated to the trier of fact that the relevant case facts and data were used reliably in those methods and principles. In addition, key assumptions are identified and explanations provided for why they are reasonable and valid.

- **Work performed by the financial expert witness**. Once the methods and principles are explained, together with the facts, data, and assumptions used, the financial expert witness will be asked to describe the work performed, the results, and the significance of such results. In addition, any work not performed that may lead to controversy in cross-examination may be explored to stunt any potential adverse effects. The work performed and the associated results lead up to the foundation for each opinion expressed.

- **The basis for each opinion expressed by the financial expert witness**. After explaining the results of the work performed using reliable methods and principles applied to the relevant facts in the case, the financial expert witness will tell the jury the basis, or reason, for each opinion.

- **Contrast the financial expert witness against the opposing expert**. The financial expert witness may be asked to compare and contrast the qualifications; methods, and principles used; work performed; facts, data, and assumptions relied upon; and opinions offered by an opposing financial expert witness. This is done to give the trier of fact a way to measure the credibility and reliability of the financial expert witness, with the objective of having the trier of fact give more weight to the testifying financial expert witness.

- **Recap the financial expert witness's opinions**. The financial expert witness is requested to provide his opinions to the trier of fact at the end of testimony. This is done to bring the testimony together and assist the trier of fact to recall the opinions to be accepted.

DIRECT EXAMINATION OUTLINE

One of the primary objectives for trial preparation is to outline direct examination for the financial expert witness. This outline can be brief and topical or excruciatingly detailed, like a script to a play. Regardless, the financial expert witness should work directly with the client legal counsel to prepare the direct examination outline. This will ensure that there are no questions asked that will come as a surprise to the financial expert witness and inquiries about technical matters will be properly posed as questions. Following are some things to keep in mind when preparing the direct examination:

- Identify and prioritize essential testimony that the financial expert witness must express on the witness stand. This requires giving up points of lesser significance and minor details in favor of mission-critical matters. As time will be limited for the financial expert witness to testify at trial, this is one of the most critical, and challenging, tasks.
- In general, the most important testimony should get the most time in direct examination. Conversely, avoid insignificant and circumstantial information.
- Get to the most important points quickly and tell the trier of fact why the material is important.
- Build in the exhibits and testimonial evidence from others that will be needed for the direct examination.
- Find a small number of themes for the financial expert witness's testimony and stick to them. It is easier for the trier of fact to recall a handful of important themes than many unstructured details.
- Begin and end key testimony themes with something memorable for the trier of fact to remember.
- Get the jury instructions and tailor the direct examination so that it uses similar wording. This will help the jury understand the relevance of the financial expert witness's testimony during deliberations.
- Reduce technical jargon and complex concepts into plain, everyday language.
- Craft metaphors and analogies helpful to the trier of fact and reinforce them with visual aids.
- Consider the psychological concept of primacy and recency. According to the National Institutes of Health, primacy and recency is a phenomenon where, "Following a single exposure to learning, recall is better for items at the beginning (primacy) and end (recency) of a list than for middle items."[1]

- Use repetition as a method for the trier of fact to retain oral testimony. According to the research of B. Price Kerfoot, ". . . if you take information in small amounts and repeat it, it encodes that information in your memory."[2]
- Carve longer direct examination themes into smaller, bite-size questions and answers that leave the trier of fact waiting for the next question.

Tell the audience what you're going to say, say it; then tell them what you've said.

—*Dale Carnegie*

TRIAL DEMONSTRATIVES

Demonstratives are visual aids used to explain the financial expert witness's testimony. Demonstratives are an excellent way to help the trier of fact grasp complexities that are difficult to explain, or to reinforce core points. The chapter on expert report writing describes some practical tips for demonstratives. In addition to these tips, there are a few things to remember about demonstratives to be used in a courtroom:

- Demonstratives should be prepared as far in advance of the trial as practical so that the client's legal counsel can review and approve the content and admissibility.
- Demonstratives should be kept to a minimum, usually no more than half a dozen or ten.
- Demonstratives should be used to reinforce critical testimony, such as opinions and key calculations.
- Demonstratives must be shared by the client's attorney with the opposing attorney in a timely manner before trial. Failure to do so may cause the court to exclude the demonstratives.
- Demonstratives must be large enough for anyone in the courtroom to read.
- Demonstratives must be free of mistakes and legible.
- Demonstratives should be uncluttered, clear, and direct.
- Demonstratives should use words sparingly.
- Demonstratives should avoid technobabble.
- Demonstratives that use images, pictures, graphs, charts, and diagrams to replace words and show concepts are more effective.
- Demonstratives should consider the psychological impact of colors and imagery.

If anything, PowerPoint, if used well, would ideally reflect the way we think.

—*Steven Pinker*

 ## PREEMPTIVE CROSS-EXAMINATION

Preemptive cross-examination is defensive direct examination. Defensive direct examination attempts to predict what the opposing attorney will likely attack in cross-examination and deal with it during direct examination. Among many other things, preemptive cross-examination can be used to defuse:

- Qualification concerns
- Shortcomings in the work of the financial expert witness
- Vulnerabilities
- Fees and billings
- Bad facts
- Shaky assumptions
- Grounds for impeachment
- Mistakes and errors

For example, if the expert has been unable to obtain information that normally would be important to the expert's analysis, the client attorney might ask the expert on direct examination whether there was additional information the expert would have liked to have, and to explain why it is still possible to reach reliable opinions and conclusions without that information. Similarly, the client attorney might elicit the fact that the financial expert has not performed a specific type of analysis before, and then allow the expert to explain that he or she has performed other analyses that are based on the same principles and provide appropriate experience and qualifications.

There are, of course, risks to preemptive cross-examination. There is the chance that the opposing attorney was not going to raise the matter in cross-examination because it was not strategic or perhaps feared to be inadmissible. Asking a defensive question in direct examination opens the door for opposing legal counsel to pounce on the financial expert witness when her turn comes. Therefore, preemptive cross-examination should only be done with the utmost caution and care.

USE OF THE EXPERT REPORT IN TRIAL

The financial expert witness is required to personally provide sworn testimony about his present knowledge, including knowledge regarding any expert report prepared in connection with the trial. The financial expert witness's report prepared during discovery and the focus of the deposition testimony is not admitted into trial evidence, except in rare circumstances. That is because it represents inadmissible hearsay. That means that the financial expert witness should not expect to read from his expert report as a means to deliver testimony in trial.

However, in cases involving multiple complex issues, large amounts of information, or when significant time has passed between the preparation of the expert report and the trial, it can be challenging to remember all the necessary information and keep the facts straight while testifying. In these situations, the financial expert witness may be allowed to use their expert report to assist with recollection if it can be legally authenticated. Generally, it is appropriate for an expert witness to say something like, "It would help me to answer that question if I looked at my report."

Authentication of a financial expert witness's report can be accomplished simply by having the financial expert identify and adopt it as being prepared by him or under his direction. Once authenticated, the expert can use the report to aid recollection on the witness stand. This is referred to as "present recollection refreshed."[3] If this effort fails to sufficiently revive the financial expert witness's present recollection, legal counsel may be allowed to have the financial expert witness provide a foundation for admissibility in order for the expert report to be read into evidence. The specific requirements of the foundation in such cases are within the purview of the judge to decide; however, it requires proof that the financial expert witness had personal knowledge of the matters in the expert report and that it accurately reflects the expert's opinions and conclusions and the basis for them. The use of the expert report as evidence when the financial expert witness has insufficient recollection to testify completely and accurately at trial is referred to as "past recollection recorded."[4]

REDIRECT EXAMINATION

After cross-examination is complete, the client attorney will have the opportunity to ask questions again of the financial expert witness in redirect examination. By court rule, the redirect is limited in scope to only those matters covered in the cross-examination. However, this can vary depending on the judge. Redirect examination is used to rehabilitate the financial expert witness. In other words, it is used to clarify, explain, and respond to points made by opposing counsel in cross-examination. During redirect examination, attempts to impeach, inconsistencies in testimony, and mistakes or errors, can be handled along with other matters. Redirect examination is the life preserver thrown to the financial expert witness after he or she falls overboard.

 ## REBUTTAL TESTIMONY

In some cases, the financial expert witness may be allowed to testify as a rebuttal witness after testimony is given by an opposing expert witness. This is more typical for a financial expert witness retained by a plaintiff because the defendant's financial expert witness testifies after the plaintiff's. The defendant's expert witness may raise issues in trial that can only be rebutted afterward, thereby affording the plaintiff's financial expert witness an opportunity to respond, if allowed by the judge. The financial expert witness should ask the client attorney if rebuttal trial testimony is expected.

 ## COMING UP

Next, we look at one of the hardest jobs the financial expert witness will ever have to do—facing a cross-examination.

 ## NOTES

1. Available at www.ncbi.nlm.nih.gov.
2. Mary Tamer, *Repetition, Repetition, Repetition* (Cambridge, MA: Harvard Graduate School of Education, 2010), available at www.gse.harvard.edu/news-impact/2010/01/repetition-repetition-repetition.
3. Bryan A. Garner, *Black's Law Dictionary, Third Pocket Edition* (New York: West Group, 2006), 558.
4. Ibid., 526.

CHAPTER EIGHTEEN

Financial Expert Witness Cross-Examination

CROSS-EXAMINATION

Cross-examination resembles a military sergeant's drill exercise. Questions are posed by the drill sergeant (i.e., the opposing attorney) that are to be answered with only "yes, sir" or "no, sir" by the soldier (i.e., the financial expert witness). Granted, the opposing attorney will rarely bark questions like a drill sergeant. Instead, opposing legal counsel will be professional and diplomatic. But, the expectation is still to elicit only a "yes" or "no" response from the financial expert witness. The answers "I don't know" or "I don't recall" will be tolerated. However, if the financial expert witness makes any attempt to stray from these limited replies, the opposing attorney will seize this as an opportunity to attempt to show the financial expert as a biased advocate, an obstructionist, evasive, uncooperative, and, therefore, lacking in credibility.

> Firstly, you must always implicitly obey orders, without attempting to form any opinion of your own regarding propriety.
>
> —Horatio Nelson

Cross-examination is the questioning of the financial expert witness in trial or at a hearing by an opposing party to the party who called the expert witness to testify. Cross-examination inquiries are generally limited by court rule to subjects brought out during direct examination. However, there is often great latitude given by the court to conduct cross-examination. For the financial expert witness, cross-examination is the opportunity for an adversarial opposing legal counsel to discredit and minimize qualifications and testimony, making it a dangerous and frightening activity.

OBJECTIVES OF CROSS-EXAMINATION

Each of the participants in the deposition has objectives. The opposing attorney seeks to learn new information about the financial expert witness and his or her opinions. The client attorney wants to identify any potential weaknesses in the financial expert witness's testimony that may result in opinions being limited in trial or cause problems during cross-examination. The financial expert witness is focused on survival.

Opposing Attorney

The objectives of the opposing attorney are not pleasant for the financial expert witness. Seen in the best light, the opposing attorney wants to marginalize the financial expert witness's testimony. In the worst case, the opposing attorney desires to crush the financial expert witness, having him crawl off the witness stand defeated. Based on a number of texts and articles, here are some of the words used to describe what the opposing legal counsel wants to do to the financial expert witness in cross-examination:

- Agonize
- Attack
- Argue
- Confront
- Control
- Corral
- Cut
- Demand
- Destroy

- Kill
- Knock around
- Impeach
- Lead
- Neutralize
- Slap

The main objective for opposing legal counsel in cross-examination is to control the financial expert witness. This is accomplished by using leading questions and techniques proven to raise concerns about financial expert witness credibility and the reliability of opinions reached. Leading questions are inquiries that imply an answer to the financial expert witness.

During cross-examination, control is evident because the opposing attorney intentionally shifts the trier of fact's attention away from the financial expert witness and onto the opposing attorney asking the questions. The opposing attorney does this by asking the leading questions that call for short answers suggested by the opposing attorney. By design, the opposing attorney will not ask any question for which she does not already know the answer. The goal is to make the financial expert witness inconsequential.

Using this technique, the opposing legal counsel will find ways to tell her storyline through the financial expert witness: Case theories will be reinforced, facts and assumptions challenged, foundations laid for new evidence, and opposing financial expert witnesses embellished. Of course, any perceived harm done by the financial expert witness on the stand will be handled, oftentimes by discrediting the financial expert witness and his testimony. Perhaps most important, "gotcha" moments will be emphasized, with a *pièce de résistance* saved for the closing.

Client Attorney

The client attorney observes the cross-examination closely to identify any damage done by the opposing attorney that requires repair in redirect examination. This requires that the client attorney listen to the questions and answers as well as watch the responses of the trier of fact. In addition, the client legal counsel pays close attention to objectionable inquiries, alerting the judge to improper questions asked by opposing legal counsel. Overall, the objective is to determine what rehabilitation of the financial expert witness is needed in redirect examination.

Financial Expert Witness

The objectives of the financial expert witness in cross-examination center around survival. Survival is best accomplished by using the TRUTHFUL trial testimony technique described in the following.

Testifying the TRUTHFUL Way

Much like the PRACTICAL approach to financial expert report writing, TRUTHFUL provides an easy-to-remember acronym to describe the process for trial testimony. The TRUTHFUL way is built on the following principles:

- **Truthful**
- **Reliable**
- **Unbiased**
- **Teacher**
- **Helpful**
- **Firm**
- **Uniform**
- **Likable**

These principles are explained next.

Truthful
The TRUTHFUL acronym and the first principle of this approach intentionally refer to being truthful. Above all else, the sworn testimony of the financial expert witness must be "the truth, the whole truth, and nothing but the truth." Without truthful testimony, the financial expert witness is of no value to the trier of fact.

Reliable
To be reliable, the financial expert witness must be qualified, credible, and trustworthy. Opinions and the foundations for them must be based on extraordinarily high levels of quality. Oral testimony must be consistent, supported by relevant foundational facts, data, and analysis, and objective and believable. Only then will the trier of fact find the financial expert witness's testimony and opinions dependable for use.

Unbiased
The financial expert witness is allowed to testify at trial, in part because it is believed that the expert is to assist the trier of fact in an unbiased manner. To

be unbiased, the financial expert witness must be objective, impartial to either disputing party, and unprejudiced about the objectives and wished-for outcome of the client. As noted above, the absence of bias is also a contributing factor for financial expert witness reliability.

Teacher

As described earlier in this book, the financial expert witness is most effective when oral testimony is given like a good teacher delivers a lesson. The testimony should be organized, clear, and based on an analytic approach. Oral testimony should be delivered dynamically, with enthusiasm, always sensitive to interactions with the triers of fact on a group and individual level.

Helpful

The financial expert witness must never lose sight of the requirement to be helpful to the trier of fact. Therefore, this principle reminds the financial expert witness to consistently attempt to assist the trier of fact to decide facts and issues in controversy. Behaviors that are unhelpful, such as obstructionism and evasiveness, can cause the trier of fact to doubt the credibility and reliability of the financial expert witness and should be avoided.

Firm

This principle refers to the conviction the financial expert witness must have when advocating opinions. The financial expert witness must be firm about this, demonstrating strong feelings that professional opinions are proper and unlikely to change. Firmness can be expressed by confidence and an unwavering allegiance to expressed opinions.

Uniform

For testimony to be uniform it must be stable and unchanging throughout the proceedings. The financial expert witness should strive to state opinions in a confident, consistent manner. Deviations from previous positions, such as waffling or flip-flopping, can seriously hurt credibility.

Likable

Likability is one of the most important, but often forgotten, principles for oral testimony. In short, if the judge or jury doesn't like the financial expert witness, it is unlikely that they will listen to testimony given and adopt opinions that are offered. To be likable, the financial expert witness must present a pleasant demeanor and be professionally friendly. The financial expert witness should avoid arrogance, stubbornness, verbal combat with the opposing attorney, and dodgy behavior.

> Arrogance is a weed which grows upon a dunghill; it is from the rankness of the soil that she has her height and spreadings: witness, clowns, fools, and fellows, who from nothing, are lifted up some few steps on fortune's ladder: where, seeing the glorious representment of honour above them, they are so eager to embrace it, that they strive to leap thither at once, and by over-reaching themselves in the way, they fail of the end, and fall.
>
> —Owen Felltham, *Resolves, Divine, Moral, and Political*

CROSS-EXAMINATION TECHNIQUES

Cross-examination is conducted using leading questions. In order to control the financial expert witness's response to leading questions, they will likely be asked using either incremental or sequential methods. The incremental method rejects broad, sweeping questions in favor of inquiries broken down into smaller parts to reduce the possibility for a lengthy response from the financial expert witness. Sequential questioning asks questions in a specific leading order, for example, a chain of events, usually moving from undisputed and irrefutable facts to more controversial ones.

Either method can be used for the "other shoe never drops" method of questioning. The "other shoe never drops" is a method by which the opposing counsel leads the trier of fact to a conclusion as a natural and evident consequence of incremental or sequential questioning methods. The magic to this method is that the final question leading to an answer from the financial expert witness about the conclusion is never asked, leaving the financial expert witness frustrated and confused.

Regardless of the type of leading question, opposing counsel will rarely let the financial expert witness answer a leading question with an unexpected, unresponsive, or rambling answer. Such responses will be dealt with by repeating the same question over and over again, until the desired answer is elicited. If the financial expert witness fails to cooperate, it may be met with a dramatic stare intended to get the attention of the trier of fact. If all else fails, the judge will be asked to instruct the witness to answer the question.

Using the methods described previously, there are several proven cross-examination techniques that may be employed by opposing legal counsel. In general, however, these techniques fall into two categories—constructive and destructive. Constructive techniques, as implied by the name, are used to build the case for opposing legal counsel. Conversely, destructive techniques destroy the financial expert witness. Both kinds of cross-examination use leading questions to accomplish the opposing attorney's objectives. The financial expert witness should be familiar with both types of techniques to effectively survive cross-examination.

Constructive

Constructive cross-examination techniques use the financial expert witness to build the case for the opposing party. This can be achieved by asking questions that effectively narrow the opinions and usefulness of the testimony of the financial expert witness. Alternatively, an opposing party's story can be told through the financial expert witness by soliciting agreement with an opposing financial expert's methods, principles, facts, and assumptions, thereby building the credibility of the opposing expert.

For example, the following set of questions and answers shows how an opposing attorney may use constructive cross-examination techniques to get agreement from the financial expert witness that an opposing financial expert witness's method and facts are reasonable:

> *Question: There are a number of factors that contribute to the success of a restaurant, right?*
>
> Answer: Yes.
>
> *Question: Menu prices can make a difference, correct?*
>
> Answer: Right.
>
> *Question: Quality of the food can make a difference, right?*
>
> Answer: Right.
>
> *Question: Advertising can make a difference, true?*
>
> Answer: True.
>
> *Question: Atmosphere can make a difference, correct?*
>
> Answer: Yes.
>
> *Question: Location is an important factor, but it is only one factor among several factors, correct?*

Answer: Yes.

Question: You criticized the other expert in this case for not adequately considering location, right?

Answer: Right.

Question: The other expert did perform an analysis of the restaurant's advertising, didn't he?

Answer: Yes.

Question: It is possible for advertising to compensate for an inconvenient location, isn't that correct?

Answer: Yes.

Question: The other expert also analyzed the restaurant's menu pricing, right?

Answer: Right.

Question: Low prices can compensate for location, true?

Answer: Possibly.

Question: So, you would agree that Mr. Dobbs considered at least two factors that could offset the location issue, correct?

Answer: Yes, he considered those factors.

Question: The relative importance of those two factors is a matter of judgment, isn't it?

Answer: Yes.

Question: You can't deny that advertising and pricing could be more important than location in some situations, correct?

Answer: Depends.

Question: In this case, you and the other expert disagree on these factors, correct?

Answer: Yes.[1]

Destructive

Destructive cross-examination is what strikes fear in the hearts of financial expert witnesses everywhere. These techniques are intended to break the financial expert witness and cause the trier of fact to disregard anything said by him. Effective destructive cross-examination techniques will raise significant doubts in the minds of the trier of fact about the credibility and reliability of the financial expert witness and the testimony given. Here are a few destructive techniques that may be used:

- **Challenge the financial expert witness's qualifications**. The opposing attorney may attack perceived shortcomings in the breadth, depth, or relevance of the financial expert witness's qualifications to testify. In connection with such attempts, the opposing legal counsel may contrast the financial expert witness's qualifications against her opposing financial expert witness, perhaps even asking the financial expert witness to confirm or endorse the opposing expert's qualifications.

- **Impeach the financial expert witness**. Impeachment of the financial expert witness is an attempt by opposing legal counsel to make the financial expert witness look like a liar, or at best a flip-flopper. Impeachment is usually performed by comparing the financial expert witness's trial testimony to the deposition, the expert report, prior case expert reports or testimony, published material, or public statements. In today's world, social media is also increasingly being used to impeach.

- **Reproach the financial expert witness's work**. Each case will have bad evidence, imperfect facts and data, and judgment calls made by the financial expert witness. Opposing legal counsel will try to expose these matters and turn them into fatal faults. Exposure areas may include incomplete data sets, untested facts and assumptions provided by client legal counsel, failure to look at alternatives, overlooking the importance of evidence, work not performed, individuals not interviewed, relevance of facts and data, alternative methods and principles, differing professional guidance, or contrary learned treatises.

- **Show that the financial expert witness lacks objectivity**. One of the easiest ways to raise issues about the credibility and reliability of the financial expert witness is for the opposing legal counsel to show a lack of objectivity. Among other ways, this can be done by demonstrating that the financial expert witness: (1) has a bias for either plaintiff or defendant work; (2) has been retained disproportionately by a single industry or organization; (3) has a prior business or personal relationship with the client, client attorney, or client law firm; (4) has charged excessive fees or has the appearance of contingent fees because of unpaid billings; or (5) has a blind spot due to prior positions taken or endorsed.

- **Demonstrate sensitivity of facts, data, and assumptions used by the financial expert witness**. An effective way for opposing legal counsel to attack the financial expert witness is to demonstrate how facts, data, and assumptions used by the financial expert witness are subject to differing interpretations. To do this, opposing legal counsel will simply replace information used by the financial expert witness with alternative facts and data that significantly change the results. This can be especially effective if the degree of certainty held by the financial expert witness is just over the line of reasonably certain.

▪ **Point out dependent opinions held by the financial expert witness**. The financial expert witness may have been asked to form opinions in reliance of the work and opinions of other experts. For example, the financial expert witness may have computed damages for an industry based on the expected future state of the industry. However, the financial expert witness was asked by the client attorney to rely on the future growth rate of that industry based on the opinion of an industry expert. If the financial expert witness does this, the opposing attorney will point out to the trier of fact that the opinions of the financial expert witness are dependent on another expert and if that other expert is wrong, the financial expert witness's opinion is unreliable.

 ## TEN COMMANDMENTS OF CROSS-EXAMINATION

Instructive to the financial expert witness are the generally accepted cross-examination principles used by attorneys. These principles are based on an address given by Irving Younger in 1975 and are commonly referred to as the Ten Commandments of Cross-Examination.

1. **Be Brief**

    Be brief, short and succinct. Why? Reason 1: Chances are you are screwing up. The shorter the time spent, the less you will screw up. Reason 2: A simple cross that restates the important part of the story in your terms is more easily absorbed and understood by the jury. You should never try to make more than three points on cross-examination. Two points are better than three and one point is better than two.

2. **Use Plain Words**

    The jury can understand short questions and plain words. Drop the fifty-dollar word in favor of the two-dollar word. "Drive your car" instead of "operate your vehicle."

3. **Ask Only Leading Questions**

   The law forbids questions on direct examination that suggest the answer. The lawyer is not competent to testify. On cross-examination the law permits questions that suggest the answer and allows the attorney to put his words in the witnesses' mouth. Cross-examination, therefore, specifically permits you to take control of the witness, take him where you want to go, and tell your important point to the jury through the witness. Not asking controlled leading questions leaves too much wiggle room. What happened next? I would like to clear up a couple of points you made on direct? These questions are the antithesis of an effective cross-examination. Any questions which permit the witness to restate, explain or clarify the direct examination is a mistake. You should put the witness on autopilot so that all of the answers are series of yes, yes, yes.

4. **Be Prepared**

   Never ask a question that you do not know the answer to. Cross is not a fishing expedition in which you uncover new facts or new surprises at the trial.

5. **Listen**

   Listen to the answer. For some, cross-examination of an important witness causes stage fright; it confuses the mind and panic sets in. You have a hard time just getting the first question out, and you're generally thinking about the next question and not listening to the answer.

6. **Do Not Quarrel**

   Do not quarrel with the witness on cross-examination. When the answer to your question is absurd, false, irrational, contradictory or the like: Stop, sit down. Resist the temptation to respond with "how can you say that, or how dare you make such an outrageous claim?" The answer to the question often elicits a response, which explains away the absurdity and rehabilitates the witness.

7. **Avoid Repetition**

   Never allow a witness to repeat on cross-examination what he said on direct examination. Why? The more times it is repeated, the more likely the jury is to believe it. Cross-examination should involve questions that have nothing to do with the direct examination. The examination should not follow the script of the direct examination.

Cross-examination commandments	Financial expert witness response
Be brief	Be brief
Use plain words	Use plain words
Use only leading questions	Expect only leading questions
Be prepared	Be prepared
Listen	Listen
Do not quarrel	Do not quarrel
Avoid repetition	Repeat key points
Disallow witness explanation	Be patient for redirect
Limit questioning	Be thankful
Save for summation	Anticipate closing statements

EXHIBIT 18.1   Response to the Ten Commandments of Cross-Examination

8. Disallow Witness Explanation
Never permit the witness to explain anything on cross-examination. That is for your adversary to do.

9. Limit Questioning
Don't ask the one question too many. Stop when you have made your point. Leave the argument for the jury.

10. Save for Summation
Save the ultimate point for summation. A prepared, clear and simple leading cross-examination that does not argue the case can best be brought together in final summation.[2]

The Ten Commandments of Cross-Examination provide important guidance to the financial expert witness. Exhibit 18.1 summarizes the response the financial expert witness might have to knowledge about these commandments.

SURVIVING CROSS-EXAMINATION

There is no secret formula for surviving cross-examination. Preparation and practice help, but only live experience can fully educate the financial expert witness about what to expect. Even with that experience, the human element makes it impossible to predict with precision what will happen in cross-examination. There are, however, a few pointers in addition to other instructions provided in this book that may help the financial expert witness survive cross-examination.

Demeanor

The financial expert witness must try to stay calm, cool, and collected during cross-examination. The general rule is to have the same demeanor in cross-examination as was displayed in direct examination. Try to be helpful to the trier of fact, remembering that any problems that surface in cross-examination can be mopped up in redirect examination. If the opposing attorney causes strife, then try to imagine her as a student who is angry because she doesn't understand the lesson. Alternatively, look at the opposing legal counsel's forehead and avoid the eyes when listening to questions. The point is to try to not make it personal. The more personal it feels, the more likely it is to affect demeanor. In no circumstances should the financial expert witness appear to be irritated, defensive, evasive, argumentative, angry, or arrogant.

Be Reasonable and Professional

One of the most difficult lessons for most financial expert witnesses to learn is to be conscious of what a reasonable professional would say or do in the circumstances. There is nothing more damaging to a financial expert witness than an illogical and unreasonable disagreement with opposing legal counsel over an obvious point. If a mistake or error is revealed, the financial expert witness has to admit it. As the saying goes, "If you mess up, 'fess up.'" In addition, if a matter is raised that calls for an obvious concession—concede. This includes hypotheticals proposed by the opposing legal counsel. In most cases, the financial expert witness can deny the relevance of the hypothetical to the case at hand and still answer reasonably. Prolonged bickering over plain-sight issues simply tarnishes the credibility of the financial expert witness.

Never Lose Sight of Redirect Examination

Inevitably, opposing legal counsel will score some points in cross-examination. The financial expert witness must resist attempts to recover from this damage during cross-examination. Instead, remember that redirect examination can be used to rehabilitate the financial expert witness. Don't worry, client legal counsel is listening and will repair any significant harm when it is her turn again. However, there are rare instances when client legal counsel misses a key point to be covered in redirect examination. With that in mind, the financial expert witness may want develop a way to alert client legal counsel about matters to be considered for handling in redirect examination.

Answering "Yes" or "No" Questions

There will be times when answering "yes" or "no" to a leading question posed by opposing legal counsel is impossible, or at least misleading. In these situations, the financial expert witness has few choices. He or she can tell the trier of fact that a "yes" or "no" response is not possible or would be misleading, and not answer. Such a response seldom works with a talented opposing attorney. Alternatively, the financial expert witness can establish a normal pattern of response that begins with an explanation and ends with the "yes" or "no" desired by opposing legal counsel. The following example demonstrates this technique.

> *Question: Did you consider the effects of competition on your work?*
> Answer: I don't believe competitive factors are appropriate, no.

Another thing for the financial expert witness to remember about a "yes" or "no" response to leading questions, often the trier of fact will fail to detect the importance of the answer if a calm and undisturbed response is offered. This is particularly true when a battery of leading questions calls for "yes" or "no" answers and the response cadence is maintained by the financial expert witness. Let's look at the next set of questions and answers to understand this idea.

> *Question: Did you look at pricing?*
> Answer: Yes.
> *Question: Did you analyze location?*
> Answer: Yes.
> *Question: Did you review personnel?*
> Answer: Yes.
> *Question: Did you look at competition?*
> Answer: No.
> *Question: Did you review products offered?*
> Answer: Yes.

Imagine these questions answered by the financial expert witness in a very confident and nonchalant manner. If so, the "no" response may not have been fully noticed or appreciated by the trier of fact. Of course, it will be rare when the "no" response is not immediately pounced on by an attentive opposing counsel. Nonetheless, this technique may be useful.

Avoid Smart-Aleck Answers

It is sometimes tempting for the financial expert witness to respond to opposing legal counsel in a smart-aleck fashion. Consider the following:

Question: The method you used was one you used before?

Answer: Yes, but I am not sure you got the concept. Can I try to help you?

Question: Did you consider competition in your analysis?

Answer: I can't answer that "yes" or "no" because we would both be wrong.

Responses like these are likely to anger the opposing legal counsel and may result in an admonishment by the judge. Neither outcome will make cross-examination any easier. Any cleverness intended by the financial expert witness is more likely to be interpreted as disrespect, which can harm the financial expert witness.

 ## RE-CROSS-EXAMINATION

After the conclusion of redirect examination, opposing legal counsel will be offered the chance to conduct re-cross-examination. Re-cross-examination is limited, by general rule, to matters brought out in redirect examination. The financial expert witness should treat re-cross-examination just like cross-examination. The only caveat is that there may not be another opportunity to repair any damage that may be done.

 ## COMING UP

In the next few chapters we discuss alternative dispute resolution, starting with mediation.

NOTES

1. Reprinted with permission from *Expert Testimony*, 2nd ed., by Steve Lubet and Elizabeth Boals. Copyright owned by the National Institute for Trial Advocacy. A full copy of this publication may be purchased at www.lexisnexis.com/nita/product.aspx?prodid=prod-US-NITA-FBA0959#table-of-contents.
2. Summarized from Irving Younger, *The Art of Cross-Examination*. The Section of Litigation Monograph Series, No. 1 (American Bar Association Section on Litigation), adapted from a speech given by Irving Younger at the ABA Annual Meeting in Montreal, Canada (August 1975).

PART FOUR

IV

Alternative Dispute Resolution

CHAPTER NINETEEN

Alternative Dispute Resolution: Mediation

 ## MEDIATION PROCESS

Mediation is like a tennis match in which the players are blindfolded. Each of the players knows how to win the game, but each does not know where the opponent is on the court. One player strikes the ball over the net in the form of an offer for compromise delivered by a mediator. However, that player does not know where on the court the opponent stands. Is he on the baseline waiting to volley right back with a counteroffer from the mediator? Or, is he at the net waiting to strike down the next offer quickly and definitively and potentially end the negotiation? In either case, swinging away is the strategy to end the dispute.

Mediation is one of the fastest-growing and increasingly popular forms of alternative dispute resolution. Mediation is a process entered into by disputing parties wherein a neutral party facilitates a nonbinding conciliation to resolve a dispute. Although nonbinding, the disputing parties' usual intent is to use the mediation agreement as the basis for formal settlement and resolution that is binding.

Entering into mediation is typically voluntary; however, it is common for the court to require mediation before trial. A pretrial conference is required under the Federal Rules of Civil Procedure, Rule 26(f), which can include mediation activities. The rule states, in part, that the purpose for such a conference is for the disputing parties to discuss the "possibilities for promptly settling or resolving the case." For example, the United States District Court, Middle District of Florida, has a local rule description of why a case is referred to mediation that states, ". . . the Court has a duty to the other cases on its docket to ensure that all possible avenues of settlement in this case are explored prior to trial."[1] Regardless of the means, the voluntary nature of mediation is important to the process, because the motivation and commitment of the disputing parties to resolve their issues out of court is critical to success.

The mediation process can take several forms. However, it generally includes the following activities:

- Introductions of the parties and the mediator
- Opening remarks from the mediator
- Presentation of each of the disputing parties' opening positions
- Private meetings between the mediator and each of the disputing parties
- The exchange of offers and counteroffers of settlement
- Agree to settlement terms, or terminate discussions
- Execution of settlement documents, or continuing conciliation dialogue between the disputing parties and the mediator

The mediation process is illustrated in Exhibit 19.1.

FINANCIAL EXPERT PARTICIPATION IN MEDIATION

Participation in the mediation process is a unique experience for the financial expert. The financial expert assists with, and attends, mediation proceedings only when asked by the client legal counsel. Mediation proceedings and the materials exchanged (i.e., settlement offers) have strict restrictions regarding disclosure and the financial expert must adhere to these restrictions. The Federal Rules of Evidence, Rule 408, prohibit the use of civil offers to compromise as admissible evidence in court. In addition, the American Bar Association has guidelines regarding the ethical use of information exchanged in settlement negotiations.[2]

Financial expert mediation assistance requests typically involve an analysis of the strengths of the client's positions and the quantification of damages. Of course, potential weaknesses are also assessed. These analyses and computations are often summarized and documented using demonstratives

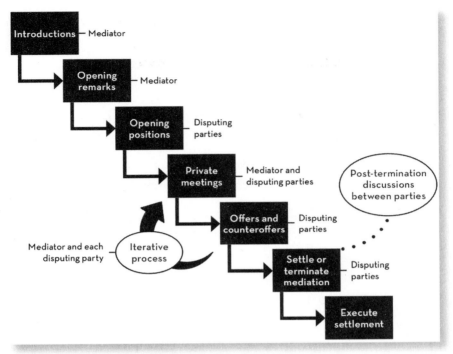

EXHIBIT 19.1 Mediation Process

that may be useful during mediation. Such work product and demonstratives should be marked by the financial expert with restricted-use legends indicating that use is limited to settlement discussions, unless otherwise instructed by the client attorney. In addition, if the mediation takes place before the disclosure requirement for financial expert witnesses, the work product and demonstrative may exclude any reference to the financial expert and his employer or firm based on the directions received from the client legal counsel.

The financial expert may be asked to attend the mediation hearing. The reason for such requests varies, but in most cases it is to provide real-time consultation about offers, counteroffers, and issue analysis. It may also be a way to let the opponent know that the client is serious about the negotiations and that capable critical resources are available here and now to drive a bargain. Therefore, the financial expert should be sufficiently prepared to immediately handle case-specific technical issues and damages inquiries. However, in many cases the client is not compelled to disclose the financial expert as a possible expert witness at the time of mediation. So, the financial expert should take precautions not to be detected, even at the mediation, without the expressed consent of the client attorney.

Mediation proceedings can be exciting at times and extremely boring at other times. After the initial introductions and the presentation of opening positions, the disputing parties are sequestered from each other by placing them in separate rooms (i.e., conference rooms, hotel rooms, etc.). The mediator then meets privately with each of the disputing parties in their separate rooms, using all ethical means to elicit an offer of settlement for the opposing party to consider. The mediator then shuttles the offers and counteroffers to the other party in hopes of closing the gap and reaching conciliation.

The back-and-forth exchange of offers and counteroffers can take a long time and be quite tedious. It is not uncommon for hours to pass between exchanges. That means that the financial expert will likely have a lot of time to get to know the client and client-associated parties in close quarters. These long, quiet periods may also allow the financial expert to undertake activities unrelated to the mediation, like handling business e-mails. Therefore, the financial expert should be prepared mentally, and have the resources available on-site, to make the most of these waiting periods.

> An ounce of mediation is worth a pound of arbitration and a ton of litigation.
>
> — *Joseph Grynbaum*

 ## MEDIATION ACTIVITIES

The activities in the mediation process may vary from matter to matter based on the facts and circumstances of the dispute, the disputing parties, and the preferences of the mediator. Putting aside for a moment these possibilities, the parties and activities in the mediation process are generally explained below.

Parties in Attendance

The parties in attendance at mediation include the disputing parties, their legal counsel, and the mediator. Depending on the dispute, an insurance representative, perhaps an adjuster, may be at the mediation to make decisions on proposed offers and counteroffers potentially covered as insured claims. It is also possible that the financial expert, or other experts, will be asked to attend by the client attorney. Mediation proceedings are not formally recorded by a court reporter, unless agreed to in advance by the disputing parties.

One of the most crucial participants in the mediation proceeding is a party legally authorized to make and accept settlement offers for each of the disputing parties. Nothing is more frustrating than to spend hours in mediation only to discover one of the disputing parties failed to bring, or have ready access to, a person with the legal authority to approve an offer of compromise and settlement.

Introductions

The mediator opens the mediation by bringing the disputing parties together for introductions. At this time, the mediator provides her credentials, experience, and qualifications to the disputing parties. Then, one by one, each party in attendance provides his or her name, title, and organization and states the party he or she is associated with, or representing. The financial expert may not be invited by the client legal counsel to join in introductions if expert witness disclosure is sensitive at the time of mediation. If invited, the financial expert should confirm in advance of the mediation what introductory remarks are appropriate. The names of the parties in attendance are usually captured and circulated to the disputing parties for use in the mediation.

Opening Remarks

After introductions, the mediator provides the disputing parties with the rules and protocols for the mediation. It is common in these opening remarks for the mediator to reiterate why the disputing parties are convened and whether they are there voluntarily, or otherwise. The mediator is provided the positions and arguments of the disputing parties before the mediation. Using knowledge obtained from studying these materials, the mediator may provide a brief overview of her understanding about the dispute. In addition, confidentiality, process, and logistics are described. At this time, the parties typically agree to use a private-meeting resolution process, during which the parties are separated and the mediator conducts private caucuses with each of the disputing parties throughout the duration of the mediation.

Oftentimes, this is the first time all of the disputing parties have been together in the same room and talking since the dispute arose, so the mediator may attempt to foster rapport and civility. The mediator recognizes the goal is to settle the matter once and for all during the mediation. In that vein, an experienced mediator will embellish common ground, stress compromise, appeal for flexibility, and ask the disputing parties to agree on a number of matters related to the mediation. Concluding the opening remarks of the mediator is a question-and-answer session that allows the disputing parties to clarify mediator comments and get answers to matters of concern.

Opening Positions

After the opening remarks, the mediator will give each of the disputing parties the opportunity to present their positions and arguments to the opposing party. This is not intended to be an exercise to convince the mediator, who has no actual authority to make any decision about the dispute. Instead, this is a pleading made directly to an opposing party in a face-to-face manner. Usually, this is the first time each of the disputing parties has heard the entire story about the dispute from the perspective of the opposing party.

This presentation may include all of the parties in attendance, or be limited to the disputing parties and their legal counsel, or just legal counsel. The financial expert should ask for instructions from the client legal counsel about the appropriateness of attending the presentation of the disputing parties' positions and supporting arguments. In many cases, the financial expert is excused from this part of the proceedings.

Private Meetings

Assuming that the disputing parties agreed to use a caucusing method, the mediator shows each of the disputing parties to separate rooms in order to conduct private meetings between the mediator and the disputing parties for the remainder of the mediation. These private meetings are used by the mediator to discover confidential information that can be used to broker a settlement. Depending on a number of things, the mediator may interact with each of the disputing parties using diplomacy, common sense, reality checks, aggression, or complacency. The mediator may try to involve the financial expert in the conversation. For the financial expert in attendance, this can be uncomfortable at times.

Exchange of Offers and Counteroffers

The result of the private meetings with each of the disputing parties is a settlement offer, an impasse, or termination of the mediation. A settlement offer is taken under consideration by each opposing party and will result in acceptance, a counteroffer, or rejection. Among other reasons, an impasse can result when the disputing parties desire a settlement, but certain tangential issues prevent it from happening at the time of the mediation. Of course, termination of the mediation indicates that the disputing parties have admitted that the mediation is unlikely to result in an agreement acceptable to both parties, thereby making continuance futile.

If a settlement offer is made, the mediator shuttles it to the opposing party and delivers it with messaging intended to facilitate agreement. After stating her thoughts, the mediator leaves the parties alone to discuss matters. Alternatively, the mediator calls the disputing parties together for the exchange of offers. The party receiving the offer considers its merits, which may include requested insights from the financial expert in attendance. Even if the financial expert is not at the mediation, it is possible that the client may need timely advice regarding these deliberations. Therefore, arrangements for on-call financial expert services should be discussed with the client attorney in advance of the mediation. If the offer is unacceptable, a counteroffer is prepared, or the mediation is stalemated and headed toward termination. In either case, the mediator is told of the decision and asked to communicate the results to the opposing party.

The negotiation process related to offers and counteroffers is part art and part science. The process is art in the sense that posturing, hyperbole, acting, and emotion may be integral to the process. The process is part science because the negotiation is a numbers game. Costs must be carefully estimated as a potential trade-off to the mediated settlement, such as the avoided costs of taking a case through litigation and to trial, the time value of money, future business relationships, and the nuisance factor.

In rare situations, the financial expert may be asked by the mediator to meet and confer with an opposing financial expert with the expectation that objective experts working together may be better able to reach an accord. If permission is granted by the client legal counsel, the financial expert may join any such requested conference. However, the financial expert must be abundantly cautious not to disclose sensitive case strategy or legal advice shared with the underlying client by client legal counsel. Participation in a joint session of the opposing financial experts should be focused on the calculation of a settlement amount, and little else.

The negotiation often comes down to a well-crafted strategy to narrow the gap of monetary offers by splitting the difference. Neither disputing party particularly likes this strategy, but it is a proven one. For example, one of the parties will send an offer to an opposing party of $1 million.

The opposing party counters at $250,000. That prompts a thoughtfully timed response of $750,000. In turn, this compels the other party to offer $300,000. A final offer is tendered of $625,000, which is accepted. In this example, each disputing party compromised $375,000. The party offering $250,000 raised its offer by $375,000 to $625,000. Likewise, the party offering $1 million lowered its offer by $375,000 to get to the agreed-upon amount of settlement.

Agreement or Termination

If the disputing parties have reached a settlement as part of the mediation, the principles of the agreement are discussed and memorialized for the formal final documents to be prepared at a later date. If termination is contemplated by either of the disputing parties, the mediator may use this as an incentive to encourage more realistic bargaining. After all, failure to mediate a settlement likely leads to an escalation of the dispute to more formal, and expensive, litigation proceedings.

Continuing Dialogue

Even if the disputing parties terminate the mediation, many mediators facilitate continued dialogue between the disputing parties afterward. The mediator will communicate with each of the disputing parties, sharing permitted information between the opposing parties in an effort to resolve the dispute. In some cases, settlement during the mediation hearing is hampered because the disputing parties learn previously unknown information about the dispute and they need time to research and contemplate this news. Regardless, the mediator knows from experience that keeping open the lines of communication will increase the chances for an alternative dispute resolution.

In true dialogue, both sides are willing to change.

— *Thich Nhat Hanh*

 COMING UP

Another commonly used method for alternative dispute resolution is arbitration. In the following chapters we explore arbitration proceedings.

NOTES

1. United States District Court, Middle District of Florida, Federal Court Mediation, Description of the Process, Rev. 2/94, available at www.flmd.uscourts.gov/forms/Civil/MedDesc.pdf.
2. *Ethical Guidelines for Settlement Negotiations*, American Bar Association Section of Litigation Special Project, ABA (August 2002), available at www.americanbar.org/content/dam/aba/migrated/2011_build/dispute_resolution/settlementnegotiations.authcheckdam.pdf.

CHAPTER TWENTY

Alternative Dispute Resolution: Arbitration

 ## THE ARBITRATION PROCESS

Arbitration is a frequently used form of alternative dispute resolution. It is less formal than litigation, but formalities are built into the process to ensure binding awards will be legally enforceable. Arbitration proceedings are often built into contracts as the agreed-upon form of dispute resolution. It is also a preferred form of resolution over formal litigation because of the perception that arbitration offers: (1) more control for the disputing parties, (2) an expeditious resolution, (3) a cost-effective solution, and (4) more privacy. However, because arbitration is less formal than litigation and the authorities of the arbitrator less powerful than a judge, arbitration can at times feel like a rodeo—hang on to that bull because it can be a fast, bumpy ride!

Arbitration is a process entered into by adversarial disputing parties wherein a neutral party, called an arbitrator, serves as the trier of fact to resolve the dispute. Arbitration awards are typically binding to the disputing parties. However, advisory awards are allowed if such treatment is agreed to in advance by the disputing parties. The arbitration process loosely follows the steps in the litigation process, with a few notable exceptions as discussed next.

STRUCTURE OF ARBITRATION

Similar to formal litigation, arbitration has a plaintiff party, called a claimant, and a defendant party, called a respondent. Although there are a number of ways to initiate an arbitration proceeding, it is common for one party to notify another of a dispute and the intent to exercise a contractual right to arbitration. Absent any contractual right, disputing parties can voluntarily agree to initiate arbitration proceedings.

Once arbitration is agreed upon by the disputing parties, a neutral third party or tribunal is sought, selected, and engaged to serve as the arbitrator or arbitration panel. An arbitration panel, usually consisting of three arbitration panelists, is often called for in larger, more complex, disputes. In many cases, the selection of the arbitrator or panel is facilitated by an organization specializing in alternative dispute resolution. Examples of U.S.-based organizations include American Arbitration Association (www.adr.org), JAMS, The Resolution Experts (www.jamsadr.com), and the International Institute for Conflict Prevention & Resolution (www.cpradr.org). Once retained by the disputing parties, these organizations provide the names of qualified neutral arbitrators to the disputing parties for consideration. In addition, they provide administrative due process for the arbitration proceedings that must be adhered to by the participating parties. If an alternative dispute resolution organization is not used by the disputing parties, private parties are selected and engaged to serve as the arbitrator or tribunal.

U.S.-Based Alternative Dispute Resolution Organizations

- American Arbitration Association (AAA)
- JAMS, The Resolution Experts
- The International Institute for Conflict Prevention & Resolution (CPR)

Once an arbitrator or arbitration panel is engaged by the disputing parties, administrative protocols are agreed upon for the proceedings. Such protocols normally include rules and procedures for preparing and serving arbitration filings, rules of evidence, discovery, pre-arbitration sessions, and the arbitration hearing.

If nonbinding arbitration is selected by the disputing parties, the arbitrator or panel hears the dispute and delivers an award that is strictly advisory. An advisory determination may be delivered orally together with arbitrator or panel commentary on the merits of each disputing parties' case. A nonbinding award is useful to narrow the issues, to show the disputing parties the strengths and weaknesses of their positions, and to drive future settlement.

If binding arbitration is the ultimate choice for the disputing parties, the arbitrator's or panel's determination and award becomes legally enforceable once issued. Binding arbitration awards are rarely appealable, with reversals typically limited to fraud or gross procedural error. Regardless, many binding arbitration awards are submitted to the court for formal confirmation and recordation in an effort to avoid future controversies and provide for formal legal enforcement, if necessary.

The activities in the arbitration process may vary from case to case based on the protocols adopted by the disputing parties. In general, arbitration activities include the following:

- Notice of demand for arbitration
- Identification, selection, and retention of arbitrator or panel
- Agreement on arbitration administrative protocols
- Demand for arbitration
- Response to demand for arbitration
- Discovery
- Pre-arbitration hearing conferences and sessions;
- Pre-arbitration hearing preparation
- Arbitration hearing
- Post-arbitration memoranda and consideration period
- Arbitration award notification

The arbitration process is depicted in Exhibit 20.1.

 ## ARBITRATION ACTIVITIES

The disputing parties enter into arbitration and agree to have the process administered by a set of protocols that control the activities in the process. Surely, these protocols and activities can vary; however, there are some common activities that are a part of every arbitration process. These activities are summarized next.

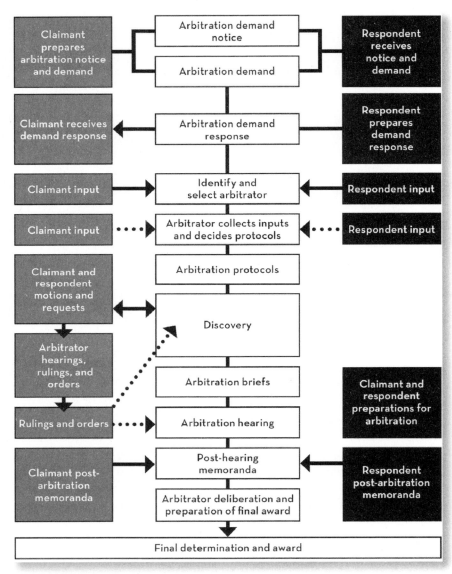

EXHIBIT 20.1   Arbitration Process

Notice of Demand for Arbitration

The initiation of arbitration usually begins with a dialog between two parties about a potential dispute. As this discussion escalates or terminates prematurely, a decision will be made to demand the commencement of an arbitration proceeding to resolve the dispute. Once that decision is made, the party to be the claimant gives the opposing party notice of the intent to file a demand for arbitration. This notice may include a brief description of the dispute and claims for relief, together with any legal basis to support the demand for arbitration and compel voluntary participation. Such a notice may be given orally; however, it is traditionally done in writing to preserve any rights related to the initiation of an arbitration demand as the claimant.

Identification, Selection, and Retention of Arbitrator or Panel

After the notice of intent to demand arbitration has been communicated, the disputing parties reach agreement to proceed to arbitration. In some cases, the prospective respondent may initiate formal litigation to affirm the legal obligation to participate in arbitration. One of the first steps in the arbitration process is the identification, selection, and retention of a neutral third-party arbitrator or arbitration panel. Whether this activity is facilitated by a professional alternative dispute organization or handled exclusively by the disputing parties, it involves sourcing qualified candidates, confirming the absence of conflicts of interest, interviewing possible arbitrators, selecting an arbitrator or panel that is mutually acceptable to both disputing parties, and engaging the arbitrator or panel. If an arbitration panel is used as the tribunal for the dispute, the panel will usually consist of three panelists, an odd number to avoid deadlocks, with one of the panelists named as the chairperson.

Agreement on Arbitration Administrative Protocols

As mentioned earlier, arbitration administrative protocols are the rules and procedures the disputing parties and the arbitrator or panel agree to follow to conduct the arbitration proceedings. If the arbitration is controlled by contractual language agreed to by the disputing parties and that language calls for the retention of a professional alternative dispute organization, the vast majority of the arbitration administrative protocols will be provided by that organization. If private arbitrators and tribunals are to be used, the disputing parties frequently make inquiries and suggestions to the prospective candidates during the selection process in an effort to influence and craft the protocols to be used. In any case, the arbitrator typically has wide-ranging authority to dictate to the disputing parties what the arbitration administrative protocols will be for the proceedings.

Commonly in an initial conference between the disputing parties and the arbitrator or panel, the arbitrator or panel will provide instructions to the disputing parties on the following types of matters:

- Form and content of written submissions and disclosures
- Arbitration scheduling, similar to a scheduling or calendaring order in civil litigation
- *Ex parte* and other communications
- Pre-arbitration sessions to hear the equivalent of civil litigation motion arguments
- Process for making rulings and issuing orders
- Evidentiary rules
- Arbitration hearing protocols, including, without limitation, location, duration, time allotments for each disputing party to present cases and limitations on the number of witnesses, and the preparation of a formal record by a court reporter
- The timing, form, and content of the arbitration award

It is well-established in the courts that a binding arbitration award is legally enforceable, with limited exceptions. These exceptions generally include any arbitration award deemed by the court to have been secured by fraud or the improper exclusion of material evidence. Of course, cases have also been made related to unjust arbitrator or panel bias, procedural failures, and overreaching authority and powers.

The following paraphrased anonymous quote demonstrates the concern seasoned arbitrators have about having an arbitration award set aside by the courts.

> I've been told that the only way an award from this arbitration can be reversed is due to fraud or by not letting evidence in. So, I am inclined to let everything in and consider the weight, if any, I give the evidence.
>
> —Anonymous arbitrator

Demand for Arbitration

Once arbitration administrative protocols are in place, much like a complaint in civil litigation, the claimant prepares and delivers a formal written demand for arbitration to the opposing party respondent. It is possible for the demand for arbitration to be prepared prior to engagement of the arbitrator or panel if the disputing parties elected to use a professional alternative dispute resolution organization with published and publicly available arbitration administrative protocols. The demand for arbitration will normally set forth: (1) the parties to the dispute, (2) the appropriateness of arbitration for the hearing of the dispute, (3) a background on the matter and a relationship history, (4) the allegations of wrongdoing, (5) all claims for relief, (6) and the legal support for allegations and claims. The demand for arbitration may be accompanied by and reference relevant documents and evidence integral to a full understanding of the demand.

Response to Demand for Arbitration

Once again, in a fashion resembling civil litigation, the respondent will formally respond in writing to the claimant's demand for arbitration. The response agrees with, or disputes, the facts asserted by the claimant and may offer affirmative defenses to the allegations. In certain situations, a counterdemand is included with the response, or it may be made using a separate written demand.

Discovery

Like the civil litigation process, there is discovery in arbitration. However, it is frequently more informal than civil litigation, partially because the arbitrator or panel lacks the legal authority to issue subpoenas or orders compelling discovery compliance. That is not to say that arbitration is free from contentious adversarial discovery disputes because it is more informal. Most large and complex arbitrations will have several discovery complaints levied by the disputing parties that require the intercession of the arbitrator or panel. Discovery in arbitration is subject to the administrative protocols adopted in the proceedings and the judgment of the arbitrator or panel. Discovery may include stipulations, interrogatories, the production of evidence, and depositions or other sworn statements from witnesses.

Pre-Arbitration Hearing Conferences and Sessions

Most arbitration proceedings have pre-arbitration hearing conferences and sessions where the arbitrator or panel hears evidence, complaints, and arguments from the disputing parties on a wide variety of matters. These conferences and sessions can be conducted in person, telephonically, by videoconference, or simply using an exchange of e-mails. The result of such exchanges can include written or oral interpretations of arbitration protocols, official rulings, admonishments, and sanctions or informational updates from the arbitrator or panel.

Pre-Arbitration Hearing Preparation

The approach to preparation for an arbitration hearing parallels the approach used to prepare for a trial in civil litigation. Among many other things, evidence anticipated to be presented is identified, exhibits are prepared and marked, disclosures exchanged, and direct and cross-examination prepared. This is also when the final case presentation and defense strategies are determined. The evidence is readied for presentation, witnesses are told the order of testimony and prepared, and opening and closing statements authored and practiced.

Arbitration Hearing

The parties attending an arbitration hearing include the disputing parties and their legal counsel, the arbitrator or panelists, paraprofessionals assisting legal counsel, and a court reporter, if agreed to in advance by the parties, which is typical. The arbitration hearing can be held in a conference room located within one of the disputing parties' offices. However, a neutral location is often chosen at the offices of a professional alternative dispute resolution organization, the neutral arbitrator, or a rented facility. The format of the hearing may vary based on the arbitration administrative protocols, the whims of the arbitrator or panel, and available space and technology. In most arbitration hearings, there are opening statements, the presentation of the claimants' positions and witnesses, the presentation of the respondents' defenses and witnesses, testimony of rebuttal witnesses, and closing arguments. Each of these matters is briefly described below.

Opening Statements

Opening statements are made by each of the disputing parties. The claimant goes first, followed by the respondent. Each of the disputing parties' attorneys put on opening statements and they have significant latitude on what can be said and presented. Opening statements are expressed advocacy for the client's case and may include demonstratives and theatrics.

Claimants Case in Chief and Witnesses

After opening statements have been delivered by each of the disputing parties, the arbitration hearing moves to the next phase, wherein the claimant puts on their case in chief and witnesses. If a counterdemand has been filed, the claimant may also address these claims at this time, although it is often prudent to wait until the counterclaimant delivers their case and witnesses before offering any such defense. The proceedings are presided over by the arbitrator or panel, who may actively ask questions directed to legal counsel or witnesses. In addition, the respondent's legal counsel may tender objections throughout the presentation.

Respondent's Defenses and Witnesses

When the claimant rests, or runs out of the time allotted by agreement to present their side of the dispute, the respondent is allowed to present their defenses and witnesses. It is possible that a version of directed verdict can be requested after the claimant completes their case in chief. But, this is extremely rare. More likely, the respondent presents defenses through witnesses and admissible arbitration exhibits. Once again, the arbitrator or panel may interject commentary and questions to the respondent's attorney or witnesses at any time during the respondent's presentation. Also, the claimant's attorney may make objections to offered testimony or exhibits.

Rebuttal Witnesses

Subsequent to the respondent wrapping up the defense, the disputing parties may be allowed by the arbitrator or panel to put on witnesses to rebut the others' witness testimony. The claimant usually cycles their rebuttal witnesses first, with the respondent's to follow. In many cases, rebuttal testimony is offered by experts, such as the financial expert witness. Therefore, the financial expert witness should discuss this possibility with the client legal counsel in advance of the arbitration hearing.

Closing Statements

Once all the evidence has been presented, the disputing parties each give a closing statement. The claimant is allowed to close and then the respondent. The closing statements are offered as a final summary of the case presented, the merits of each disputing party's positions and claims, and the reasons the arbitrator or panel should rule in favor of each client. The arbitrator or panel can then award either full relief in the case of the claimant, or dismissal or reduced award, if the respondent.

Post-Arbitration Memoranda and Consideration Period

At the conclusion of the arbitration hearing, the arbitrator or panel will notify the disputing parties about any other materials needed to render a decision and award, and the expected time needed to complete deliberations, prepare the written determination, and issue the final award order.

Arbitration Award Notification

Once a decision is reached by the arbitrator or panel, it is communicated to the disputing parties in a signed written opinion. Such rulings are typically less detailed than a trial decision, with some as brief as one page. There are a few unique types of decisions that can be agreed upon by the parties in advance of the arbitration proceeding. One is called baseball arbitration and another high/low.

Baseball

Baseball arbitration is a specialized form of arbitration agreed to by the disputing parties in advance of the initiation of arbitration proceedings. In baseball arbitration each of the disputing parties submits an award amount to the arbitrator or panel. The arbitrator or panel is then bound to make an award limited exclusively to one or the other submitted award amounts. Baseball arbitration has its roots in professional baseball player contract negotiations; hence the name.

High/Low

High/low arbitration is another form of specialized alternative dispute resolution. In this type of arbitration, each of the disputing parties submits an award amount, with one award representing the "high" end of the range of award and the other the "low" end. The arbitrator or panel is obligated to make an award determination that falls only within the "high" and "low" range.

 ## FINANCIAL EXPERT PARTICIPATION IN ARBITRATION

The financial expert may be asked to serve as a consultant or an expert witness in arbitration. In the role of a consultant, the financial expert performs many of the same services that would be performed in formal litigation. As an expert witness in arbitration, the financial expert witness serves the client in a manner closely approximating formal litigation. In fact, the disputing parties often agree to abide by the Federal Rules of Civil Procedure and Federal Rules of Evidence to govern the administration of the arbitration. Reference should be made to other chapters in this book that more fully describe the responsibilities and considerations for serving as a financial expert consultant or witness in deposition and trial.

Financial Expert Consultant

The consulting services provided by the financial expert in arbitration proceedings are similar to those provided for formal litigation. The financial expert may be asked to assist with the drafting of the demand for arbitration, preparation of an early case assessment, or calculation of preliminary damages. After the proceedings have started, the financial expert is likely to be asked to assist with discovery, especially the identification of financial facts and data to be produced by an opposing party, the analysis of the produced materials, and the drafting of questions for the deposition of opposing expert witnesses. In anticipation of trial, the financial expert usually assists with preparations, including the creation of demonstratives, the drafting of direct and cross-examination questions, and the preparation of witnesses. During the arbitration hearing, the financial expert may be required to be on-call to field real-time issues and questions.

Financial Expert Witness

As an expert witness in an arbitration proceeding, the financial expert witness must treat the event as if it is a litigated bench trial. The financial expert witness's testimony is allowed to assist the trier of fact, in this case the arbitrator or panel. Testimony is still sworn, but delivered outside a courtroom in a conference room, or other suitable location. The activities to be performed by the financial expert witness in arbitration closely follow what is to be done for formal litigation. The preparation, demeanor, dress, and performance of the financial expert witness in arbitration should be similar to deposition or trial. Accordingly, the chapters of this book dedicated to these subjects should be referred to for important considerations.

 COMING UP

There are matters for which the financial expert may be asked to serve as the trier of fact. In these cases, the financial expert may serve as a neutral arbitrator. Chapter 21 delves into neutral arbitration services.

CHAPTER TWENTY ONE

Alternative Dispute Resolution: Neutral Accounting Arbitration

 ## NEUTRAL ACCOUNTING ARBITRATION

Neutral accounting arbitration is a form of alternative dispute resolution. In a neutral accounting arbitration the disputing parties agree to engage an independent financial expert to serve as a trier of fact. As the fact finder, the neutral accountant makes binding determinations about the accounting treatment for submitted issues in controversy. The determinations made by the neutral accounting arbitrator are usually communicated to the disputing parties in a written decision. The written decision letter may be provided to the disputing parties with or without reasoning based on the engagement terms.

Although there are a wide variety of disputes giving rise to the need for neutral accounting arbitration, the discussion herein is limited to accounting disputes that arise in connection with mergers and acquisitions. These are commonly referred to as post-acquisition disputes. Post-acquisition disputes may arise from the following types of accounting disagreements, among others:

- Final calculation and settlement of a purchase price, especially one based on a determination of working capital.

- Treatment of contractually defined accounting items that vary from, or reference, generally accepted accounting principles (GAAP).
- Computations based on earnings before interest, taxes, depreciation, and amortization (EBITDA).
- Accounting for earn-out provisions.

The selection of a neutral accounting arbitration process to resolve accounting controversies is normally made by the disputing parties at the time the merger and acquisition written agreements are prepared. Specific language about accounting disputes and the associated resolution process agreed to by the parties will be memorialized in the agreements. In some cases, a neutral accounting arbitrator will be named in the agreements, as well. If so, an agreed-upon protocol will be used to notice a dispute, retain a neutral accounting arbitrator, and deliver a final determination.

 NEUTRAL ACCOUNTING ARBITRATION PROCESS

Neutral accounting arbitration proceedings require due process to reach dispute resolution. That due process may be defined in the merger and acquisition agreement; however, this is uncommon. It is more typical for the disputing parties to engage a neutral accounting arbitrator and then work together to reach a mutually agreeable due process for the proceedings. In most cases, the proceedings start with a formal dispute notice and work through a schedule of calendared activities, concluding with a final determination letter. Common steps for neutral accounting arbitration are described next and in Exhibit 21.1.

Accounting Dispute

Every neutral accounting arbitration proceeding begins with an accounting dispute. Once a dispute surfaces, the disputing parties try to work out their differences before turning to arbitration. It is possible that the disputing parties will engage a financial expert to help with these negotiations. However, in order to preserve typical contractual rights related to accounting disputes, one of the disputing parties must give formal written notice of the disputed accounting issues to the other party in the form, and prior to a date, specified in the agreement. This notice of accounting dispute will refer to the neutral accounting arbitration requirements spelled out in the merger and acquisition

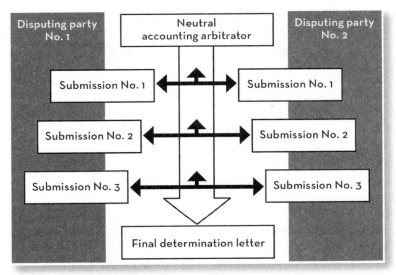

EXHIBIT 21.1   Neutral Accounting Arbitration Process Flow

agreement. After a time agreed upon in the agreement, negotiations subside and the neutral arbitration process is initiated.

Common Accounting Disputes

- Materiality
- Liability, loss, and asset value estimates
- Cut-off
- Expense allocations
- Taxes
- Disclosures
- EBITDA, a non-GAAP measurement

Selecting a Neutral Accounting Arbitrator

If a neutral accounting arbitrator is not named in the merger and acquisition agreement, the disputing parties begin to identify viable candidates. This search may be conducted using methods similar to those used to locate a financial expert witness, with one exception. The neutral accounting arbitrator is to be neutral regarding both disputing parties. Initially the search focuses on qualified prospects having relevant industry, accounting, and dispute resolution experience. After the initial search, the disputing parties can jointly agree on a neutral arbitrator and move forward, or each of them can submit a handful of names for examination.

If an examination is called for, the financial expert may be questioned by each of the disputing parties and requested to provide information. The queries and produced materials are used by the disputing parties to evaluate candidate qualifications and vet any potential conflicts of interest. Any actual or perceived conflicts of interest can be waived by the disputing parties. This should be done in writing, perhaps as part of the engagement letter, to protect the financial expert serving as a neutral accounting arbitrator. At the conclusion of the candidate evaluation, the disputing parties mutually agree on a single neutral accounting arbitrator. The chosen neutral accounting arbitrator is then notified and formally engaged to serve.

Scheduling and Protocols

Concurrent with engagement contracting, the disputing parties and the selected neutral accounting arbitrator initiate discussions about scheduling and governing protocols for the proceedings. In a few cases, the scheduling and protocols are set out by prior agreement. Even so, these matters are often changed based on a subsequent agreement of the disputing parties or the wishes of the neutral accounting arbitrator.

If the schedule and protocols are not previously agreed upon by the disputing parties, the neutral accounting arbitrator works with the disputing parties to prepare these items. To do so, the neutral accounting arbitrator should read the merger and acquisition agreement so that any specified scheduling and protocols are considered. Protocols for neutral accounting arbitration should cover communications with the neutral accounting arbitrator and the form of the final determination to be issued.

One of the priority items to make initially clear to the disputing parties is the limitation that the neutral accounting arbitrator is not qualified to make decisions concerning legal issues. The neutral accounting arbitrator is only qualified to make decisions about accounting issues in dispute. These issues can only be based on the neutral accounting arbitrator's financial, accounting, and business knowledge and experience. This fact is important for the disputing parties to understand because the neutral accounting arbitrator will be required to read and interpret the merger and acquisition agreement and decide discovery disputes that may arise, among other duties.

Communication protocols should address oral and written exchanges between the disputing parties and the neutral accounting arbitrator. In the vast majority of neutral accounting arbitrations, *ex parte* communications are prohibited between a single disputing party and the neutral accounting arbitrator. That creates a requirement for the disputing parties to provide copies of all written or electronic communications to the opposing party when it is given to the neutral accounting arbitrator. In the same vein, oral discussions between the disputing parties and the neutral accounting arbitrator must be in the presence of both disputing parties.

The final determination of the neutral accounting arbitrator can be delivered orally or by a written decision. In either instance, the final determination will set out the neutral accounting arbitrator's decisions on the disputed accounting issues for the disputing parties. In addition to this information, the disputing parties and neutral accounting arbitrator may agree to have the final determination supported by the reasons for the decisions. The neutral accounting arbitration protocols should reflect any agreement about the form and content of the final determination to be made by the neutral accounting arbitrator.

Following is an example of what scheduling and protocols might look like for the submission of the disputing parties participating in a neutral accounting arbitration:

1. **January 1—Initial Submission** due, limited to 25 pages in length, but unlimited supporting documents allowed.
2. **February 1—Response Submission** due, limited to 15 pages in length, but unlimited supporting documents allowed.
3. **March 1—Final Reply Submission** due, limited to 10 pages in length, but unlimited supporting documents allowed.
4. **March 15—Oral Hearing**, limited to one hour for each party.
5. **April 15—Final Determination Letter** to be issued by neutral accounting arbitrator.

The scheduling dates used in the example above may be reasonable for a number of disputes. However, it should be obvious that scheduling is subject to significant variability based on the disputing parties' needs, the complexity of the accounting issues in dispute, the availability of the neutral accounting arbitrator, and other factors.

Discovery

As the neutral accounting arbitrator, the financial expert will also be responsible for discovery decisions when disputes arise. This responsibility is often uncomfortable for the financial expert. In some cases, it will involve issues that come close to the line of being legal in nature. However, the neutral accounting arbitrator has no subpoena power or legal standing to compel production. Therefore, the neutral accounting arbitrator should make it clear to the disputing parties that any such decisions are based solely on the expertise of the neutral accounting arbitrator as a financial expert. Undoubtedly, the neutral accounting arbitrator will be in the middle of adversarial disputing parties arguing over discovery disputes.

Submissions

Prior to providing the positions and supporting arguments submissions, the disputing parties produce foundational materials to the neutral accounting arbitrator. These materials include the merger and acquisition agreement, accounting items in dispute, and any other relevant documents and correspondence previously exchanged between the disputing parties. If the initial disclosures of the disputed accounting items differ between the two disputing parties, which happens frequently, the neutral accounting arbitrator should request that the disputing parties reconcile any differences. It is critical that the neutral accounting arbitrator have a clear and irrefutable understanding of the matters subject to final determination and the governing agreements for dispute resolution.

The positions and arguments, together with support, are submitted to the neutral accounting arbitrator for consideration based on an agreed-upon schedule. The schedule is designed to allow sufficient time for each of the disputing parties to reasonably prepare submissions and respond to an opponent's offerings. In addition, the schedule provides adequate time for the neutral accounting arbitrator to research and contemplate the submissions before a final determination is rendered. Schedules for a neutral accounting arbitration proceeding can range from as little as 60 days to more than a year, depending on the facts and circumstances.

Submissions to the neutral accounting arbitrator are prepared and delivered in a prescribed manner. The manner of the submissions is negotiated by the disputing parties and the neutral accounting arbitrator and may include considerations about the form, content, length, and transmission of submitted materials. Agreements about the manner of submission may limit the number of pages for each submission, dictate the format of the documents, or address supporting evidence. In many cases, the initial submission is allowed to have the most pages, with subsequent submissions reduced in size to expedite the resolution process. However, it is uncommon for supporting evidence to be limited due to the voluminous and electronic nature of accounting books and records.

Written submissions will always include an initial submission from the disputing parties. The initial submissions lay out the accounting disputes, positions, and arguments for each disputing party. Initial submissions may also be accompanied by relevant supporting documents, like accounting books and records. Following the initial submissions there may be a response and final reply. The response submission is used to address any new information disclosed by the opposing party in the initial submission. The reply is usually the final submission. It rebuts new information reported in the response and provides a final opportunity for the disputing parties to make arguments.

Oftentimes, a client will need assistance researching and preparing submissions for the neutral accounting arbitration. The financial expert (but, not the neutral accounting arbitrator, of course) may be engaged to assist the client with this work and reporting in the role of an accounting consultant. The retention of the accounting consultant may be kept secret from the opposing party and neutral accounting arbitrator. However, it is not uncommon for the accounting consultant to be disclosed and for submissions to be marked as the work product of the accounting consultant. In doing so, the client hopes to convince the neutral accounting arbitrator that their work product, which has been prepared by a qualified accounting consultant, is reliable and credible.

Hearings

In a neutral accounting arbitration proceeding, hearings can range from casual phone dialog with the disputing parties to a formal oral presentation of each party's positions and arguments in front of the neutral accounting arbitrator. The number and type of hearings is determined exclusively by the neutral accounting arbitrator, although some merger and acquisition agreements may call for a formal hearing. The purpose of any hearing is to allow the disputing parties the opportunity to present unsworn oral arguments, facts, and evidence to the neutral accounting arbitrator. Hearing testimony may be considered by the neutral accounting arbitrator in making final determinations or in reaching decisions on issues arising during the course of arbitration.

Accounting Research and Analysis

Throughout the arbitration proceedings the neutral accounting arbitrator will perform independent research and analysis concerning the disputed accounting items and the facts, data, and evidence produced. This work tends to be technical in nature. For example, the neutral accounting arbitrator may evaluate the proper application of available GAAP to a set of facts. The progress of this work can be discussed with the disputing parties, but in no case should preliminary results be disclosed.

At times, it may be necessary for the neutral accounting arbitrator to contact the disputing parties during deliberation to ask questions, request additional details, or clarify positions. This can be accomplished using e-mail, teleconference, or more formal written correspondence. Once again, *ex parte*, or single-party contact, with the neutral accounting arbitrator should be avoided in connection with these exchanges of information.

In some cases, the evidence produced by a disputing party will be inadequate to support a position. This can happen in a number of different ways. It may occur when insufficient evidence has been produced. It can also be the result when the neutral accounting arbitrator deems the reliability, weight, or source of the evidence to be inferior. It is not the responsibility of the neutral accounting arbitrator to point out such deficiencies, or to recommend sources of evidence that may be compelling. To do so could impair impartiality, in fact or appearance.

Final Determination

After deliberations are complete, the neutral accounting arbitrator makes a final determination on each of the accounting items in dispute and subject to arbitration. In some situations, the neutral accounting arbitrator may also be asked to reflect the impact of the final accounting determinations on a contractual amount, such as a final purchase price or earn-out payment. This decision is delivered to the disputing parties in written form, except in unusual cases. The contents of the final determination letter are subjective; however, the following sections are typically helpful to the reader:

- Introduction of the parties and scope of neutral accounting arbitration
- Background of the dispute
- Description of disputed items
- Itemization of facts, data, and evidence considered, including the disputing parties' submissions to the neutral accounting arbitrator

- Summarized positions of the buyer and seller
- Final determination for each accounting issue in dispute

The written decision can be delivered with, or without, the reasoning for each determination. If the written decision is without explanation, the final determinations may be expressed simply as the decision and an amount. An example of this type of decision is reflected next.

> I find in favor of the Seller on Accounting Dispute item No. 1, in the amount of $1,000,000.

For final determinations requiring that the reasons be set forth, the neutral accounting arbitrator should provide explanations in reasonable detail. Such explanations may include descriptions of the evidence relied upon, the result of independent research and analysis, interpretations of agreements, and citations to applicable accounting standards. In most cases, a final determination on an individual item in dispute can be explained in a handful of paragraphs. Occasionally, complex matters may need several pages to describe the reasoning for a decision. The example that follows shows how a reasoned final accounting determination might be explained for an accounting dispute over the computation of net working capital.

> My final determination on the accounting matter in dispute favors the Seller. Net Working Capital is to be reduced by $1,000,000 as of the Closing Balance Sheet Date.
>
> Net Working Capital is clearly defined and unambiguous in the Purchase Agreement. The computation of Net Working Capital under the terms of the Purchase Agreement must include all current liabilities reported on the Seller's balance sheet as of the Closing Balance Sheet Date. Net Working Capital is to be determined in accordance with U.S. GAAP applied consistently with the Seller's audited financial statements dated December 31, 2013. The Seller's accounting for the Disputed Items was determined in accordance with U.S. GAAP, as defined in the Purchase Agreement.
>
> The Financial Accounting Standards Board (FASB) Accounting Standards Codification (ASC) is the source of authoritative U.S. GAAP for the relevant period in this matter. FASB ASC Section 210–10–45–8 discusses items which are to be classified as current liabilities on a company's balance sheet. ASC 210–10–45–8(b) states that current liabilities include "[c]ollections received in advance of

the delivery of goods or performance of services. Examples of such current liabilities are obligations resulting from advance collections on ticket sales. . . ."

 ## IN CLOSING

I hope you found this book useful for its practical tips and techniques on serving as a financial expert in civil litigation and alternative dispute resolution. My hope is that you are able to take away just a few of my personal lessons learned to become a more effective and valuable financial expert. Now comes the hard part—doing it yourself. Just remember, making mistakes is human and humans acting in the role of financial expert witnesses and consultants play an important role in our society. Good luck and best wishes.

Bibliography and Suggested Reading

AICPA Forensic and Valuation Services Section in partnership with the Institute for the Advancement of the American Legal System. "Another Voice: Financial Experts on Reducing Client Costs in Civil Litigation." AICPA, 2012. Accessed January 3, 2014. www.aicpa.org/interestareas/forensi candvaluation/newsandpublications/advocacy/downloadabledocuments/ financial-experts-on-reducing-client-costs%20in-civil-litigation.pdf.

AICPA Forensic and Valuation Services Section. "The 2011 Forensic and Valuation Services (FVS) Trend Survey." AICPA, 2012. Accessed January 3, 2014. www.aicpa.org/InterestAreas/ForensicAndValuation/Resources/Pract AidsGuidance/DownloadableDocuments/2011%20FVS%20Trend%20 Survey.pdf.

Barrett III, William C. "Alternative Dispute Resolution Services, A Nonauthoritative Guide." AICPA (1999).

Davis, Charles, Ramona Farrell, and Suzanne Ogilby. "Characteristics and Skills of the Forensic Accountant." AICPA FVS Section. AICPA, 2010. Accessed January 3, 2014. www.aicpa.org/InterestAreas/ForensicAndValua tion/Resources/PractAidsGuidance/DownloadableDocuments/Forensic AccountingResearchWhitePaper.pdf.

Dunbar, Michael K., and Roman L. Weil. "Ex Ante versus Ex Post Damages Calculations." Accessed January 3, 2014. booth.chicagoexec.net/public/ public_files/Ex%20Ante,%20Ex%20Post%20Damage%20Calculations.pdf.

"Ethical Guidelines for Settlement Negotiations." American Bar Association Section of Litigation Special Project. ABA, August 2002. www.american_ bar.org.

"FVS: Sales Presentation Skills." The Rainmaker Academy. Nashville, TN, 2013.

Garner, Bryan A. *Black's Law Dictionary, Third Pocket Edition.* New York: West Group, 2006.

Garner, Bryan A. *Legal Writing in Plain English: A Text with Exercises*. Chicago: University of Chicago Press, 2001.

Hildebrand, M., R. C. Wilson, and E. R. Dienst. *Evaluating University Teaching*. Berkeley, CA: UC Berkeley, Center for Research and Development in Higher Education, 1971.

Honore, S., and Paine Schofield, C. B. "Generation Y: Inside Out. A Multi-Generational View of Generation Y—Learning and Working, Preliminary Report." Ashridge, 2009. Accessed January 3, 2014. www.ashridge.org.uk and www.theguardian.com/teacher-network/teacher-blog/2013/mar/11/technology-internet-pupil-attention-teaching. Also www.nimh.nih.gov/health/topics/social-phobia-social-anxiety-disorder/index.shtml.

Keeton, W. Page, general editor. *Prosser and Keeton on the Law of Torts*, 10th reprint. St. Paul, MN: West Group, 2004.

Lubet, Steven, and Elizabeth Boals. *Expert Testimony: A Guide for Expert Witnesses and the Lawyers Who Examine Them*. Boulder, CO: NITA, 1998.

Lubet, Steven. *Modern Trial Advocacy: Analysis and Practice*, 2nd ed. Boulder, CO: NITA, 1997.

Lloyd, Robert M. "The Reasonable Certainty Requirement in Lost Profits Litigation: What It Really Means" (April 5, 2010). University of Tennessee Legal Studies Research Paper No. 128. Available at SSRN. http://ssrn.com/abstract=1584710 or http://dx.doi.org/10.2139/ssm.1584710.

Lyons, Ian M., and Sian L. Beilock. "When Math Hurts: Math Anxiety Predicts Pain Network Activation in Anticipation of Doing Math." PLoS ONE: 7(10) e48076. doi: 10.1371/journal.pone.0048076.

Malone, David M., and Paul J. Zwier. *Effective Expert Testimony*, 2nd ed. Boulder, CO: NITA, 2006.

Malone, David M., and Paul J. Zwier. *Expert Rules: 100 (and More) Points You Need to Know about Expert Witnesses*. 2nd ed. Boulder, CO: NITA, 2001.

Preber, Bradley J. "Introduction to Civil Litigation Services, Practice Aid 09–1." AICPA, 2009.

PricewaterhouseCoopers LLP. "*Daubert* Challenges to Financial Experts 2012." PricewaterhouseCoopers LLC, 2013. Accessed January 3, 2014. www.pwc.com/en_US/us/forensic-services/publications/assets/daubert-challenges.pdf.

Tamer, Mary. "Repetition, Repetition, Repetition," Harvard Graduate School of Education, Winter 2010. www.gse.harvard.edu/news-impact/2010/01/repetition-repetition-repetition/.

Thompson, Debra K., et al. "Serving as an Expert Witness or Consultant, Practice Aid 10–1," AICPA, 2010. www.aicpa.org/InterestAreas/Forensic

AndValuation/Resources/PractAidsGuidance/DownloadableDocuments/ preview-pa-expert-consultant-1pp-2.pdf.

U.S. Federal Rules of Evidence, December 1, 2012. www.uscourts.gov/uscourts/ rules/rules-evidence.pdf. U.S. Federal Rules of Civil Procedure, December 1, 2012. www.uscourts.gov/uscourts/rules/civil-procedure.pdf.

Younger, Irving. "Irving Younger's 10 Commandments of Cross-Examination." 1975. Summarized from *The Art of Cross-Examination* by Irving Younger. The Section of Litigation Monograph Series, No. 1, published by the American Bar Association Section on Litigation, from a speech given by Irving Younger at the ABA Annual Meeting in Montreal, Canada, in August 1975. www.dayontorts.com/uploads/file/Younger%20on%20Cross—10%20 Commandments.pdf.

About the Author

B RADLEY J. PREBER IS THE U.S. national managing partner of Grant Thornton LLP's Forensic and Valuation Services practice. Mr. Preber formerly served as the office managing partner for Grant Thornton's Desert Southwest cluster of offices and the U.S. national leader for Litigation and Dispute services. For more than 30 years, Mr. Preber has served as an expert witness, litigation consultant, financial forensic investigator, and neutral accounting arbitrator. He specializes in complex claims and disputes, with an emphasis on "bet the company" civil litigation and alternative dispute resolution. His clients have included the U.S. Department of Justice, Department of the Treasury, Department of the Interior, New York Office of the Attorney General, Special Trustee of the Securities and Exchange Commission, state gaming authorities of California, Nevada, and Mississippi, and a number of the largest global and domestic law firms.

Mr. Preber frequently writes, speaks, and presents on leadership, litigation, and alternative dispute resolution services, and the provision of neutral accounting arbitration services. He authored the American Institute of Certified Public Accountant's special report entitled *Introduction to Civil Litigation Services* in 2009 and assisted with the development of that organization's professional training on expert witness testimony. Mr. Preber and Grant Thornton LLP coauthored "Hear That Whistle Blowing," a model accounting complaint-handling process that was published as part of the *Anti-Corruption Handbook* authored by William P. Olsen. In addition, Mr. Preber has instructed courses for Arizona State University, the Thunderbird International School of Management, the American Institute of Certified Public Accountants, and the Institute of Internal Auditors.

Mr. Preber is a Certified Public Accountant licensed to practice in Arizona, Mississippi, New Mexico, and Texas. In addition, Mr. Preber is Certified in Financial Forensics by the American Institute of Certified Public Accountants and is a Certified Fraud Examiner as sanctioned by the Association of Certified

Fraud Examiners. Mr. Preber received a BBA with honors from the University of New Mexico, with an emphasis in accounting. Mr. Preber was inducted into the University of New Mexico's Robert O. Anderson School of Management Hall of Fame in 2008, in recognition of his postgraduate contributions to business, community, and charitable causes.

• • •

The people in the independent firms of **Grant Thornton International Ltd** provide personalized attention and the highest-quality service to public and private clients in more than 100 countries. Grant Thornton LLP is the U.S. member firm of Grant Thornton International Ltd, one of the world's leading organizations of independent audit, tax, and advisory firms. Grant Thornton International Ltd and its member firms are not a worldwide partnership, as each member firm is a separate and distinct legal entity. Grant Thornton's Forensic and Valuation Services practice includes financial investigations, anticorruption services, litigation and dispute resolution services, forensic technology services, and valuation services.

About the Website

THIS BOOK HAS A COMPANION website, which can be found at www.wiley.com/go/financialexpertwitness.

The companion website provides helpful information, tips, and techniques in addition to those included in the book. It includes a description of the differences between audit and forensic procedures, a Model Accounting Complaint Handling (*MACH*) process developed by the author, commentary on post-acquisition disputes, and a handy presentation model that can be used by the financial expert witness in court. The website also provides an unpublished U.S. Court of Appeals decision regarding one of the author's cases.

The password to enter this site is: preber123.

Index

NOTE: Page references in *italics* refer to figures.